Meanwhile, Back at Café Du Monde...

The "Meanwhile, Back at Café Du Monde . . ." show premiered May 16, 2010 at the Myrtles Plantation, St. Francisville, Louisiana.

We had a wonderful NOLA Visit. December, 2014 ♡

Meanwhile, Back at Café Du Monde...

Life Stories about Food

Created and Edited by Peggy Sweeney-McDonald
Photography by Troy Kleinpeter
Foreword by Karen Benrud

PELICAN PUBLISHING COMPANY
Gretna 2013

First printing, September 2012
Second printing, September 2013

ISBN 9781455616602
E-book ISBN 9781455616619

Printed in China
Published by Pelican Publishing Company, Inc.
1000 Burmaster Street, Gretna, Louisiana 70053

I dedicate this book to my beloved parents, Myles and Sherry Sweeney, who have been my greatest fans and taught me to shine. And to my cherished husband, James McDonald, who has taught me that the joy really is in the journey and to keep the train moving forward despite all of life's obstacles.

Bert Fife 1951-2011
In loving memory of Bert Fife, who shared her life, stories, smile, and light with us.

Contents

Foreword

The Café Du Monde is something I have grown up with my entire life. My grandfather, Hubert N. Fernandez, purchased the eighty-year-old café on May 6, 1942. It was our family business, and the entire family pitched in. If my daddy didn't come home from work smelling like beignets, I knew something was wrong! I also know that most New Orleanians will agree with me in saying that many special occasions and fond memories have been created in the café throughout the years. We have had everything from weddings to jazz funerals, from late-night after-prom dates to early risers looking for their predawn cup of café au lait. Several celebrities, athletes, politicians, and even a U.S. president or two have stopped in while in town. Countless commercials and movies were filmed under the famous green and white awning. We even had a baby born in the ladies' room!

If you do the math, the year 2012 is doubly special for us. It is the seventieth anniversary of the Fernandez family (now fourth generation) as owners and operators of the café, and the café itself celebrates 150 years in existence. Wow, that's a lot of beignets!

One of the strangest times for me was during the aftermath of Hurricane Katrina. We had to close our 24-hour-a-day/364-day-a-year business for more than ten weeks. To walk on Decatur Street and not hear jazz music playing or smell beignets frying was so sad. It just wasn't right. We had a huge celebration when we were able to reopen, with a banner that said it all, "Beignets are Back!"

In June of 2010, I was in the audience for the New Orleans premiere performance of "Meanwhile, Back at Cafe Du Monde . . ." at the House of Blues. The show was amazing! It was so much fun to listen to the stories and realize that we are all connected through our different food experiences. I know that my grandfather probably had no idea that the Cafe Du Monde would grow into the world-famous icon it has become, and I am sure that he was smiling down on us that night.

When Peggy asked me to write the foreword to this awesome book, I was both honored and overwhelmed. How does one fit a lifetime of experiences into a few words? Let me just conclude with my one wish: that we will always be able to say, "Meanwhile, back at Café Du Monde . . ."

Karen Benrud
Owner, Café Du Monde

Karen and Burt Benrud at House of Blues Premiere Show, June 22, 2010

Karen and her grandfather Herbert N. Fernandez at Mardi Gras

The Fernandez grandchildren, from the left: Jay, Celeste, Karen Denise, Nicole, and Colleen, circa 1970

Karen, Burt, and Peggy greeting Leah Chase and Jackie Toledano at the House of Blues Show

Sylvia Fernandez Maher and Cynthia Fernandez Roman

Karen and Peggy Sweeney-McDonald at Café Du Monde

Owners and operators Burt Benrud, Jay Roman, and Scott Escarra

Acknowledgments

Where do I begin to thank everyone who has supported me in following the dream called "Meanwhile, Back At Café Du Monde . . ."? I am forever grateful for the love and endless support I have been given by my family: my husband, Jimmy; my parents, Myles and Sherry Sweeney; my three sisters, Shannan Rieger, Erin Segrest, and Dr. Kelly Clements; brothers-in-law; and nieces and nephews, especially Myles Rieger, my talented nephew who helped me with the editing. My family has been there from the beginning and at most shows cheering me on. I could not have done any of this without them.

To Café Du Monde, Karen and Burt Benrud and the Fernandez family for letting us use the Café Du Monde name, writing the foreword, and including the history and vintage pictures in the book, as it adds so much "Café Du Monde" flavor!

To Troy Kleinpeter, who became the official photographer from the first show, traveled with us, and helped create the book. He has captured the heart of the show with every picture he has snapped, and I'm so grateful for his dedication and talent. To Jay Basist, my co-producer for the Louisiana and Mississippi shows. He believed in the idea, stepped up to make it happen, and was there for me in countless ways. To Thom Ward, my co-producer for the great San Francisco shows. To Jeanne Vidrine, my cousin and friend, who not only appeared in the shows as headliner and an emcee, but who helped guide the shows in New Orleans. To Diana Zollicoffer and Tom Pace who stepped up to take additional great pictures of the recipes. To the talented artist Christine Ababon, who designed our fabulous logo and event posters. To Todd and Lanya Grammer, who sponsored the audio/visual in Baton Rouge, and Mike Ryan, who sponsored the audio/visual for the Los Angeles shows. To my dear friends who assisted with the events: Teeta Moss, Daron Stiles, Claudia Wong, Melanie Elliott, Lisa Singer, Danielle Hunter, Kim Biel, Janet Thorne, Tom and Judy Young, Missy Crews, Scott McEuen, Steve Lytle, Jemi Jeffrey, Mary and Lance Spellerberg, and all the other friends who supported me and came out to the show.

To all the venues who partnered with us: the Myrtles Plantation and Carriage House Restaurant, the Lyceum Ballroom, House of Blues (New Orleans and Sunset), Ralph & Kacoo's, Juban's Creole Restaurant, the Southern Food and Beverage Museum, Ernest's Orleans Restaurant, Boutin's, the Razz Room at Hotel Nikko, SOUTH, Sonoma Wine Garden, Lumpkins Barbeque, and Dunleith Historical Inn.

To Clint Crisher, who designed the amazing website and helped us with marketing. To Bob Mazza, for publicity. For the wonderful team at Pelican Publishing—Dr. and Mrs. Calhoun, Nina Kooij, Kathleen Nettleton, Heather

9

Green, Sally Boitnott, Antoinette de Alteriis, Scott Campbell, Katy Doll, Kevin Johnson, and Terry Callaway—who made this book possible and held my hand as I learned the process of publishing. To my literary agent, Anna Olswanger, at the Liza Dawson Agency, and my attorney, Jeff Spellerberg, for guiding me into a new world. To the team who produced the TV pilot Sizzle Reel: Vinni Villicano, Giovanni Jackson, Smith Glover, Angela Gervasio, Gary Nelson, Caleb Michaelson, Craig McGraff, Jeff Kleinpeter, Melinda Walsh, Drew Ramsey, Jay Ducote, Liz Williams, and Honey Labrador.

To our audience members—thanks for sharing the show with us and spreading the word. Your feedback is what kept us coming back for more!

And to all who shared their talent and enthusiasm in the shows: the wonderful emcees Whitney Vann, Scott Rogers, Jeff Kleinpeter, Paul Arrigo, Donna Britt, Tom Pace, Sonya Bailes, Ed Walsh, Carolyn Roy, Chris Russo, Eric Paulsen, Becky Allen, Jay Ducote, Christine Devine, Carolyn Cicero, Jeanne Vidrine, Poppy Tooker, Beth Schnitzer, William Annesley, Lynn Curtin, and Tom Ramsey. And a huge heartfelt thank you to the "headliners" who shared their amazing personal stories of life about food; without them, we would not have the show or the book and "Meanwhile . . ." would just be an idea, not a delicious reality.

I am especially grateful to my beautiful friend Lisa Annitti, who inspired the show. If she hadn't shared her "Coconut Pie and a Bottle of Red Wine" story, the show may have never been born. I tell her she was my muse.

Everyone above has held my hand and pushed me forward. I am forever grateful and filled with love for all of you. I can't begin to thank you for making me shine!

Introduction

It was Thanksgiving 2009, and I was "home" in Baton Rouge visiting my family. I wasn't grateful for much this particular Thanksgiving and was in the "depths of despair," as I like to say, as I am a bit of a Southern belle drama queen, maybe more than a bit. I was a very creative event producer living in Los Angeles and, with the recession, had few events in sight.

The day after Thanksgiving, my friend Lisa Annitti came down from Shreveport to visit me in Baton Rouge. When I asked her how her Thanksgiving was, she rolled her eyes and told me her "Coconut Pie and a Bottle of Red Wine" story. I laughed and then throughout the weekend asked her to share the story with my mom, family, and friends; they all laughed hysterically. I said, "This is like one of those monologue shows, but with food stories and everyone has a food story!" I stayed up most of the night thinking of people coming together to share their stories about the universal language, *food*, and how our lives revolve around it.

The next day, I told Lisa I wanted to produce the show, and since it would be about food, you have to eat and drink so it's really an event—a celebration of how food is so important in our lives. These stories would be endearing life stories with a thread of food. I now had an event, and I started to get excited, inspired, and jazzed and felt I was coming alive again!

What would I call it? When I lived in New Orleans, I had coined the phrase "Meanwhile, back at Café Du Monde" on one of our many visits there. My husband, Jimmy, said to me "everyone has their own Café Du Monde, as it is a metaphor for the place you always go to, your own comfort food place."

Back in Baton Rouge, I told my parents and sisters. They loved the idea and made suggestions—local TV anchors, chefs, restaurant owners, business owners, and foodies. I now had a wish list of potential headliners to invite to share their personal food stories. I drew up an outline with the vision of the show. I then called Café Du Monde to get permission to use their name. I spoke to Burt Benrud, vice president of Café Du Monde, and told him the working title and sent him the outline of the show. Within 15 minutes, I received an e-mail granting me permission to use their name. I will be forever grateful to him and his lovely wife, Karen, who have since become dear friends.

My friend, Teeta Moss, owner of the Myrtles Plantation in St. Francisville, suggested we do the premiere show there with a cocktail party. We sent out the request for monologues to our wish list. "Meanwhile, Back at Café Du Monde . . ." premiered on Sunday, May 16, 2010. It was a beautiful event on a hot, humid summer evening. The Carriage House Restaurant catered the delicious cocktail party and guests mingled while Steve Bing and the Bayou Hot Shots played festive Cajun music. Friends came from nearby in Baton Rouge, as well as all the way from Atlanta and Tampa. A portion of the proceeds benefitted the West Feliciana Parish TRIAD Program for the Elderly. After the cocktail party, the guests began gathering in the living room and parlor of the historical plantation for the show. Headliners included Lisa Annitti, Paul Arrigo, Chef Don Bergeron, Donna Britt, Daniel Brockhoeft, Todd Graves, Ruffin Rodrigue, Leah Simon, Daron Stiles, Michael Scott, Peggy Sweeney-McDonald, and Jim Urdiales. Whitney Vann was the emcee.

We were so lucky to have everyone jump on board that we decided to add another show at a second venue, the Lyceum Ballroom, in downtown Baton Rouge, three days later. Many of the headliners from the Myrtles show reprised their food monologues along with new headliners Jeff Kleinpeter, Leo Honeycutt, Chris Russo, Paul Gates, Jim Overby and Sister Judith Brun. Whitney Vann was the emcee. A fabulous cocktail buffet was served, which included food dished up by the headliners—duck empanadas from Jim Urdiale's Mestizo Louisiana Mexican Restaurant, chicken fingers from Todd Graves' Raising Cane's, shrimp and grits from Ruffin Rodrigue's Ruffino's Restaurant, and crawfish étouffée from Chef Don Bergeron's Mid-City Market. Jeff Kleinpeter of Kleinpeter Farms Dairy provided delicious ice cream for dessert. A portion of the proceeds benefited the Baton Rouge YMCA Strong Kids Program.

The two shows were a hit and the journey of "Meanwhile, Back at Café Du Monde . . ." began. The New Orleans premiere show was held at the House of Blues in the French Quarter on June 22, 2010. House of Blues served a delicious buffet and Chef Matt Murphy provided desserts. Headliners included Leah Chase, Jeremy Davenport, Chef Matt Murphy, Chef Michael Regua, Davis Rogan, Jeanne Vidrine, Lisa Annitti, and Peggy Sweeney-McDonald. Scott Rogers of the *Around Town Show* was the emcee. The owners of Café Du Monde, Karen and Burt Benrud, were honored guests and were presented with a poster of the event signed by the cast members. Beignets, compliments

of Café Du Monde, were served with coffee. Jeremy Davenport closed the show with his food story and ended by playing his trumpet while the audience waved their napkins in the air second-line style. It was a night to remember!

I like to say the show has snowballed and the beignet has become bigger and sweeter. My life has changed so much. It has been a spirit-driven show, with all the right people and talent stepping up to create the most amazing events. On May 12, 2011, we celebrated the one-year anniversary of the show at Juban's Creole Restaurant in Baton Rouge. The evening began with cocktails and red carpet interviews by Jay Ducote. Many of the original headliners from the first show returned to reprise their original food monologues, including Paul Arrigo, Chef Don Bergeron, Daniel Brockhoeft, Jim Urdiales, and Whitney Vann. Popular emcee, Scott Rogers was back to lead the evening, and for the first time, Baton Rouge mayor Kip Holden was on board to share his food story, along with Missy Crews, Nancy Litton, and Dave Wright.

Mayor Holden presented us with a proclamation naming May 12, 2011, "Meanwhile, Back at Café Du Monde . . ." Day in Baton Rouge! It was an honor! During the dinner, we projected pictures on the wall from the past events from Louisiana, Mississippi, and California, and it was astonishing when we stopped to realize how far the show has come in just one year. It was our thirtieth show, and more than two hundred people had shared their life stories around food.

The show has brought so many old friends back into my life, and I've made so many new ones. The joy, laughter, and tears that happen night after night are pure magic. We do not rehearse and, many times, do not even get to read the monologues beforehand. Each story is a sparkling jewel and loved by all as they warm your heart and feed the soul. I am so grateful to have the book published by Pelican Publishing, to continue sharing the stories. I have no idea where this journey will take me or when it will end. I have learned to enjoy the sweetness of life, and I finally understand the meaning of "the joy is in the journey." For this, I will always be in thanksgiving!

The 2010 Premiere Shows in St. Francisville, Baton Rouge, and New Orleans, Louisiana

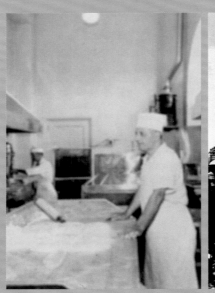

The History of Café Du Monde

In May 2012, Café Du Monde celebrated its 150th anniversary. When the original location in the French Quarter opened, electricity was still a decade away. Café Du Monde sits just off the Mississippi River in the New Orleans French Market. The French Market dates back to the Choctaw Indians, who used this natural Mississippi River-level location to trade their wares with travelers along the river. The French Market is comprised of seven buildings and is anchored at the Jackson Square end by Café Du Monde and on the other end by the Farmers Market and flea markets.

The café is located at the corner of St. Ann and Decatur in the building known as the Butcher's Hall. This building was built in 1812, after a hurricane destroyed the original. It has undergone a number of renovations over the last two hundred years, including major changes in 1930 and 1975.

Café Du Monde is world renowned for its café au lait and beignets. The signature drink is a blend of coffee and chicory, which is the root of the endive plant. Once the coffee and chicory have been roasted and ground, the two are mixed together prior to packaging. The chicory is added to dark-roasted coffee to soften its bitter edge. Once brewed, the coffee is mixed with heated milk to make the perfect cup of café au lait.

The Acadians, who were expelled from France in the mid-1700s, introduced coffee with chicory and the beignet to New Orleans. Their version of the beignet was a fried fritter, sometimes filled with fruit. Today, the beignet is a square piece of dough that is fried and then covered with powdered sugar and is served in orders of three.

In 1942, Hubert Fernandez purchased Café Du Monde. Since then, four generations of the Fernandez family have joined together to serve their guests. They have expanded to nine different locations in New Orleans and the surrounding areas, while remaining family owned and operated.

Images Courtesy of Café Du Monde

Lisa Annitti
Actress, Los Angeles
A Coconut Pie and a Bottle of Red Wine

"If I were a food, I'd be a chocolate Ding Dong, hard on the outside and oh so soft and sweet in the middle. I'm from Jersey...what do you want?"

So it was the night before Thanksgiving, and I found myself lonely and depressed, in my corporate apartment in Shreveport, Louisiana, trying really hard to overcome a devastating break up. If you're wondering why I was in Shreveport, it's because I was on location working on a feature film. Actually, that's not the whole truth. I had run away from Los Angeles, which is where I live, because my heart was broken. The love of my life had broken up with me. (You know the kind of guy I'm referring to—the guy who when you meet him you know you are "done with searching" and you thank God that you will never have to date again.) I needed to put some distance between us.

Now mind you, I was invited to a wonderful Thanksgiving family dinner in Baton Rouge (thank you Sweeney family), but I was coerced by my boss to attend a dinner for orphans (you know what I mean, right? People with no other place to go—very depressing!) at her home in Shreveport.

It turns out that my boss's mother is a gourmet cook, and I thought maybe this wouldn't be so bad. I quickly changed my mind when I heard the menu, which, although it sounded delicious, didn't include the most basic Thanksgiving fare, mashed potatoes. The dessert menu was even worse! No pies! How do you have Thanksgiving dinner with no pies? They had no pumpkin, no pecan, and not even my all-time favorite coconut cream pie. So being the generous person that I am, I offered to bring a

coconut cream pie. If looks could kill, I would be a dead woman. However, my boss, ever polite, said that that would be fine.

So it was the day before Thanksgiving, and I ran out of my office to Strawn's Eat Shop to get my pie. I was so excited. When I returned to the office, to my utter disbelief, the "powers that be" announced that the office would be closing early for the holiday. I was almost reduced to tears. You're probably wondering why I was so upset. It sounds great, right? Well, remember I was in Shreveport, and dinner wasn't until 5:00 P.M. the next day! What was I supposed to do alone for the following twenty-seven hours?

I took a few moments to compose myself, and being ever resourceful, I decided to run a few errands. I went to the grocery store and bought myself some beautiful pork chops, Brussels sprouts, and a bottle of wine. I then headed home to make myself a very fine home-cooked meal. Sounds good, right? This was not so great because it brings me right back to the beginning of my story. I was trying really hard to get over a devastating breakup, lonely and depressed, in my corporate apartment in Shreveport, Louisiana. Oh, and did I mention, I have two cats?

So now, it was only 5:30 P.M., and I was home in my pajamas, with pork chops marinating, when I decided that it was not too early to open a bottle of wine. We've

16

all been there, right? Uh huh. The next thing I knew I had practically licked my plate clean and had almost polished off the entire bottle of wine. In my slightly drunken haze, I really wished I had something sweet to eat. All of a sudden I heard this little voice calling me from the kitchen, "Lisa, Lisa, eat me, eat me!" And that's when I remembered that I had pie!

Okay, so I know what you're thinking. The pie was for Thanksgiving. But remember I was drunk, and drunk people can rationalize almost anything. So I headed to the refrigerator and removed my beautiful pie, and it was beautiful. I told myself that if I only have one piece, I could cut the pie in half and still bring it to dinner. I cut myself a piece of pie. I took my first bite, and it was glorious, rich, and creamy. It was so cold and smooth in my mouth. I almost didn't want to swallow it. But swallow it I did, and the next thing I knew the pie was on the coffee table. I was no longer cutting slices but eating it out of the tin with a fork, still rationalizing that I could bring the pie to dinner. I wouldn't cut it in half though. I would cut it in slices and arrange it on a plate. I mean after all, they didn't even want me to bring it anyway, right?

Then the phone rang, and it was my friend Sheri from Los Angeles. Before I could even begin to speak, she blurted out, "I am so depressed! They let us out of work early, and I had nothing to do, so I came home and opened a bottle of wine. Now I'm lying on the couch, and I'm really drunk!" Well, they say misery loves company, so I told her she was not alone. I was in the same boat as her, lying on my couch and drunk off my ass. But at least she was not alone in Shreveport. Then I began to tell her about the pie.

I'm not a minute into the story when she screamed in my ear, "You can't bring that freaking pie!" I started to tell her that I thought I could cut it into pieces and arrange it on a plate. "Are you kidding me?" she screams again. "You can't bring that freaking pie!" And then the realization hit me. She was right. What the hell was I thinking? I couldn't bring that pie. Was I out of my mind? So then she asked me what I was going to do. Stumped for only a second, I said, "Well if I can't bring it with me, I am going to finish eating it!" And that's right. I ate that pie, every last bit of that pie, and it was good!

I woke up the next morning hung over, still depressed, and with no pie to bring with me. When I finally peeled myself off the couch to leave for my boss's house, I realized I couldn't go empty handed, so I grabbed a bottle of wine as I headed out the door. Yes, I managed not to drink all the wine in the house. Anyway, I drove myself to my boss's house, and when she opened the door, I said in my most non-hung-over voice "Happy Thanksgiving" and handed her the bottle of wine. She looked at the wine and looked at me, and she said "Lisa, where's my pie?"

Signing event poster at House of Blues with Jay Basist

Lisa's Coconut Cream Pie

My real recipe is as follows: Go online and find a flight to Shreveport, Louisiana. Book it. Drive to the airport and get on the plane. Upon arrival in Shreveport, rent a car, and drive as fast as you can to Strawn's Eat Shop. Get a table and order a coffee and a slice of their amazing coconut cream pie. Die and go to heaven. If you are unable to fly to Shreveport, check out my recipe below. It will make you want to die and go to heaven too!

1 cup white sugar
½ tsp. salt
¼ cup cornstarch
4 tsp. flour
3 cups whole milk
4 egg yolks, beaten
3 tbsp. butter
1 ½ tsp. vanilla
1 cup shredded, sweetened coconut, plus ½ cup for toasting (optional)
9-inch pie crust
Whipped cream

In a medium saucepan, combine sugar, salt, cornstarch, and flour. Gradually stir in 3 cups of milk. Cook over low heat, stirring constantly until mixture becomes thick and boils. Boil for 1 minute, still stirring. Remove from heat.

Place egg yolks in bowl. Whisk constantly, while combining with 1 cup of hot milk mixture. Mix egg mixture with remaining milk mixture. Bring mixture to slow boil. Boil for 1 minute and remove from heat.

Stirring constantly, combine butter, vanilla, and coconut into the hot mixture. Pour mixture into pie shell. Chill for at least 3 hours.

Top with whipped cream and toasted coconut (optional).

Toasted Coconut

Preheat oven to 350 degrees. Spread ½ cup of unsweetened coconut shavings, sweetened, shredded, or flaked coconut on a rimmed baking sheet and bake, stirring once or twice, until golden, about 5 to 10 minutes. If toasting sweetened coconut, check and stir more frequently because the added sugar causes irregular browning.

The famous Strawn's Eat Shop Coconut Pie

Photography by Diana Zollicoffer

Lisa with her mother, Ellie, and her grandmother, Catherine celebrating Catherine's one hundredth birthday; Lisa at 2010 Endymion Parade; The Myrtles Plantation Premiere Show, May 16, 2010; Strawn's Eat Shop in Shreveport; House of Blues New Orleans Premiere; Lisa and Peggy at SOUTH Santa Monica Show; Academy Award Party; Thanksgiving with mom

Peggy Sweeney-McDonald
President, Superstar Events—LA, Los Angeles
Meanwhile, Back at Café Du Monde . . .

"If I were a food, I'd be a gourmet chocolate. I'd come in a shiny gold box with a ribbon on top, sometimes sweet, sometimes bitter, or sometimes nutty or a tasty combination, but always a treat!"

In May of 1992, I moved back to Louisiana with my New Yorker fiancé, Jimmy McDonald, who came kicking and screaming. I had left Louisiana twelve years before after graduating from Louisiana State University with stars in my eyes and dreams of being an actress, but after struggling as a legal assistant with the occasional acting job, I was ready to go home. The last year in New York had been a tough one. Jimmy had been laid off as a result of the stock market crash and then was shot in the eye by a twelve-year-old kid with a pellet gun, while walking out of our apartment on the Upper East Side. I suggested a move to Louisiana might be good for us. He told me I was out of my fricken mind if I thought he would move to fricken Louisiana (well, that's the PG version). But, after lots of fights, tears, and threats, Jimmy went out to Rockaway to talk to his mother. She told him that if he couldn't imagine his life without me, then that was his answer—a wise woman!

The day we left New York, we made a final important stop at Carnegie Deli, our favorite, to pick up one more mile-high pastrami sandwich, pickles, coleslaw, spicy brown mustard, and extra rye bread. As we drove through the Lincoln Tunnel, I took the giant sandwich apart, divided the delicious, mouthwatering pastrami into smaller sandwiches with the extra bread—making it easier to "inhale" in the car—and headed south. This Southern belle was going home!

The first week in Louisiana, we found a great apartment in the warehouse district, found jobs, traded in the old Monte Carlo for a brand new Honda Accord, and set a date for our wedding at the St. Louis Cathedral.

The day the movers delivered our furniture to our fabulous apartment at 700 South Peters we were totally overwhelmed, surrounded by boxes, and didn't know where to begin unpacking. Jimmy was having a low blood sugar moment and looked at me and said, "I need to eat, let's get out of here"—so much for unpacking and getting settled. I suggested we go to the famous Camellia Grill for a great breakfast. It's a small diner where you sit at the counter, and I hadn't been there in years. The line was out the door and down the sidewalk, but I convinced him the amazing pecan waffles would be worth the wait. However, being the impatient New Yorker that he is, he just kept getting more annoyed! We were finally close to getting in the door when some college student rudely stepped in front of us to look at the menu on the wall. Jimmy looked at me and said "Damn tourist!" We had only been residents of New Orleans for a couple of hours and already considered ourselves locals.

Six months later on a cold, clear November day, with trumpets playing, the big doors of the St. Louis Cathedral opened up. On the arms of my daddy, I sashayed down the aisle as only true Southern belles can do, slowly stopping for pictures whenever I saw a camera. At that same moment, Jimmy, overcome with emotion, started tearing up. His dad saw this and got up from his pew to hug his son. Those who witnessed this special moment between father and son couldn't keep the tears back. After the wedding, we climbed into one of those grand, white mule-drawn carriages and headed to the reception at the Bourbon Orleans Hotel. Lots of delicious Creole food was served, cocktails flowed, and Joe Simon's jazz trio kept everyone on their feet dancing. The New Yorkers didn't know what hit them and were soon up on their feet joining in the New Orleans second line around the room, waving their napkins in the air!

Later that evening, we met all of our out-of-town friends at Pat O'Brien's patio bar, and around midnight, we ended up at Café Du Monde stuffing our faces with delicious beignets and café au lait, laughing at memories of the day and wiping powdered sugar off our faces, hands, and clothes. As we were peeling ourselves off those sticky green chairs, we saw Mike Spiro, a friend from New York at the takeout window. Mike and his wife, Lori, had decided this three-day wedding extravaganza was a nine-meal trip! "No sightseeing just let us know all the best restaurants in town!" They had been to dinner at Brennan's that night, and now he was picking up beignets to go, as the day would not be complete without beignets in bed! He had five orders to go. His wife is a size 2. So unfair!

With all this great food around, I knew I needed to find a walking buddy fast, and I did—Alden Lovelace, a Southern belle from Gulfport, Mississippi—practically "dripping from the magnolias." We would meet at 6:15 A.M. in the lobby of our building and walk briskly over by the aquarium, along the Mississippi River, around Jackson Square, and back. The smell of beignets frying would hit us as we passed Café Du Monde. The first time she said, "Smell the beignets. I could eat a dozen of them." "Yes," I replied, "It's heavenly. I think of them as little pillows of decadence, and one of these days, we should bring some money, stop, and order some to go." Although we craved that indulgence, we realized that would defeat the purpose of the early morning walks, so we never gave in to our beignet power-walk fantasy. Instead, we'd walk and discuss our favorite New Orleans restaurants and recipes. I remember one recipe she shared with me—Easy Delicious Crawfish Pasta, made with pasta, a bag of crawfish tails, a can of spicy tomatoes, and a block of cheese. She told me her guests flipped out over it, and all but licked the pot clean. They begged her for the recipe, but she claimed it was a secret family recipe. Funny thing about Alden and this recipe is that years later, she married a famous New Orleans chef. I have yet to ask her if she ever shared or made her easy crawfish pasta for Emeril!

Anytime Jimmy and I were in the French Quarter, we would always end up at Café Du Monde. Morning, noon, or night! We never discussed it. It was calling our name. We would automatically start walking there. Even if we had just finished a big, fancy dinner at NOLA, Antoine's, the Palace Café, sandwiches from Masperos, jambalaya from the Napoleon House, or gumbo from the Gumbo Shop, we were headed to our place. Even full, we could always find room to throw down a few beignets and delicious café au lait.

At one point, Café Du Monde started making iced café au laits! If you haven't dipped a hot beignet in an iced café au lait on a hot, sticky day, you haven't lived the whole Café Du Monde experience. It takes those little "pillows of decadence" to a whole new level.

Six years later, my wanderlust kicked in, and I decided it was time to move to Los Angeles. Jimmy's response was, "You're fricken kidding me, right?" The New Yorker had fallen in love with life in Louisiana, had learned to play golf, had his favorite cigar shop in the Quarter, made great friends, and loved all the great food. However, being the persuasive Southern belle that I am, he finally gave in and moved to Los Angeles, kicking and screaming! Before moving, we were at Café Du Monde one night, and I lifted my coffee cup, toasting my friends, and said, "Meanwhile, back at Café Du Monde." We all started laughing. The next time we were visiting, I said the same thing. Jimmy and our friends joined in by the time I got to "Café Du Monde," and we clinked cups on the dot, dot, dot. I remember saying, "One day that will be the name of a book, movie, play, or the story of my life."

So here I am thirteen years later, back home in Louisiana, where I have created a festive event celebrating our food experiences with the people I love!

No matter where I live and no matter what happens in my life, I always end up at Café Du Monde. You know what you are ordering, those little pillows of decadence. You know how it will taste, delicious. You know you can afford it, cheapest meal in New Orleans. And you know you are having a great time with good friends or family, and for a brief hour, you are totally in the moment—taking life one beignet at a time. So lift your glass, pretend it's one of those famous white porcelain cups and join me in saying, "Meanwhile, back at Café Du Monde . . ."

Peggy's Jammin' Jambalaya

When I lived in New York, every time I would visit my family in Baton Rouge, I would return to New York with Louisiana coffee, jambalaya mix, creole seasoning, red beans, and black-eyed peas. Once back in New York, I would invite my friends over for a great Louisiana dinner, and everyone raved about my jambalaya. Jimmy will tell you that I make the best jambalaya he has ever tasted! Yes, I cheat and use a jambalaya mix to start, as it makes a good base. I claim this is an award-winning recipe because I once won a company cook-off at one of my corporate jobs. Everyone knew the senior vice president did not like me, and I loved it when he realized he had just awarded my recipe the prize! I serve the jambalaya with coleslaw or green salad and hot French bread. It's even better the second day, so make enough for leftovers.

2 8-oz. packages Louisiana Jambalaya Mix,
or 1 12-16-oz. package family-style mix
1 large onion, chopped
1 bunch green onions, chopped
1 medium green bell pepper, chopped
1 medium red bell pepper, chopped
3 stalks celery, chopped
1 14.5-oz. can crushed tomatoes with juice (spicy/hot optional)
1 package beef or turkey sausage (spicy sausage optional)
1 lb. chicken breast, cut in bite-size pieces
Low-fat chicken broth, as directed for water on jambalaya package
Creole seasoning and hot pepper sauce, to taste

In large pot, sauté vegetables in cooking spray or butter until softened. Add the can of tomatoes with juice.

In separate frying pan, sauté sliced sausage. Remove. In same pan, sauté chicken until cooked. Add sausage and chicken to pot with vegetables.

Add Jambalaya Mix. Add chicken broth as directed for water on jambalaya package. Stir, bring to boil, turn to low, and cover. Cook per directions on package (usually 25 to 30 minutes).

Photograph by Diana Zollicoffer

Peggy and Jimmy McDonald at the Lyceum Show

Remove from heat and let sit for 30 minutes (to absorb extra fluid). Add hot sauce or Creole seasoning, to taste.

Serve with green salad or coleslaw, French bread, and butter.

Serves 12 to 15.

Peggy eating a beignet at Cafe Du Monde; Peggy with Leah Chase, New Orleans premiere show at House of Blues; Peggy and James "Jimmy" McDonald, Jr. wedding at St. Louis Cathedral, November 14, 1992; Peggy with her parents, Myles and Sherry Sweeney, at the premiere show at the Myrtles Plantation, May 16, 2010; Peggy and Jay Basist at Café Du Monde; Peggy and Baton Rouge Mayor Kip Holden; Peggy at the Santa Monica Show at Sonoma Wine Garden, February 2011; Peggy, Jimmy, and Nanny, Peggy's grandmother, second lining; The Sweeney Family, Christmas 2011

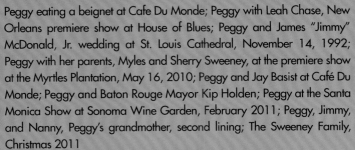

Jeff Kleinpeter
President, Kleinpeter Farms Dairy, Baton Rouge
Mooving Stories from a Fourth-Generation Milkaholic

"If I were a food, I'd be Crème de la Kleinpeter Caramel Pecan Fudge Ice Cream because why not be the best of the best!"

As a boy growing up within walking distance of our dairy farm, I grew to be very comfortable around cows. Often sitting on the cows' backs while they rested in the fields, my sisters, brothers, and cousins would pass the time talking about life, school, and things to come.

We were unaware that our farm life would change soon, mostly due to the growth of Baton Rouge. Little did we know or care that the lifestyles we led back then would become so very cherished before too long. And, little did we know that the things we learned would stick with us and become a way of life and a way of business.

Back then, we all learned to stick together and to rely on each other. We had some great times swimming in the lake behind our house with our horses. The first person would hold on to the horse's tail, and the second person would hold on to the first person's feet, and so on. If one person let go, the entire line following would have to swim to catch up to the horse again.

Growing up, we also learned that we rely on our cows to give us the best milk in the world. We rely on them, and they rely on us to feed them quality feeds, to take care of them when they are sick, and to always treat them well.

When the idea of having our own ice cream hit me—like a ton of you know what—it was a natural step to use local ingredients, such as Ponchatoula strawberries, Louisiana cane sugar, and Bergeron's pecans.

I would never dream of using anything other than Louisiana products. You see, reflecting back to my childhood, we "had to" rely on each other. There was no one else; we were out in the middle of nowhere, and all we had was each other. So now, fast forward to ice cream, and there you have it, relying on each other once again.

And what's not to love? Ponchatoula has the best-tasting strawberries in the world! Louisiana cane sugar is produced right here, and it's awesome! Bergeron's pecans have the greatest taste ever! And, as we all know, we've expanded our line to twenty-four flavors now, and each of them uses "something Louisiana."

And now, we even have a Super Premium Ice Cream line, called Crème de la Kleinpeter. Our trip to Bora Bora for our twenty-fifth wedding anniversary inspired this line, because while there, Debbie and I tasted Tahitian vanilla, and that flavor is dedicated to her inspiration.

And believe me, I'll stand up and fight for what's right at the drop of a hatpin. I'll do what's right for our company, for our neighbors, for my family, for Louisiana, and for our providers of Louisiana ingredients, and our entire team will go that extra mile for our customers.

Funny how those great things I learned as a kid still stick with me today, and I am passing them on to my daughter, Taylor. I guess it's called "values," and they are a part of me now. Even though the farm is now in Pine Grove, Louisiana, the values are still with me, right here in Baton Rouge, right where our family has been since 1774.

Vinni Villicano, Jeff, and Peggy with "Sweetie Pie" at pilot shoot; Kleinpeter Ice Cream; Peggy, Don Gerald, Jeff, Vinni, Melinda Walsh, Jay Basist, "Meanwhile, . . ." television pilot shoot; Grandfather, Leon R. "Papa" Kleinpeter, Sr.; "Sweetie Pie" born November 28, 2009, with natural heart on her forehead (the Kleinpeter logo); Shelly, Debbie, Jeff, Peggy, and Candy at Denims & Diamonds, Jeff as emcee at Baton Rouge Show; Jeff and his dog on the farm; Jeff and his wife, Debbie Kleinpeter

Chef Don Bergeron
Owner, Chef Don Bergeron Enterprises & Mid-City Market, Baton Rouge
Cooking on the Bayou

"If I were a food, I would be a crawfish, of course! Why? Because you get your tail pinched and your head sucked."

I guess I first learned you can create some magic in a kitchen at my Grandma Tute's house in Belle Rose, Louisiana, about five miles down the road from the big city of Donaldsonville. At Tute's house, everything was homemade, such as cream cheese, chicken pie, cakes, and jelly rolls. She even made her own ketchup. Can you imagine how cool you are to a five-year-old kid if you know how to make ketchup? And those jelly rolls were so good that my cousin and I hid in the bathroom with Grandma Tute's mixer and tried to make our own. They didn't exactly turn out the same.

Then one day, I went to Bellina's Grocery, our local Italian grocery, and I poked my head over the counter. I proudly explained to the store clerks that I intended to bake a cake just like Grandma Tute. The clerks loaded me up with all the ingredients I needed, and I baked a batch of cupcakes. Then I took them back to the store and presented them to the store clerks. I guess you could say it was the first time I catered. I was five. I'll never forget the look on their faces. It's a thrill that I still feel when I cook for people.

Grandma Tute passed her love of cooking down to my dad, Donnie Bergeron, and he passed it down to me. I started working in this business when I was fourteen at John Folse's restaurant, Lafitte's Landing. It's where I had my first cup of coffee. I had my first scotch there, too. I started out as a bus boy and a bartender. Yeah, I know I said I was fourteen—but hey, it's south Louisiana, what

can I say? And pretty soon, I was filling in when one of the cooks was out. As John Folse's business grew, so did my responsibilities. I even cooked all of the employee meals, and I have to say my daddy's meatballs and spaghetti were everyone's favorite.

It was at the restaurant where I met another incredible inspiration in my life. She was a retired schoolteacher and an artist named Marion Goodwin. Marion ate lunch at Lafitte's Landing every day, and she hired me to be her chauffeur. From the time I was about fifteen years old until I finished college, I drove her down to New Orleans to go to concerts and to go eat in all the best restaurants. What an education that was!

I spent fifteen years working for John Folse. I went on to be a managing partner at Jumelle's Restaurant in Baton Rouge, and then I left to pursue my gourmet catering business full time. It was what I really wanted to do. Things were going pretty well until Hurricane Katrina hit. When you run a small business and your customer base is wiped out, the business comes to a halt. One morning, I received a call asking if I could make one hundred sausage biscuits to feed the first responders who were rescuing people out of New Orleans. I said, "You bet I can." Soon I was cooking two thousand meals a day, working sixty-two straight days. At one point, I worked fifty-two straight hours without sleep, until I literally passed out in my office.

I could tell you some crazy stories about catering, like

the time I catered three parties on game day at Louisiana State University, and I took my bike with me so I could run from one party to the next. Just as I was speeding across campus to arrive at one of the parties, the Tiger Band started down the hill to the stadium and cut me off. Well, I had to get to my party, so I stashed my bike behind the Indian Mounds, sneaked over them, and worked my way down through the crowd. Then I arrived and found out we were running out of rib-eyes. And since we were right in the middle of campus and couldn't get in or out to go to a store, I called someone to go buy some more and meet me on the levee. So I biked to the levee, met the guy with the rib-eyes, stuffed the rib-eyes in my backpack, and pedaled my way back to the party, flying down Skip Bertman Drive! No one ever knew what I went through just to make sure everyone had a great steak before that game.

Oh, I've had plenty of great catering moments, such as cooking Gov. Edwin Edwards's farewell dinner before he left for prison. I prepared Beef Tenderloin with Caramelized Onions and Horseradish Cream as his entrée. After he finished enjoying his meal, his comment was "Son, your roast beef was as tender as the bun!"

In 2006, I traveled to Switzerland to cook for the closing soiree at the World Economic Forum in Davos, so we could remind people from around the world about New Orleans after Katrina. I was invited to cook there by the CEO of Zurich after he enjoyed my Speckled Trout with Jumbo Lump Crabmeat at a private party during the Zurich Classic. It was quite an honor! We had to send our list of ingredients over in advance, go through an extensive background check, and even wait through vehicle searches when we got there. We cooked all of the food offsite at a country club and then brought fifteen hundred meals through X-ray machines to the party. Zurich hosted this great party! We had cooked all day and hadn't eaten a bite, and the only thing left was some jambalaya. So we sat on the side of the road and ate jambalaya out of a bucket and drank Dom Pérignon. It was an experience I'll never forget.

I've traveled a lot with the Louisiana Office of Tourism, introducing Louisiana cuisine to people everywhere. I've visited Canada, Colombia, France, Germany, Korea, Mexico, Switzerland, and Taiwan, not to mention hundreds of places across the United States to promote Louisiana food.

Two days after Hurricane Gustav hit Baton Rouge in 2008, we opened our Mid-City Market on Jefferson Highway. I leased the space joining my office and catering kitchen to open a storefront. My plans were in progress when Baton Rouge was devastated by the storm. We were on generator power again, just like Katrina, and had entered disaster-feeding mode to supply meals for the hundreds of emergency responders. The energy company had been working to clear the trees and power up areas of Baton Rouge, and I was cooking as fast as I could! One day, while the energy crews were working, my "Open" sign came on during a power surge, and people began lining up outside the door. That was my first day of business, and we haven't closed the doors since. We do hot plate lunches and dinners every day for takeout, like Tute used to cook. We also make "take and bake" casseroles, soups and gumbos, appetizers, and my famous Mid-City Market Chicken Salad. We also have this great Catering-to-Go option that's been a great success.

In 2010, I received an honor that made me feel as if I had finally arrived. It's something of which I am very proud. I was named 2009 Chef of the Year by the American Culinary Federation's Baton Rouge Chapter. This year, I was named Baton Rouge's Best Caterer by the readership of 225 Magazine. I'm pretty proud, and I think Grandma Tute is proud, too.

My dad was probably my greatest inspiration, and it's not easy to talk about. Along with Grandma Tute's and a few favorites from my mama, I still use many of my daddy's special recipes in my business every day. When he got sick, I thankfully had the opportunity to move home. I cooked for him every day before he passed away. The last meal I prepared for him was crawfish stew. Although he wasn't well, I think he enjoyed it.

One of my greatest childhood memories is of the trips he took us on to Grand Isle, where we literally slept on the beach. The girls slept in tents, while the boys slept on cots under the stars. We caught all of our food, and we cooked it right there. It really was the best of times. I remember my dad taught us to bury a watermelon in the sand to keep it out of the sun because the water would keep it cool. So we buried our watermelon and marked the spot where it was with a big X. Then the tide came in and washed the X away, and we never could find that watermelon. Every year when we went back to Grand Isle, my dad would say, "Better look for that watermelon." I can't go to Grand Isle without thinking of those summers.

I have a great family. There are thirty-five people in my immediate family, so let's face it—any time we get together for dinner, it's a catered event and guess who ends up cooking? But it's what I love to do! I've got wonderful friends, fantastic customers, and a terrific staff at Chef Don Bergeron Enterprises and Mid-City Market. I'd like to think that all the love that has come my way over the years is somehow passed along to you in the food that I cook, thanks to the inspiration from Grandma Tute and Daddy!

Grandma Tute's Pecan Kisses

I thank Daddy and Grandma Tute for their cooking inspiration, and I think about them all the time, especially around the holidays. I still make one of their favorite desserts around the holidays—something Grandma Tute called "Kisses"—which are similar to sea-foam divinity—little meringue treats with fresh pecans. Enjoy!

2 egg whites, room temperature
½ tsp. cream of tartar
Pinch of salt
¾ cup sugar
1 cup chopped pecans
½ tsp. vanilla

Beat egg whites with cream of tartar and salt until stiff peaks. Blend in sugar until well incorporated. Fold in pecans and vanilla. Spoon out onto parchment paper a nice dollop about the size of a walnut. Bake in a preheated 250 degree oven for about 30 minutes.

Turn oven off and leave in oven another 30 minutes.

Chef Don with Linda Price-Thomas, director of sales and marketing at Chef Don Bergeron Enterprises; Sammy, Don, Amy, Rick, Michael; Chef Don and sister, Amy, and the bread pudding; Carving for family Christmas dinner; Uncle Bud, Aunt Joyce, Betsy (mom), Don, Aunt Judy, and Amy; Chef Don Bergeron at the one-year anniversary show at Juban's Restaurant

Drew Ramsey
Owner, Hubig's Pies, New Orleans
Da Pie Man

"If I were a food, I'd be a diabetic- and vegan-friendly, fat-free, sugar-free Hubig Pie, and I'd make a fortune!"

I am a simple man. I enjoy the simple pleasures in life. I make pies five days a week with the ingredients of sugar, flour, fruit, and fat—the good 'ol fat—lard. My father taught me to make them, and his father taught him. The same machines have been used to make these pies in the same factory for about a century. Some of the employees have worked with us for fifty years. These longtime employees occasionally work alongside their spouses and their grown kids.

Simon Hubig was a German baker who learned the trade from his mother. He had a string of bakeries in the southeast, and all but the New Orleans bakery failed in the depression. My grandfather, Otto Ramsey, owned part of that bakery and taught the trade to my father, Toby. I started out as a delivery driver, waking long before dawn to deliver warm pies to the customers on my route. I worked every station in the factory from dough, filling, fry duty, and wrapping. I'm a few decades into the position I call "passe-par-tout." The literal translation is "all-purpose" or "key for all locks," which means when the dough man doesn't show-up—I make dough. Work in a bakery is never done.

Our pies have long been a staple in local homes, gas stations, and other pit stops. They're even served to inmates in the Orleans Parish Prison. In 2005, Hubig's joined forces with the Police Association of New Orleans to hand out pies to the officers who were on Mardi Gras parade duty.

Something you may not know that Hurricanes Betsy and Katrina have in common is that Hubig's Pies were readily available immediately after the storm passed and were given away to those in New Orleans when the rain let up. The pies were made in advance of each storm's landfall and have the shelf life of about one week. What we didn't realize while handing out pies to those folks at the Superdome one day post-Katrina was just how long it would be before we had the ability to make another one—132 days after Hurricane Katrina.

It's funny what comforts people. Savory Simon, the bakery mascot, emblazons the T-shirts the employees wear, from the low man on the totem pole on up. After Katrina, my father was driving back into New Orleans. He didn't have any official capacity and others were getting turned away, unable to get past the blockades. What he did have on was a Hubig's T-shirt. The Kansas National Guardsmen at the Orleans/Jefferson line were directing him back to where he came from when an NOPD officer walked up and asked, "Are you the man who gives us the pies?" And in he was ushered.

Of course, life, in and out of the factory, has not been the same since that time. Hubig's launched a website in late 2005, kicking and screaming its way into the digital age but we were incredibly grateful that post Katrina we were able to sell our T-shirts online and survive the months before we could make pies again.

I am a simple man, making simple pies; I am a simple man who was amazed and astonished that on our first trip back down the parade route in 2006, people clapped, cheered, and cried when they saw us handing out our little fried pies.

Drew with his wife, Kathleen, and daughters, Margo and Grace; Drew at work; Drew in the New Oleans show at Ralph & Kacoo's Restaurant, October 2010; Margo Ramsey; Drew, Vinni Villicano, and Peggy at "Meanwhile, . . ." TV pilot shoot; Hubig's pies; Drew with his wife, Kathleen, and their daughters, Margo and Grace; Hubig's Pies on conveyor belt; Drew with Hubig's team members packing pies.

Leah Chase
Owner, Dooky Chase Restaurant, New Orleans
"I Say Like This"

"If I were a food, I'd have to pick something that everyone liked, so I would pick a good chicken breast stuffed with oyster dressing or a shrimp Clemenceau or meatballs and spaghetti, because that's my all-time favorite!"

I grew up in the country in Madisonville, Louisiana, across the lake from New Orleans. My mother did not like to cook, and I can't blame her as there were eleven of us, so it was like cooking for an army every day. She did love to make homemade bread every day. It was delicious bread and cinnamon rolls, but we would always ask for store bought bread! We didn't have pain perdue (French toast) because there weren't any leftovers in my family. These days, I hear all the time that children can't learn because they aren't eating a balanced breakfast. Well, we learned and all we had to eat for breakfast was bread, butter, jam, and a big cup of cocoa. On Sunday, we would have a big breakfast. We had our big meal for lunch and at night a light supper with toast or jam. We sat down for every meal with the family at the table, and it could have been a simple meal like beans, rice, and a piece of bread. We didn't have meat or chicken every day.

We grew up growing strawberries, and we would take the culls (which are the strawberries that were too ripe to ship—but were dark red and delicious) and my Daddy would make the best strawberry wine. We would enjoy it with every meal. We didn't have root beer, soda, or iced tea, maybe lemonade every now and then, but we had delicious strawberry wine often. Even when we were young, our parents would put a couple of tablespoons of the wine and sugar in water. As we became older, they would add more wine and less water.

I came to New Orleans when I was thirteen to live with my aunt and go to high school. After high school, most girls my age were working at a sewing factory, but I wanted to work in the French Quarter. I went to work at the Colonial Restaurant, and I loved it. I fell in love with the restaurant business and with my customers. I've waited on everyone from Tennessee Williams to Lena Horne.

When I started waiting tables, I didn't know it was going to be the beginning of my life in the kitchen. I met my husband, Edgar Dooky Chase, Jr. in 1945. He was a musician, and we were married within a couple of months. He had his own band and was a trumpet player and composer. His family had opened a small sandwich shop in 1941 that sold po' boys. Dooky and I both ended up working there, and I started cooking in the kitchen.

The restaurant would soon become a very popular Creole restaurant, and I've been there ever since. At that time, people were cooking in their homes; they didn't go out to eat. If you came out, it was to have a few drinks and to have an oyster sandwich or something you didn't typically eat at home. Once wives started working, people started going out to eat more, and I think that's when everyone left the table and stopped having dinner together. This is one of the reasons I started a takeout business here at the restaurant; I wanted people to be able to pick up a quart of gumbo or meatballs, go home, and enjoy dinner together with their family—at the table with their little children. It is so important for families to dine together.

President Bush came in to eat at the restaurant. He was such a nice man even though I didn't agree with his politics. President Obama came here before he won the election. Dr. Norman Francis brought him in, and he wanted fried chicken but was in a hurry. I said, "Mr. Obama, sit down and I'll serve you some gumbo while we cook the chicken, and you can take it with you on the plane." So I served him some gumbo and what did he do, he reached for the hot sauce! I immediately said, "Mr. Obama, nobody puts hot sauce on my gumbo!" I guess that was my first falling out with the president.

During Hurricane Katrina, we had five feet of water in the bar and two and a half feet of water in the restaurant. We lost everything—except the art. The New York Fire Department came, and they were lifesavers. By the time they got to New Orleans, our fire department and police department were exhausted. The New Yorkers helped load the art and moved it to Baton Rouge. I have collected art since the seventies and was so blessed and overjoyed that we didn't lose it. We were closed for two and a half years after Katrina. I first went to Birmingham to stay with my granddaughter, and I cooked in her kitchen every day. At one time, we had fifty people in her house—my family, her husband's family, and more. Cooking was my therapy. My son and daughter-in-law rented a house in Baton Rouge, so we moved there, and at one time, they had fifteen people living there. I cooked there too.

There was a lovely woman in Baton Rouge, Lynn Mitchell, who wrote a story about me in the paper and introduced me to a woman who owned the Pan Handler, a store that sold kitchenware and had space for cooking demonstrations. She let me come in and do demonstrations, and I was able to keep all of the money. I'll never forget it. I would cook and serve ten people three times a week. I remember doing BBQ ribs over sweet potatoes and a delicious quail. I met some lovely people in Baton Rouge, and they were so kind to me. They all helped me out. Cooking has always brought me happiness.

The day we reopened Dooky Chase is one of the happiest days of my life. Chef John Folse helped me to reopen my restaurant.

He said, "Leah, we are going to make Gumbo Z'herbes, and we aren't going to charge a penny, and I'm going to bring in everything—china, linens, glasses, and the ingredients for the gumbo." He said, "We will cook and just give it away!" It was so wonderful to see people come after the storm. People came from all over to help us. Now you don't need to help us clean up, but just come help give us the push forward! We are going to do alright in this city. Every day I get up and say, "Thank You God, I'm up!" When I go to sleep, I say, "Thank You God for this day!"

What I love about New Orleans is that there is at least one good cook in every family, so every family has someone to cook good food. That's why New Orleans people love their food, and if you go to their homes, they will prepare you something nice to eat and will do it with all their heart. That's in all the homes here—rich, poor, white, black. We enjoy cooking and we enjoy inviting people to our homes. I like people coming to the table and sitting together to eat.

Don't think you are going to come eat in five minutes and run. We want you to sit down, savor your food, and enjoy it. We "sit to the table" and enjoy the company we are in. You could have a zillion restaurants in New Orleans, and they would all do well, because people here love to go out to eat. I love to go out, to be waited on, and to pretend I'm a queen. You could feed me wood, but as long as you served me properly, I would love it. I don't think you can find a bad meal in this city, and I never go to a restaurant where you don't see the owner. The owners are always there so I get to see my friends!

The first time I went to Café Du Monde was when I was young and working in the Quarter, and we went late at night after work. My problem is I can't eat just one beignet. It's hard to stop. If I ordered a dozen, I would eat every one of them! I tell people don't worry about the powdered sugar; it's going to get on you, your clothes, and all over the floor. Just eat the beignets and enjoy them because they are really a great thing. The funny thing is that you can't replicate them at home even if you try to make them because they just don't taste the way they do when actually at Café Du Monde! It's amazing!

Shrimp Clemenceau

I created this recipe about forty years ago. You may find many Clemenceau recipes in New Orleans restaurants with different vegetables. Most of the time, I don't use wine, but sometimes I add it to kick it up. You can substitute chicken instead of shrimp. It's a simple and delicious recipe. You can cook it in ten minutes, and your guests will think you were cooking all day long.

1 stick butter
2 medium potatoes, peeled and diced small
2 lb. small or medium shrimp, peeled and deveined
2 cloves garlic, finely chopped
½ cup button mushrooms
1 cup green peas
¼ tsp. chopped fresh parsley
½ cup white wine (optional)
Salt and pepper, to taste

Melt butter in 2-qt. saucepan. Add potatoes. Cook 5 minutes. Add shrimp, garlic, and mushrooms. Cook until shrimp are tender. Add peas, parsley, and wine. Salt and pepper to taste.

Cook for 5 more minutes. Serve with a nice green salad and French bread.

Serves 4.

Leah Chase with grandson Edgar Chase IV, and his wife, Gretchen Fauria at the House of Blues Premiere show; Leah in the New Orleans House of Blues premier show, June 2010; Leah in the Dooky Chase dining room; Leah with her daughters Leah (left) and Stella (right); The Leah Chase Gallery at the Southern Food and Beverage Museum; House of Blues Show July 2010; Frying chicken; Greeting guests from Washington, D.C.; Leah Chase with Peggy and Jay and friends at Dooky Chase the day after the New Orleans premiere

Edgar Chase
Graduate, Le Cordon Bleu Paris, and Chef,
Dooky Chase Restaurant, New Orleans
Introduction to Leah's Kitchen

"If I were a food I would be gumbo, because you get a taste of everything and it never misses a holiday!"

Growing up in a family-owned business, every child, grandchild, and cousin's first job was at Dooky Chase Restaurant. Whether it was a bus boy, waiter, or dishwasher, you name it and family members did it. I started as a bus boy, but my main interest was in the back, so I started washing dishes. I would receive my opportunity to join the kitchen when my grandmother, Leah Chase, would say, "Trevor, Travis, Rob, Wayne . . ." None of those are my name, but then came "Lil Boy, bring me a pot from over there." I was excited to grab the pot.

Let me briefly describe Mrs. Chase's kitchen. It has about twenty-five to thirty pots that are older than I am and they all look brand new. I had no clue; I grabbed one and brought it to her. "This boy don't know which pot to boil rice in." Eventually, I learned.

Then it was utensils. She would say "Dook, bring me a chef's knife." I thought this was an easy one. She's a chef and these are her knives. So I guess these are chef knives. Boy was I wrong! After learning all sorts of knives, she threw a curve ball at me. "Get me a China cap." In my mind, I was like "A what? China cap?" I didn't know what to look for. So I walked to another kitchen and asked my cousin Cleo. "Cleo, I need a China cap," and she showed me a coned-shaped strainer. So now I had the pots and utensils down, and I was feeling good.

Next came the ingredients. "Dook, bring me the onions, garlic, bell pepper, celery, parsley, basil." Then on to the spice rack—"Bring me some ground thyme, look for it in a jar that says 'I'm Ground Thyme!'" Things are going well, but I still had not received the official introduction to Leah's Kitchen. It's not the pots, utensils, or ingredients. It's a phrase and not said much, but everyone who works there knows it. When you hear it, you smile and say, "Thank you, Mrs. Chase." One summer day, I was helping in the kitchen for a party. She came over, looked at what I was doing, and said, "You stupid jackass." There was the official introduction. I smiled, said thank you, and knew whatever I was doing not to do it again.

Years later, I headed to Paris, France, to attend Le Cordon Bleu Culinary Arts School. I enrolled in the intensive program, and I was pretty much in school from 8:00 A.M. to 8:30 P.M. Being ambitious and wanting to experience working in a French restaurant, I worked Friday and Saturday, which were the days I was out of school. I lasted a month before I decided to start visiting Europe on my days off, so there went the job. After I graduated, I returned home to work full time with my grandmother at Dooky Chase Restaurant or as she would put it "Le Cordon Noir."

Recently, my new lifetime job and the best thing I could ever imagine is my family—my wife, Gretchen, and our baby girl, Sydney Vaughn Chase. Coming from such a big family, Sydney makes number twenty-one of my grandmother's twenty-two great grandchildren, which means we have a lot of first-time jobs coming up and a few more official introductions to Leah's Kitchen.

Edgar Chase in House of Blues New Orleans Show, July 2010; Edgar Chase with wife, Gretchen Fauria; Edgar with Gretchen watching his grandmother, Leah Chase, at the New Orleans premiere show, June 2010; Leah Chase, Gretchen, and Edgar at premiere show; Edgar at Le Cordon Bleu class making duck; Edgar, wife, Gretchen Fauria, and daughter, Sydney Vaughn

Nell Nolan
Social Columnist, *New Orleans Times-Picayune;*
Actress and Educator, New Orleans
Pineapple in a Can

"If I were a food, I would be peanut butter. It is tasty, nutritious, good on almost everything, and you don't have to cook it."

Until I was ten years old—maybe twelve—I thought pineapple came in a can, only in a can, in little yellow slices. That was part of the meal my sister, Margie, and I prepared for our younger siblings on almost every Sunday night—pineapple in a can and spaghetti in a can. We would turn on the gas stove and dump the latter contents into a pot. We stirred it up, added the pineapple and a bit of parsley on the plates, and fed T., Phil, Jerry, Betty, and Nancy, our brothers and sisters. Sunday night was the date night for my beautiful mother and handsome father, who would go out to eat with the likes of Bunny and Eddie or Jackie and Walter, and Margie and I fixed dinner.

My mother didn't cook. I never remember her in the kitchen, and our kitchen, in a huge house, was relatively tiny. With seven children all within ten years, my mother told my father that she could either take care of the children or cook. She believed she couldn't do both. And what she really wanted to do, and did lovingly, was to care for us. So we had cooks at various times by the names of Geneva, Carrie, and Annie Lee. Carrie was a puzzle. She called my distinguished grandfather "Popie" and the epileptic dog, "Mr. Ace." *Mister Ace!* One day I entered the kitchen to see her looking out over the backyard, most intent. When I asked her what she was looking at, Carrie turned to me and said, "Mr. Ace trowing a fit." Ah! Tales of the kitchen.

Years later, when I was about to be married, I told my mother that I didn't know how to cook. "Don't worry," she said, "You can read." And so I did in the early stages. I read and prepared such fabulous dishes as beef Wellington, etc., etc. My attitude now follows the philosophy of "been there, cooked that."

Now I know why God invented restaurants. Praise be the Lord!

Children didn't go out to eat when I was growing up like they do now. We were numerous and the Frostop was about the most kid-friendly, affordable spot for a brood. But on special occasions, our parents would take us to a restaurant. They would bring just one child to accompany the two of them. How special it was to be one on one with a mother and father and to see the excitement of a lively eatery! However, I couldn't understand why Galatoire's didn't have the grilled cheese sandwich that I wanted, which had become another item I could cook, as was egg-milk. (Well, I really didn't "cook" it, the egg-milk.) Getting all seven of us off to school in the morning was a feat, and Margie and I concocted sort of a smoothie with milk, eggs, and vanilla or Ovaltine and whirred it all up in a blender. To this day, I'm still quite dexterous breaking an egg with one hand and plopping it into a pot or pan.

Another restaurant that figured in my early life was Commander's. We referred to it as Commander's, never Commander's Palace. It was on the same block in the Garden District as our family home, and once in a blue moon, when an aunt or relative would visit, I would be included with the grown-ups in their dinner party. Our family house, which we had since 1872, and which was the third "star" in the film *The Curious Case of Benjamin Button*, along with Brad Pitt and Cate Blanchett, was sold very recently. I heard from the realtors that as they showed the house to prospective buyers that a couple of them asked, "Where's the kitchen?" Sure, we had the smallish actual kitchen, but then there was the pantry, the breakfast room, and the butler's pantry, all in a unit. My response to that stupid question would have been, "Just eat at Commander's."

My grandmother, my mother's mother, loved to cook. She was creative and energetic, and when Margie and I would visit her and our grandfather each summer at their ranch-style house in Clinton, Kentucky, we had fabulous food. There was one exception for me—peaches. I just couldn't do them; they didn't work for me. I would sit at the dining room table for what seemed like hours, and when Mom, our grandmother, wasn't looking, I'd mash the peach to the underside of the table. Not liking peaches, or for that manner any kind of cooked fruit (except Bananas Foster), I found a sweet balance in Mom's chocolate-chip cookies—the best I've ever eaten and, as a cookie, only rivaled by Miss Cathy's Brownies at Holy Name of Jesus School.

In my own way, I was adventurous and became the first in my young high school crowd to try an oyster. Loved it! You can just imagine how some of my buddies described them. (Let your imagination come up with the adjectives.) After I finished college in three years, I raced to Paris to live and eat, and the culinary adventures continued.

The widow in whose household I lived was the cooking editor for *Elle* magazine, and we dined like little monarchs. I remember one special assignment that she had—to prepare a spectacular meal with all the proper place settings and to photograph it as a slide so that housewives could pop the picture into some device to see how the completed meal should look. We can't fathom that nowadays, especially the time spent and the fuss. But Mme. Valluet plugged ahead and son Bruno dutifully took the pictures every night. Then we sat to supper. One day, I returned to the house to find her really, really upset. Bruno's camera had been on the blink and none of the photos came out. All that work was for nothing! I also learned a few new French words that don't figure in most dictionaries. Ahem!

I admire my family and buddies who take great joy in the kitchen, and I duly appreciate what they create for both pleasure and for necessity. One does have to feed one's family. I enjoy reading recipes and imagining the delicious results, and, of course, as a New Orleanian, I can't get enough of our good restaurant food and the pleasures of eating out.

But my mind often wanders back to myself as a youngster— sort of like Proust and the madeleine—when the can opener and the can of pineapple made me feel like a great chef.

Pineapple Upside-Down Cupcakes

I am not a cook and certainly not a baker, but with my story being titled "Pineapple in a Can," I thought it would be appropriate to have a recipe for a pineapple upside-down cake—the cake that was very popular growing up in the sixties! This is an updated version in a cupcake form, which seems to be all the rage these days. Everyone loves a cupcake almost as much as a beignet!

Topping

    1 stick of unsalted butter, melted
    ¾ cup light brown sugar, firmly packed
    1 20-oz. can crushed pineapple, drained, juice reserved
    1 cup of chopped pecans
    12 maraschino cherries, drained and halved

Cupcakes

    1 18.25-oz. box yellow cake mix
    1 cup sour cream
    1 small box of instant vanilla pudding mix
    ½ cup pineapple juice, reserved from crushed pineapple
    ⅓ cup vegetable oil
    4 large eggs
    1 tsp vanilla extract

Place a rack in the center of oven and preheat to 350 degrees F. Lightly mist 24 cupcake cups with cooking spray and dust with flour.

For the topping, measure 1 tsp. of melted butter into each cupcake cup. Sprinkle 1 heaping tsp. of brown sugar on top of the butter. Spread about 1 tbsp. pineapple on top of the sugar, 1 tbsp. of chopped pecans, and place a maraschino cherry half in the center of the pineapple, pushing it down so the cherry touches the pan. Set pans aside.

For the cupcakes, blend cake mix, sour cream, pudding mix, pineapple juice, oil, eggs, and vanilla in a large bowl with an electric mixer on low speed for 30 seconds, increase the mixer speed to medium and beat for 2 minutes more, or until batter is thick and smooth, scraping sides of bowl, if needed. Spoon ⅓ cup batter onto the topping in each of the cupcake cups.

Bake until cakes are golden, 18 to 20 minutes. Immediately run a knife around the edges of the cupcakes to loosen. Invert onto a platter and cool for at least 15 minutes before serving.

Serve each cupcake with a scoop of vanilla ice cream.

Serves 24.

Nell Nolan with emcee Eric Paulsen at the New Orleans show at Ralph & Kacoo's Restaurant, October, 2010; Dancer in *The Merry Widow*, April 2005; Saints fan; The Nolan Children: Nell, Phil, T., Margie, Jerry, Betty, and Nancy (Photography by Gittings); Commander's Palace Restaurant; The former Uptown Nolan Family Residence; The Nolan Family: Mary Nell Nolan with Nancy on lap, Margie seated and standing: T., Phil, Jerry, Nell, and Betty. (Photography by Gittings)

Melvin L. "Kip" Holden
Mayor, City of Baton Rouge, and President,
East Baton Rouge Parish, Baton Rouge
The Mayor's Food Memories

"If I were a food, I'd be a peach, because it's warm and fuzzy."

I have had the wonderful opportunity to welcome people from all over the world to Baton Rouge, and what I hear from almost everyone who visits here is that the friendly people and delicious food make them want to come back often. From our fantastic restaurants to our cultural heritage festivals to tailgating at Louisiana State University and Southern University football games, Baton Rouge brings people together around good food to create lasting memories.

When I think of some of my memories of family dinners, I begin with my days growing up when we really didn't have a lot of food. My dad was a hunter, and in the afternoon, he would come home, grab his gun, go out hunting, and come back with a bag full of squirrels, rabbits, or possums. Those animals were the main staples on our dinner table, and my mom would cook delicious mustard or collard greens, sweet potatoes, and cornbread to round out the meal. We also ate a lot of grits. Even on those days when we didn't have enough to eat, we still had one of my favorites, mayonnaise sandwiches. Trust me, the mayo sandwich is not a building block for a healthy diet, but as a kid, I liked it just fine.

When I was first running for mayor, I wanted to hold a fundraiser that would highlight our food culture in Baton Rouge, bringing soul food and seafood together. So we created "Chitlins on the Half Shell." To raise money, we sold dinners of fried chicken, fried fish, and "chitlins."

When I was reelected in 2008, I spent my last day campaigning before Election Day with Mama Marino, the matriarch of Gino's Italian Restaurant, "*where mama still does the cooking,*" and spent the day in the kitchen with her learning how to make a perfect sauce before hitting the campaign trail for some last-minute stops. It was a wonderful way to relax at the end of a political campaign, with great friends, great food, and a reminder of what makes Baton Rouge so special.

When I go grocery shopping these days, some people seem to think it's funny. I can see them thinking, "What is this guy doing in the grocery? You mean he cooks, too?" The truth is, I've been doing the grocery shopping for my family for thirty years. When you go home, the mayor title goes away, and you're just a husband and a dad. I also do a lot of the cooking for our family dinners, tailgate parties, and holiday meals. It's something I have always enjoyed.

My favorite thing to cook are Kippy Burgers, and I'll share my secret recipe with you. I use fresh ground meat and add garlic and onion powder, and then I add teriyaki sauce, some dried onion and mushroom sauce, and fresh-cut onions. I mix it all up, make my hamburger patties, and throw them on the grill, and there you have my famous Kippy Burgers.

For almost every fond memory I have of times spent with family and friends, I can think of a good meal we shared. It just seems to be a part of our culture in Baton Rouge. Whether it's a simple home-cooked meal or dinner at one of our finest restaurants, we make memories that last a lifetime when we serve up something tasty to spice up the conversation.

Mayor Kip Holden enjoying the Anniversary show, May 12, 2011 at Juban's Restaurant; At Gino's Italian Restaurant with Matriarch Mama Marina; Presenting his monologue at the anniversary show; At the Healthy Baton Rouge Farmers Market event with NBA star Glen Davis and wife, Lois; With friends at the show: John and Janet Young and Bob and Alice Greer; With wife, Lois, and sons, Myron and Brian, being inducted into the LSU Hall of Distinction; Kip and his wife at the Bayou Country Fest in Baton Rouge

Marlyn Monette
Cookbook Author, *So Good . . . Make You Slap Your Mama!* *Volumes I and II,* and Columnist, *Times of Shreveport,* Shreveport

The Joys and Woes of the Southern Freezer

"If I were a food, I would be a watermelon. There's nothing prettier or more refreshing than a slice of pink watermelon on a hot summer day! Watermelon is healthy, a natural diuretic, and is rumored to enhance the libido. Watermelon is the life of the party!"

Growing up in South Louisiana is the ultimate "food" experience, for everyday life revolves around the kitchen table and what's for dinner.

Also playing a major part in this wildlife paradise is the freezer! Yes, it is a status symbol. How big is your freezer? Show me yours, and I'll show you mine. Ever ride through the streets of a small Cajun town, such as Grand Isle or Golden Meadow? Their chest freezers are proudly displayed on the front porch. It could be pride, or it could be that there's no room in the house for it.

When my kids were young, our two freezers were always filled to capacity with the bounty of the fishing and hunting season—shrimp, crabs, speckled trout, ducks, geese, deer. Believe it or not a freezer played a part in the property settlement of my first marriage. My husband got the wildlife, and wouldn't you know it, I got the kids!

I believe the old neighbors are still talking about divvy-up day when he walked to his car with a frozen alligator tail tucked under his arm! Definitely a Kodak moment!

In July we had a freezer malfunction—an experience that most freezer owners have had at one time or another. These episodes are "silent destroyers," for they often go unnoticed until it's too late and all your precious bounty from sea and shore is no more!

That fateful morning began as usual, with my husband, Ed, waking me at 6:00 A.M., as he left to work out. Within seconds, he was back saying, "You won't believe what's happened!" What a wake-up call!

I sleepily followed him to the garage where our full-to-capacity freezer was emitting water that smelled like the Gulf of Mexico. My astute better half commented, "Food's thawed," and with that, he flipped the breaker back on and shut the freezer! Out of sight, out of mind! He then climbed into his shiny red convertible and took off as I stood there in my nightgown! My first thought was "Surely, I am hallucinating. He is not leaving me with this dilemma." I won't share my second and subsequent thoughts.

Now, it's a known fact that a gal who hails from south Louisiana (aka hurricane alley) knows exactly what to do in a case like this.

The food that is still icy cold must be cooked—and soon. In our case, there was lump crabmeat, fresh Gulf oysters, sixteen pounds of shrimp, salmon, and speckled trout. And that's only the seafood. There was also venison, beef, pork, and chicken.

I quickly disposed of the bad food and refrigerated the good. When the freezer was clean as a whistle, I sat at my computer to compose an e-mail to friends and family. I'm a writer, and I needed to vent! This resulted in many offers of help, plus stories of personal freezer experiences.

I also got a call from Ed, telling me he felt awful about deserting me and was coming home to help me cook. I declined, knowing that any prolonged togetherness that day would be "too much sugar for a dime!"

My daughter Debbie called with advice: "Mom, when my freezer in the garage went out, I didn't replace it but instead use only the freezer of the refrigerator. Right now, it contains four bottles of vodka (Absolute, blueberry, Kettle One, and pepper) and a bag of chicken breasts." Way to go, Deb!

One friend suggested I "roll up my sleeves, cook it all, and send out invitations to a pot luck dinner at $40 per person contribution to Marlyn's Cook-Off Philanthropy." Deb countered this plan, stating hers was better. She could cook her chicken breasts and throw a martini party with less labor.

What I did at that point was what any prudent woman would do. I rolled up my sleeves and headed for the kitchen, where I stayed for two days preparing dishes that could be cooked and refrozen.

I began by peeling the sixteen pounds of shrimp, and then made seafood gumbo, shrimp Creole, and a gourmet company seafood casserole. For dinner we had scalloped oysters, Ed's favorite dish. Since this dish cannot be frozen, we ate it hot and bubbly from the oven. The poor man was relieved my early morning madness was over, and he gladly washed the dishes.

Day two produced a double batch of Crabmeat Elegante, MeMe's French Daube and Spaghetti, and baked Cornish hen with an apricot, honey, and sherry glaze. I cooked pork loins, tenderloins, and rump roast.

On the third day, I rested.

The Good Book teaches us not to worry about "what we will eat" and assures us "life is more than food." Goodness knows I was swollen up with pride over the treasures in that freezer. There's a load off my mind now for I have taken Debbie's sage advice and scaled down.

Life is simple now that Ed and I have come to an agreement that in the future the only "goose" to be found in our freezer is the grey kind that's 100 proof and comes in a bottle!

Tequila Shrimp

This simple to make recipe, served with fluffy long-grain rice or angel hair pasta, is a delectable entrée for any meal—a luncheon for the ladies or dinner party for twelve. Serve with steamed fresh asparagus and/or Caesar salad.

2 lb. large fresh shrimp, unpeeled
1 large onion, finely chopped
2 cloves garlic, minced
2 jalapeño peppers, seeded and minced
2 tbsp. pure olive oil
¼ cup orange juice
¼ cup lime juice
½ tsp. salt
¼ tsp. ground cumin
¼ cup tequila
½ cup whipping cream
1 tbsp. tomato paste
¼ cup chopped fresh cilantro
Hot cooked rice or thin spaghetti

Peel shrimp and devein.

Sauté onion, garlic, and jalapeño peppers in hot olive oil in a large 5-qt. sauté pan over medium heat for 5 minutes or until tender. Add shrimp, orange juice, and next 3 ingredients; sauté 3 minutes.

Stir in tequila and next 3 ingredients and cook until slightly thickened. Serve over rice or pasta.

Serves 4.

Lime Parfait

For dessert, keep it light with my prizewinning Lime Parfait. Not only is it mouthwateringly delicious, it also makes a beautiful presentation in a stemmed cocktail glass. Dollop with whipped cream and garnish with strawberry, kiwi slices, and a touch of mint. This luscious treat will please even the most discriminating palate.

1 14-oz. can condensed milk
5 egg yolks
4 oz. Key lime juice
1 8-oz. pound cake
⅔ cup whipping cream
2 tsp. powdered sugar
8 strawberries
8 slices peeled kiwi

In a medium-sized mixing bowl with an electric mixer, combine milk and egg yolks; blend at low speed. Slowly add lime juice and continue mixing until blended.

Slice pound cake into 1-inch slices and cut to fit inside wine glasses. Pour Key lime filling over pound cake and refrigerate for at least 2 hours.

Whip cream with powdered sugar and put a dollop in each wine glass. Garnish with a fresh strawberry and a slice of kiwi.

Serves 8.

Family and friends at Baton Rouge Show, October 2011. *First row, from left:* Carol Ann, Sara, Marlyn, Jill and Judy. *Back row, from left:* Ed, Judy, Carol, Adam, Tripp, Deb, Donna, Nick and Kelly; Marlyn with husband, Ed, son, Danny and his wife, Carol at the Shhreveport premiere show, September 2010; With husband, Ed, and Jackie and Edwin Jones and Ann Calhoun at the Shreveport October 2010 show; Shreveport show, October 2010; Marlyn and Peggy with Marlyn's Tequila Shrimp

Todd Graves
Founder, CEO, Chairman, Fry Cook, and Cashier, Raising Cane's Chicken Fingers, Baton Rouge
One Love

"If I were a food, I'd be a chicken finger, because that is my One Love!"

My love of food started early. Growing up in my mom's kitchen, learning to make a roux and the basics of true Louisiana cuisine are some of my fondest memories.

By college, I was working in a restaurant, and I absolutely loved everything about it—the fast pace, the fun environment, the people I worked with, and the customers I served.

It was about that time that I had a dream. It kept me up at night and consumed my thoughts. My dream was so clear—I could actually taste it. Naturally, it tasted like chicken.

I wanted to return home to Baton Rouge and Louisiana State University to open a restaurant that focused on quality chicken finger meals served by a great crew in a fun environment. I thought it was a great dream. Unfortunately, very few people agreed with me.

My partner was taking a business-planning course at LSU, so we wrote our business plan and he submitted it for his class. Our business plan received the lowest grade in the class.

But that didn't deter me. Armed with a cheap suit and my imitation leather briefcase with a brass combination lock (to keep my business plan secure), I went to every bank in town looking for financial backing.

Many banks, one conversation:

Banker: Do you have any experience running a restaurant?

Me: No.

Banker: Do you have any money?

Me: No.

Banker: Do you really think a restaurant selling only chicken fingers will work?

Me: Yes! So . . . will you lend me the money?

Banker: No.

The more I heard "no," the hungrier I became. I knew if I just had the money, I could make my dream a reality. So, I traveled to California and worked as a boilermaker, doing turnaround work at the refineries.

From there, I hitchhiked to Alaska and slept in a tent on the tundra for a month, until I was hired on as a salmon fisherman. It was dangerous but prosperous, and it gave me the seed money I needed.

I returned to Baton Rouge, and we found the perfect location at the North Gate of LSU, and we worked day and night fixing it up. And while I originally wanted to call it Sockeye's Chicken Fingers—named after the Alaskan salmon—my friends convinced me instead to name it after my yellow Labrador retriever, Raising Cane.

Finally, my vision of one restaurant became a reality. We call it "the Mothership."

And it was the beginning of One Love®.

As we grew, my vision grew with it: to have restaurants all over the world and be the brand for quality chicken finger meals, a great crew, a cool culture, and active community involvement.

But no matter how much we grow, we will still concentrate on one thing: quality chicken finger meals. And doing it better than anyone else. Because that is our One Love®.

Alaskan salmon boats; Todd with wife, Gwen, and children, Sophia and Charleton; Todd with Cane at Raising Cane's; Todd at Raising Cane's; Todd with Ruffin Rodrigue at the Myrtles Premiere Show; Todd with Cane; Todd in the show at the Myrtles, May 16, 2010; Cane at the Myrtles show

Jeanne Vidrine
Hair Stylist, Make-Up Artist, and Bon Vivant, New Orleans
Cooking the Competition

"If I were a food, I'd be salad dressing as I mix well with others and can put interesting ingredients (people) together for some wonderful and successful results."

I love to cook and entertain.

Sometimes I just love to cook. Growing up in New Orleans where we love good food, it seems that whatever we cook, we cook a lot of it. There is no such thing as a small pot of gumbo or red beans. And if you are going to go to the trouble of stuffing bell peppers or mirlitons, you're gonna make enough to feed an army!

My reason for telling you this is to make a point—when I need to provide for the masses, I can. Anyone that's been to my house during Mardi Gras season can attest to this. Every year the big Endymion parade rolls a block away from my house. Up until parade time, I have a full house of people, hungry for gumbo, red beans, étouffée, fricassee, you name it. All cooked by me over the days leading up to the Saturday Super Parade.

But before Mardi Gras season, we have football season. I'm a huge Saints fan. I've been a season ticket holder since the Dome reopened in 2006 and never miss a home game. Which means what's a Who Dat to do on game day for away games? My favorite place to watch the away games is in my neighborhood, Mid-City, at a bar called Finn McCool's. It's a wonderful Irish pub with genuine Irish proprietors, who have actually moved here from Ireland. Every week during football season, there is a friendly cooking competition encouraged by the owners, so that there is a huge, delicious, and, best of all, "free" spread of food for us patrons to feast on at halftime.

Pauline Patterson, who owns and runs the bar with her husband, Stephen, is an incredible cook and provides the majority of the dishes on this buffet. She usually prepares both Irish and Louisiana favorites—curries, cabbage, potatoes, seafood, and casseroles, all cooked in so many delicious ways. But week after week, to mix it up, they hold a game-day competition with a fun theme to keep it interesting. When we play the Falcons, it's a Dirty Bird Cook-Off; the Buccaneers, a BBQ and Pirate Party; for the Vikings, a Smorgasbord. You get the idea. We "cook" the competition.

The winner is chosen during the third quarter by popular vote. Everyone in the bar who has eaten gets a vote, and the winning dish is announced during the two-minute warning break at the end of the fourth quarter.

As you can imagine, this is a wildly popular event. There is this great sense of community, as everyone is decked out in black and gold and as hungry for a win as they are for the Halftime Buffet.

One "away week" we were playing the Philadelphia Eagles and a Wing Cook-off was set. I decided to give it a shot. Why? I don't know. I mean, how many ways can you cook wings? And sometimes it seems like there's two hundred people in the bar, so that's a lot of wings!

It took a good bit of brainstorming. What kind of sauce? How should they be seasoned? How should they be cooked? And, lordy, how many wings do I need to cook? Everyone in line for food is going to want to sample every dish up for the vote.

I finally decided to go "outside the lines" a bit. As I mentioned before, I have a lot of gumbo-cooking experience. So instead of a sauce, why not have a big pot of gumbo to feature my wings?

I went to the grocery and bought all my ingredients for the richest, most delicious chicken and andouille gumbo that I would ever cook. Plus, I bought four dozen chicken wings. The plan was to season them well with a traditional Cajun mix of salt, black pepper, cayenne pepper, and garlic powder, then slow roast them in the oven until golden brown and crispy.

But wait a minute. We were playing the Eagles, and I wanted to win this thing. Back to the grocery I went; this time I picked up every pack of turkey wings they had. I had maybe thirty or forty humongous wings! I seasoned them the same way as the chicken and had to bake them in several batches before they were all done to perfection. Meanwhile, the gumbo bubbled and simmered in my huge cast iron kettle. In fact, I let it simmer all night long.

The next morning I warmed the wings, which was quite a majestic pile of crispy deliciousness. I transferred the gumbo to a Crock-Pot and off to Finn McCool's we went.

The competition was fierce. It seemed like everyone came up with a tasty way to cook his wings. I must say I was a little less confident of winning after tasting some of the challengers. I hoped the novelty of my dish pushed it up a notch with the voters.

Well, I loved the looks on everyone's faces when they came out of the buffet line with a plate of mostly chicken wings and sauces and a bowl of my gumbo with the gargantuan "Eagle" wing balanced on top!

Call it a gimmick, call it sly planning, but what I'd call it was pure deliciousness and impressive. I mean, who gets a big golden roasted turkey wing with their gumbo? In all of my time in New Orleans and all throughout Louisiana, I've never seen it served this way in anyone's home or restaurant.

Lucky and happy me took home the Golden Spoon Trophy and drank up the $20 winner's bar tab. I bought a round of shots for my friendly competitors, and we toasted to each other's good cooking!

Jeanne and cousin, Peggy, at October 2011 show.

Jeanne and her father, Louis Vidrine, Herbsaint Bar and Restaurant

51

Turkey, Chicken, and Andouille Gumbo

This is the recipe I prepared for the event at Finn McCool's and is now my standard way of preparing gumbo. The large roasted turkey wings are not included here, but could easily be added. After cooking too many roux to count, I let Creole Instant Roux Mix do the work. It cuts way back on fat and calories. This is a great dish for a big crowd for a tailgate party, Mardi Gras party, or any fun occasion, or to make on a cold winter night and freeze for future dinners.

1 pack smoked turkey wings
5 lb. leg quarters, or 1 5 lb. chicken, cut up
3 tbsp. oil
4 stalks celery, chopped
3 cloves garlic, chopped
1 small bell pepper, chopped
1 large sweet onion, chopped
1 bay leaf
Salt, pepper, and cayenne, to taste
1 cup Creole Instant Roux Mix
2 cups stock, plus more for cooking
1 lb. andouille sausage, chopped

Prepare stock by placing turkey wings in pot with 1½ gallons of water. Bring to boil and simmer for 2 hours. Remove wings and let cool. Remove skin of wings, pick meat off bones, chop, and set aside. Throw away bones and skin. Strain liquid. The smoky, salty water is your stock.

Preheat oven to 300 degrees.

While stock is boiling, bake the chicken in oven until fat is rendered and skin crisps, approximately 45 minutes. Remove from oven, remove skin of chicken, and discard it with all rendered liquid. Set aside.

In a very large, heavy bottom pot (cast iron preferred), heat the oil over medium heat and then add all seasoning, except bay leaf and salt and pepper. When onions start to become translucent, add sausage and turkey meat; cook for 10 minutes.

Prepare roux mixture by mixing 1 cup of roux mix with 2 cups of stock, whisk to blend, and add to pot, stirring well.

When this heats, add chicken and enough strained stock liquid to cover. Add bay leaf and stir to blend ingredients.

Bring to boil, then reduce heat again to simmer for approximately 2½ hours. Be sure to stir occasionally and add more stock if necessary. A dark, stew-like consistency is desired.

Before serving, remove bones from pot and check seasoning. There may be enough salt from stock.

Serve over rice. Add a few dashes of your favorite hot sauce if you like. *Bon appétit!*

Helpful hint: To make the most of your time, put the stock on first while roasting chicken. Chop vegetables at this time, throwing in scraps of celery, bell pepper, and onions to stockpot for flavor.

Serves 12 to 15.

Photograph by Diana Zollicoffer

House of Blues show with trophy and turkey wing

52

Saints fan; At work; New Orleans premiere show at House of Blues with Finn McCool's Cook-Off Trophy; Jeanne with emcee Eric Paulsen at October 2010 show; Jeanne and her dad, Louis Vidrine, and sister, Barbara Hathorn, with Edgar Chase, his wife, Gretchen, and Leah Chase; Jeanne and Pauline Patterson, owner of Finn McCool's; With friends, Rachael Kravets, Suzy Moran, and Mary Vidrine Sullivan at the October 2011 show at the Southern Food and Beverage Museum; New Orleans October 2010 show at Ralph & Kacoo's

Jay Basist
Event Producer and Interior Designer, Baton Rouge
Country Comes to Town

"If I were a food, I would be a fried pickle. It is definitely most Southern, a bit naughty, very strange, and it leaves one coming back for more."

I graduated from Louisiana State University in 1976, not knowing what I was going to do with my bachelor's degree. I went to law school for a year, hating every damn minute of it. I dropped out and thought, "Now what?" My dream was to go to New York City, so I accepted a job offer with Merrill Lynch, Pierce, Fenner, and Smith. I was on my way to the Big Apple! I thought, "This is it. I have finally found myself."

I could hardly believe it. I could go to all those famous restaurants that I had read so much about. Lutece, Sardi's, the 21 Club, and Tavern on the Green were all calling my name.

It was the summer, and it was hot as blazes in Manhattan. Since my training class was to be at the Merrill Lynch Building at 9:00 the next morning, I decided to go to Sardi's and hang out. I'll never forget it. I ordered steak tartare because I thought it sounded "sophisticated." I had never eaten it before and had no clue what it was, but I loved it!

The next morning, I grabbed a cup of coffee, ran over to Penn Station in my poplin suit, and met my classmates for the first time. They were questioning which subway to take. I spoke up and said, "Just follow me!" I figured that would impress them. Well, we got on the E train, there was no air conditioning, and it was hot; 8:45 arrived and people started to wonder when we would arrive. "Not yet," I said. The next stop took forever. It was well after 9:00. I headed to the street level and asked the first person I saw, "Can you tell me where the Merrill Lynch Building is on Liberty and Church Street?" He looked bewildered and said, "Son, you're in Hoboken, New Jersey."

You can imagine the cool reception I received. We eventually got to class and no one was speaking to me. At lunch, I sat with the others, but it might as well have been Siberia.

I woofed down a hot dog topped with everything but the kitchen sink and washed it down with nine glasses of iced tea. Boy, was I thirsty! Well, the check came. Everyone else's bill was around $7. Mine was $22. "There must be a mistake," I said to the waitress in my Southern drawl, trying to charm her. She replied (with her hands on her hips), "Honey, this ain't the South. We charge for each glass of tea up here in the North." From then on out, I stuck to iced water.

At the end of that humiliating hot day, I reluctantly joined my classmates at Windows on the World next door at the World Trade Center. Looking to somewhat redeem myself, I ordered an extra-dry gin martini straight up with an olive and an order of sushi, trying desperately to prove that I was sophisticated after all. I'd never tried sushi in my life.

When my order arrived, I figured I'd start with that interesting green ball on my plate. I confidently sipped my martini, picked up my chopsticks, and plopped that big green ball into my mouth. Yes, it was Japanese wasabi—hot as all get out! I yelled some obscenities, jumped to my feet, and got the hell out of there while my classmates were laughing hysterically. Yep, country had definitely come to town.

Jay, Peggy, and Troy Kleinpeter; Jay at Café Du Monde with beignets; The Alta Vista Club's Academy Award's party. *From left:* Richard Flicker, Nancy Litton, Carolyn Cicero, Bert Fife, Jay, Whitney Vann, Scott Rogers, Elizabeth Dent, Judi Anderson; Jay and Peggy at Café Du Monde; Jay at the one-year anniversary show, May 12, 2011; Jay at Café Du Monde; Jay at Baton Rouge Show; Jay with mom at bar mitzvah; Jay with his sister, Beverly; Jay with Kleinpeter Ice Cream at TV pilot shoot

Savannah Wise
Actress, New York
Life of the Party

"If I were a food, I'd be a wasabi pea because I may be small, but you should never underestimate me because I pack a punch!"

Let's face it y'all, Southern ladies know how to throw parties! I come from a long line of New Orleans party-throwin' ladies. My grandmother, Moe, was an incredible cook and an amazing hostess. Her New Year's Eve parties were legendary. Born out of a desire to keep her seven children from leaving the house to go to crazy parties, the event grew every year. By the time I arrived on the scene, it was an affair with a guest list in the hundreds. Days before the event, we lined up parades of meatballs, made tubs of Moe's special horseradish sauce, and shaked up her secret Chex Mix recipe. There was also roast beef, ham, and, lest we forget, the fancier Creole fare: crawfish elegante and crab marnier. The party culminated with a display of fireworks. It was a grand night full of food, fun, friends, and family.

Me? I'm following in her footsteps with a less lavish, enjoyable Mardi Gras in New York tradition. In February 2007, I was living in a 180-square-foot studio apartment on the Upper West Side of Manhattan. This was not a space for entertaining. The "kitchen" consisted of two burners, a sink, and a mini fridge. We'll call it "quaint."

So there I was—in the thick of my first year in New York City as a struggling actress with auditions by day and working as a restaurant hostess at night. It was Mardi Gras, and to celebrate, I wore beads along with a mask and a purple, green, and gold outfit. The plan was to do something Mardi Gras-like after my long day. However, having worked late the night before, all I could do was crash when I got home.

I awoke groggy to a phone call. It was Barry.* He and I had gone on a date the week before, a date I felt had been pretty chemistry-free, but now he was inviting me out for some Mardi Gras revelry. I made a lame half-asleep "I'm so tired" excuse, thinking that would be the end of it. Oh no, friends! He said, "That's okay, I'll just come over." It all happened so fast; I was so sleepy and shocked that he had the nerve to invite himself over that I didn't protest. I did not want another date with him but telling him he couldn't come over hardly seemed the Southern belle thing to do. Clearly, my only option was to throw a party. I figured a date wasn't a date if there were other people around. Right?

Armed with a box of Café Du Monde beignet mix, which my mother had sent in her care package, I began creating my party. I sent a text to everyone I knew in Manhattan announcing a party in two hours. Five friends came to my crazy "party," and we had a blast. My "date" becoming a "non-date" was a complete non-issue, because we were all having such a good time. Now, in the style of Moe's New Year's Eve party, my Mardi Gras party has become a legendary annual tradition. The guest list grows every year, as does the menu (one year it included Popeyes fried chicken and that dangerous drink the Hurricane). The venue improves with each year (last year we were at a bar with a DJ and a brass band!), but the tradition remains the same: good people getting together to celebrate and eat good food—and get out of bad dates, just kidding, kind of.

*Name changed to protect from embarrassment.

56

Savannah making beignets; Walking the red carpet at the premiere of *Ragtime*; Peggy, Savannah, and Lance Spellerberg on red carpet at Santa Monica Show, February 2011; Savannah in her NYC kitchen; With friends in her NYC apartment for 2007 Mardi Gras party; Walking the red carpet at the premiere of NBC's *Smash*; Making her Mardi Gras beignets; Savannah with cousins, Tiffany and Jason Picus, and Jennifer Collins; Making her Mardi Gras beignets; Savannah with her grandmother, Patricia "Moe" Morvant Junius; Savannah at 2011 Mardi Gras party

Daniel Brockhoeft
Sales Manager, Omni Royal Orleans, New Orleans
A Julia Journey

"If I were a food, I would be a hot buttered Southern biscuit. For me, there are few simple pleasures more delicious or more Southern than fluffy biscuits right out of the oven with butter and homemade jam or jelly. Who would not like me if I were a hot biscuit?"

Like for many foodies the world over, *Mastering the Art of French Cooking, Vol. 1*, by Julia Child, changed my life. I was fourteen years old when I read that cookbook, really savoring it, page by page, cover to cover. I was a bit intimidated by the procedures of many of the recipes, but fascinated by the process. I knew then that cooking would be a large part of what I would do. Up to the point of reading this life-transforming book, I must admit my adventurous culinary exploits involved making a roux, while my mother cut up ingredients for a gumbo or stew. Mysterious items like Mousse de Foies de Volailles and Tarte au Citron seemed like items from another planet, but fascinating and imaginative items. I was hooked on cooking.

Through the years, I cooked more and more. When Mom and Dad came home from work, dinner was ready to be put on the table. My neighbors also enjoyed my early attempts at baking breads, cakes, and tarts (including Tarte au Citron). This all progressed into me being a caterer and cooking my way through college at Louisiana State University. I converted a Volkswagen Super Beetle into a catering mobile. My dad and I took out the back seat and installed a two-tiered shelf with locks and straps to hold down pots of gumbo and platters of grilled vegetables. You name it; it got locked down in the back seat. I did all my own shopping, cooking, florals, and centerpieces. I had a blast and paid my way through LSU. There was a full-page article on me in 1983 in the

food section of the *Times-Picayune*. Of course, they had heard about me through my mother. Only a mother would call the paper and tell them they needed to do an article on her son.

While at LSU, I had interned for Jim Brown when he was secretary of state. Jim knew I cooked since I made a monthly birthday lunch for his support staff. Everyone pitched in a dollar or two. I was great at stretching a few dollars, and the meals were great monthly events that the whole staff enjoyed.

Jim was often in celebrity-cooking contests for one cause or another, and for one event for the March of Dimes, he took me with him. Basically, he told me to cook something and then he would meet me in the hotel's ballroom before the event began. I cooked Lump Crabmeat in a White Cheddar Sauce and filled large patty shells, garnished with a little chopped chive. My neighbor had a dogwood tree that was in bloom, so I took some sprigs with me and garnished the edge of the display plate with the dogwood blossoms. Our booth was in the shape of a pyramid, and we were between Ms. Lindy Boggs in a tepee and Lt. Gov. Bobby Freeman in a swamp hut. A number of celebrity chefs were the judges. Quite unfortunately, Jim and I won first prize. Unfortunate since Jim was stuck in traffic, and no one had any clue who I was at this celebrity event. I did confess to Ms. Lindy Boggs what had happened (she made an oyster pie), and she thought it was a hoot. The cameras were headed my way, and I told Angela Hill that Jim was working the room and then quickly explained our dish. Jim finally arrived and I told him we had won first prize, and he burst out laughing.

One of the celebrity judges at the event that night was Bernhardt Metz, the president of the Culinary Institute of America at Hyde Park, New York. Chef Metz asked me if I ever considered attending the CIA at Hyde Park. He said I should, and I started to think about it.

More years passed, and I was twenty-eight, thinking about the CIA and thinking I must be crazy, but there was a strong feeling of now or never. I found the application kit, wrote my required essay about how I was transformed by *Mastering the Art of French Cooking* and the movie *Babette's Feast*, crossed my fingers, and dropped the application in the mail.

To my slight surprise, I was accepted. So I cancelled my lease, quit my job, and packed my knives. I thought I had completely lost my mind, as did most of my family and friends. But nothing ventured, nothing gained. I went off to one of the greatest and most fun experiences of my life. The CIA at Hyde Park was like Valhalla for foodies.

I worked and studied hard. I also had a fun time going down the snow-covered hills on campus in the very large roasting pans we had temporarily "borrowed" from the kitchens. We had snow for six months out of the year, torture for a boy from the Deep South. There were so few students from the southern states and only two from New Orleans. We were like celebrities. Everyone, including Master Chef instructors, wanted to know all about making gumbos and étouffées. I also have to say that the aprons my mother made and sent to me to wear in cooking school were quite the *envie*, as she had embroidered a border of shrimps, crabs, and oysters on them. All my chef instructors wanted them, but she made them only for me.

In the middle of the program, they throw you out to do a six-month externship at a restaurant to make sure this is the business for you before you spend $30,000 more dollars. I had the great fortune to do my externship at Commander's Palace. That experience alone could fill a book. I will say that the Brennan family is quite incredible, especially "Miz" Ella who wanted her bread pudding soufflés to be high and airy. I knew quite quickly that I was not cut out for restaurant work and that I would return to the life of the happy caterer after CIA graduation.

A few months prior to graduation, I was selected as one of the Top Ten Student Chef's in America for 1991 and was sent with a CIA team of chefs to the Aspen Wine and Food Festival as a student assistant to the celebrity chefs. The list of celebrity chefs was a stunner. It was all of my favorites and more. I baked pizzas with Jacques Pépin, made a fall vegetable cobbler with Ms. Fanny Farmer, drizzled olive oil over clams with Penelope Casas, and chopped onions with the very delightful and wonderful Julia Child, who was as tall as I was. It was a dream week for a foodie at an incredibly beautiful location. The week ended with a lavish reception prepared by all of us, where Julia Child presented all the Top Ten Student Chefs with a trophy magnum of Sandeman Port. I was lucky. I got the bottle, a hug, and kiss from Julia—nothing was better than that!

My trophy magnum of Sandeman Port from Julia now hangs in a prominent spot in my restored 1880 Eastlake Victorian side-hall home on Esplanade. On the same wall in my kitchen, I have my photo of Julia and my Culinary Institute of America diploma. Guests to our home—and we often entertain up to one hundred people—love to come in and ask the story behind the photo and the trophy, and I am always glad to tell them.

After graduation from the CIA, I worked in a wide range of food and beverage related fields, from chef at a catering company to director of sales for food and beverage at the Ernest N. Morial Convention Center. After nearly thirty-five years working in food and beverage, I now am in hotel room sales and enjoy the heck out of my weekends off!

Easy Fruit Cobbler

This cobbler recipe comes from a very dear friend of mine, "my Mississippi momma" Dorothy Gray, in Osyka, Mississippi. Dorothy's family has been in the area since the 1850s. She serves this incredibly delicious fruit cobbler that she has been making for years with blackberries that are picked around the large pond behind her home, Evergreen Oaks. It's delicious, easy, and always a big hit!

1 stick butter or margarine
1 cup self-rising flour
1 cup whole milk
2 cups white sugar
1 tsp. vanilla
2 cups fruit or berries, fresh or frozen

Preheat oven to 375 degrees.

In a 9x13-inch pan—glass, metal, or foil—melt butter and swirl around on bottom and sides of pan. Whisk together flour, milk, 1 cup sugar, and vanilla and pour in pan.

Mix the fruit or berries with 1 cup sugar and pour down the middle of the pan. Do not mix or stir. Bake for 45 minutes until golden brown.

Serve with vanilla ice cream or whipped cream. Delicious!

Serves 8.

Daniel's house on Esplanade; Daniel at one-year anniversary show, May 12, 2011; Daniel at the Myrtles Plantation premiere show with Peggy, Barbara Anne Eaton, and Rannah Gray; Daniel with dear friend Dorothy Gray; Daniel with CIA classmates; Daniel being interviewed by Jay Ducote at anniversary show; Daniel with Chef Paul Prudhomme at the Aspen Food and Wine Festival, 1991; Daniel with Julia Child at Aspen Food and Wine Festival; Daniel with Baton Rouge mayor Kip Holden and Rannah Gray at anniversary show

Mike Theis
Lifestyle Reporter, ABC 26, and Columnist,
Where Y'at Magazine, New Orleans
Front of House at Restaurant August after Katrina

"If I were a food, I'd be a fast food French fry as it's cheap and delicious, and since I grew up Catholic, I always feel guilty after eating them!"

I arrived back to New Orleans after Katrina on Friday, October 7, 2005. When I first returned, I went to Restaurant August to see my friend Chef John Besh. He was there with Chef Alon Shaya. I gave them both big hugs and asked, "Where the hell is everyone?" John replied, "Where have you been? Nobody is back yet!" I told him that I had been a horrible maître d' in college, but I'd love to volunteer and that I had a tuxedo. He said, "Mike, look pretty, drink white wine, and help us seat people tonight!" I thought to myself that this would be the most fabulous gig I would ever do in my life.

Restaurant August is one of the finest restaurants in the world, and tonight they were having linens delivered so it was a big night. However, the only food they could get delivered was frozen chicken and red beans, so they were going to serve fried chicken and red beans and rice! My assistant that night was the general manager's wife, who had never set a table before. So not only am I just greeting people and showing them to their seats, but I was also setting tables.

I kept getting the glasses mixed up. I was bussing bar glasses to the back, and the dishwasher got upset with me and threw a wet towel at me and said, "Mike, never bring these bar glasses back to me into the kitchen, they need to be cleaned at the bar!" I thought, "Are you kidding me?" Chef Alon told the dishwasher to be nice to me since I was only helping them out.

Now Friday night was crazy because I was just getting used to my "new job," but Saturday was worse because everyone Uptown had heard Restaurant August was open. I arrived there at 5:30 P.M., and the reservations were through the roof. This was one of the only restaurants open at this time, and we couldn't turn a table to save our life that night. If you had a reservation at 6:00 P.M., you were still at that table at 9:00. At 7:00, we had one hundred people waiting in the bar and overflowing to the Windsor Court lobby. I would call the Windsor Court and ask them to send over the party.

I was standing up by the bar, and I heard a car honking outside on the curb. I went outside to see a very large black Mercedes with the window rolled down, and the woman asked, "Where's your valet parking?" I said, "Excuse me, have you heard of Katrina?" The woman parked at the Windsor Court, walked in, and was furious that her table wasn't ready. Angela Hill was sitting at the bar, so I went up to her and said, "Angela, I will buy your dinner, if you will give this bitch your table." Angela, said, "Sure!"

Despite the craziness, that weekend started to feel like there was some normalcy to life in New Orleans. All of us who worked together bonded in some special way. After the last person left at 3:00 A.M., John, Alon, and Steve came out of the kitchen, and John gave me a hug and said, "Thank you for saving me this weekend!" And that is what New Orleans is all about. It's about community, and I'm so grateful to be a part of this great city!

Mike Theis in the French Quarter (Photograph by David Tomkins); Mike with Chef John Besh and Paula Deen at the Gulf Restoration event at Restaurant August (Photograph by David Tomkins); Mike with Mario Batali and Emeril Lagasse at Emeril's Carnivale du Vin Fundraiser (Photograph by David Tomkins); Mike with Chef John Besh (Photograph by David Tomkins); Mike at Galatoire's with Leslie Stokes, Gerri Valene, and Jude Swensen (Photograph by David Tompkins); Rita Benson Leblanc, Mike, and Gumbo emcee at YLC Wednesday Concerts in the Square; At Cafe Du Monde; Mike and Chef Alon Shaya in New Orleans show, October 2011

Gen. Russel Honoré
Retired U.S. Army Lieutenant General, Writer, and Speaker, Baton Rouge
Two Hundred Years of Taste

"If I were a food, I would be gumbo because it's a little bit of everything, and you can't go wrong."

I was about eighteen years old before I made my first trip to Café Du Monde, but it wasn't my first time having a food concoction similar to a beignet. I was raised in Pointe Coupee Parish near Lakeland. We were a family of twelve and living on a subsistence farm. Every morning my mom would make something called Le Pot. It was heavy dough that didn't rise very much, which she would cook in lard in a black iron skillet. When it came out, it was golden and would have puffs in the middle filled with air. We would have it with homemade fig preserves or cane syrup made from the sugar farms right there in Lakeland. Le Pot was a great dish for breakfast, as it would give you all the calories you needed to keep you going all day picking cotton or working the sugar cane fields. I thought it was strange when I first saw beignets with powdered sugar, but it tasted great even without the fig preserves.

My wife, Beverly, and I raised four children, and when we left Louisiana, we left in a '68 Cutlass Supreme with a few suitcases in the back. Almost forty years later, after moving twenty-four times, we came back to Louisiana with two moving vans of stuff.

In April 2012, we celebrated the bicentennial of Louisiana's statehood. We have a deep rich history, and people from around the world come to Louisiana to taste the food, listen to the music, and see the diversity. Many of them become hooked and keep coming back. This is the key to our economy.

I go around the country talking about preparedness based on the lessons we learned from Hurricanes Katrina and Rita. On any given day, Mother Nature can create an event that can cause you to be a victim. I encourage people to be prepared, as a disaster can happen at any time, and we need to build a culture of preparedness. You need to have an evacuation plan, three days' supply of food and water, and a battery-operated weather radio. We need to spread the word. Everyone needs to be prepared.

I was born two days after the great storm of 1947. When my daughter was twelve years old, we were visiting in Louisiana, and the story came up around the kitchen table. She asked how we survived without electricity and running water. We had food from our garden, pigs on the farm, and food we had jarred. People in rural areas knew how to survive. We need to learn from the resiliency of our ancestors.

A couple of months ago, we had the floods, and I had gone down to the bluffs by Southern University to be interviewed by CNN. While I was waiting, I noticed a young lady sitting on a bench looking at the Mississippi River. A frog jumped on the bench and said, "If you kiss me, I'll turn into a general, and I'll serve you for the rest of your life." So she took the frog and put it in her backpack. A few minutes later, the frog jumped out and said, "Remember, I'm a famous general, and if you kiss me, I'll turn into a general and serve you for the rest of your life." Frustrated, she said to the frog, "A talking frog is worth a lot of money, a talking general is not worth much!"

With grandson, James Russel; General Honoré's deceased parents, Marie Udell St. Amant Honoré and Lloyd Charles Honoré; General Honoré in the Baton Rouge show, October 2011; General Honoré and family. *From left:* Steven, Michael, Beverly, Stefanie, Kimberly, and General Honoré; General Honoré with President Bush after Katrina; Gen. Russel Honoré with wife, Beverly; her mom, Anna L. Darensbourg; and her sister, Sandy K. Darensbourg; General Honoré with his grandsons, James Russel and Jackson; With President Bush and Mayor Ray Nagin after Hurricane Katrina; Signing his book after the Baton Rouge Show; Gen. Russel Honoré with wife, Beverly Russel

Jay Ducote
Food Writer, Blogger, Radio Host, and Chef, Bite and Booze, Baton Rouge
Bite, Booze, and Beyond

"If I were a food, I would be a Louisiana-cane-syrup-glazed pork belly—a bit sweet, a bit fatty, and always amazing!"

The question I am asked most often is "How did you get started?" For me, my career just emerged from my daily life. I looked at my credit card receipts in September of 2009 and thought, "Man, I spend a lot of money eating and drinking." However, I knew those habits weren't about to change. So instead, I decided to make my consumption productive. I started writing about everything I ate and drank!

I spent the first eight years of my life in Baton Rouge, Louisiana, before being relocated to Sugar Land, Texas, for my father's career. I stayed there through high school but always knew I wanted to come back to Baton Rouge to be a Louisiana State University Tiger like my mom, dad, and brother before me. While growing up in Texas, I fondly remember hunting with my dad near the Mexico border. The prickly pear cacti and mesquite brush littered the south Texas landscape. It was there, at the deer camps, that I have my first memories of barbeque and cooking over open fires. The taste and smell of burning mesquite brings me right back to those frigid January nights in the desert after the hunt.

In 1999, I arrived at LSU for my first year of college. Before I could attend my first class, my cousin Travis placed our grandfather's old barbeque fork and spatula in my hands and said, "Here freshman, you're in charge of the grill now." I took it more as a rite of passage than as getting put to work, which is probably for the best. Years of being in charge of and cooking for massive LSU tailgate parties gave me the foundation for my outdoor cooking skills. I learned the grill, of course, and also the large cast iron pot and the deep fryer. I learned the countless different ways you can cook on a pit. I'd come to realize that direct heat is for the impatient.

One football season we decided to build our own barbeque pit and smoker. A couple of us skipped a fair amount of classes during the first week of school to get the pit ready in time for the first tailgate party. We constructed "the monstrosity," a massive cooking contraption on casters with an attachment to hook into the back of a truck. The pit is made from a full-size aluminum keg, turned on its side. Sitting off to the side is a normal half-barrel beer keg that has been turned into a smoker. From that moment on, we did more than just grill—we barbequed! Brisket, pork shoulders, ribs, salmon, venison, elk, boudin, andouille—you name it, and we cooked it!

One year we brought our pit with us to Little Rock for an LSU game against Arkansas. Since the game was played the day after Thanksgiving, we figured it would be appropriate to cook a turkey. We actually smoked it hanging upside down in the keg, with smoke billowing out of the top all night long, and continued to smoke the bird as we drove onto the Memorial Golf Course on game day. It sure hit the spot when we took it out of the smoker at about 11:00 A.M. On our way home, my buddy Matt and I decided to smoke a couple racks of ribs. We started early in the morning, had our fire burning hot, and put the ribs in the smoker. As we were driving home somewhere right around Lake Providence, we experienced some vehicle troubles. The catalytic converter on the truck plugged up, and the exhaust wasn't able to leave the engine. We pulled over and had to remove the converter with a hacksaw, but it was so hot that we had to let it cool down first. As we waited, we realized we had pulled over right next to a pecan grove. Naturally, we took the liberty of gathering some fallen limbs to stoke the fire for our smoker. We finally got back on the road in my dad's hand-me-down camouflage 1984 Toyota 4x4 pickup, which had an elaborate barbeque pit billowing smoke off the back and a straight exhaust with no muffler coming out the engine. It was quite a sight to see—and to hear. But for the record, when we made it to Baton Rouge and took those ribs out of the smoker, they tasted really damn good!

I graduated from LSU in 2004 with a degree in economics and political science. I went back to school and earned a master's in political science from LSU in 2007. I learned that I neither wanted to be a politician nor a political scientist for the rest of my life. From 2007 to 2009, I taught math and coached baseball at an inner-city Baton Rouge high school. My time at Lee High School served as one of the most rewarding experiences that I've ever had, but when they closed the school down in May 2009, I decided not to continue my teaching career. By the end of the summer, I had landed a job with the Louisiana Department of Health and Hospitals to assist a nonprofit, the Louisiana Health Care Quality Forum, with some research, coordination, and writing of several federal grant opportunities in the health information technology field. Shortly thereafter, the real fun began.

I returned to Houston in September for the wedding of one of my best friends from high school. While preparing for the festivities in honor of Tyler, the groom to be, I overheard my buddies John and Chetan discussing a memorable meal of Texas barbeque and how John had written about it on his blog. Intrigued, I worked my way into the conversation. I had no idea about John's blog and was curious as to how he went about casually writing about food. When I returned to Baton Rouge and settled back into my already routine and monotonous nine to five, I scoped out John's website. He didn't post often. He didn't write to build an audience. He just wrote so that he and his closest friends could share an occasional journey through food. I thought the idea consisted of pure brilliance, so I decided that I should do the same thing about the food and beverages that I ate and drank in Louisiana. Bite and Booze was born!

Bite and Booze began without a thought or idea that it would ever be more than a way for me to write about my passions of eating and drinking. However, my short, one-picture posts about random Baton Rouge restaurants would soon morph into something much, much more.

By November 2009, I already had decided that I wanted to grow my audience and do something bigger and bolder. Baton Rouge needed a food voice, and I wanted to share mine. I attended the first ever Foodbuzz Blogger Festival in San Francisco, California, with my good buddy Chef Eusebio Gongora. We went to play, eat, drink, and generally soak up San Francisco culture, as well as a little knowledge from some experienced food bloggers. I learned one thing that truly stuck with me: get on Twitter! I returned to the hotel and created my account, @biteandbooze, that night.

After just a couple more months of blogging, I received an opportunity to write a monthly restaurant feature for *Town Favorites* magazine in Baton Rouge. I also began writing more about dishes that I cooked and food-based events and festivals, instead of relying only on restaurants for my material. I entered my first barbeque competition in March 2010. I also participated in "Meanwhile, Back at Café Du Monde . . ." as a headliner. Later I would also serve as a red carpet host and emcee, and appear in the television pilot for a show based on the monologues. In August 2010, I had another really big break—my recipe for Blackberry Bourbon Bone-In Boston Butt was selected to represent LSU in a tailgating cook-off. The pork shoulder is injected throughout with a mixture of honey, bourbon, and blackberry jam then rubbed with a blend of creole seasoning and brown sugar before smoking over Louisiana pecan wood for up to twelve hours. It develops a wonderful bark on the outside, while the inside is fork tender and packed with a unique flavor! My recipe ended up winning the contest, but something even bigger was about to happen.

On the same day as the cook-off at LSU in November 2010, I also drove to New Orleans to go to a casting call for the reality show MasterChef on FOX. Two months later, I flew to Los Angeles for ten days of filming. Upon my return, I began publishing my work in Baton Rouge's *225 Magazine*. In April 2011, I started *Bite and Booze*, a radio show on the brand new Talk 107.3 FM. MasterChef aired in June 2011, and I got my first bit of national television exposure. More would come November 2011, on *Eat Street* on the Cooking Channel. That same month the Baton Rouge Business Report named me to their Top Forty under 40. I quit my day job and now focus on the blog, radio, and other adventures full time. Some of those include producing and starring in a Louisiana lifestyle and culture documentary and working on a cookbook of my own. The first two years of Bite and Booze have been absolutely tremendous. I'm really even more excited to see where it takes me from here!

Blackberry Bourbon Boston Butt

My recipe represented LSU in a tailgating contest and won! I created it because of my love for combining fruit and pork, as well as cooking with booze! The blackberry, honey, and bourbon injection keeps the inside moist and flavorful while the brown sugar and Creole rub on the outside creates a sweet and spicy bark after hours of smoking!

1 large bone-in Boston butt pork shoulder
1 cup bourbon
1 cup blackberry jam
⅓ lb. local honey (about ½ cup)
2 tbsp. fresh ground black pepper
1 cup dark brown sugar
1 cup Creole seasoning

Trim the pork shoulder, removing excess fat from the outside.

In a small mixing bowl or even a food processor, blend the bourbon, blackberry jam, honey, and black pepper together. Inject the mixture into the pork shoulder on all sides, getting it around the bone and throughout the meat.

Combine the brown sugar and Creole seasoning in a mixing bowl and whisk together. Rub the outside of the pork shoulder with the mix making sure to coat all sides liberally with the rub.

Smoke the pork shoulder over Louisiana pecan wood for up to 12 hours at around 225 degrees. The pork shoulder can also be roasted in the oven for around 6 to 8 hours, depending on size, at 275 degrees.

Allow the pork to cool until it is comfortable enough to handle. Using forks or your hands, shred the pork. Serve it as main meat dish or serve on buns as pulled pork sandwiches. Enjoy!

Jay Ducote at cast party and TV pilot shoot

68

Jay Ducote in the Baton Rouge Show, October 2010; Jay Ducote with Mayor Kip Holden on red carpet at anniversary show; Jay filming at LSU Tailgate Cook-Off; Jay Ducote with his mother Phyllis Ducote at *225 Magazine*'s 2011 Forty under Forty Awards; Jay with Mike the Tiger, Jay with friends Curtis and Shoshana Gibbs and Lauren Michaud; Jay with Peggy at November 2011 Baton Rouge Show; Jay Ducote on MasterChef on FOX (Photo courtesy of MasterChef on FOX).

Elizabeth Pearce
Culinary and Cocktail Historian and Tour Guide, New Orleans
Bywater Hospitality

"If I were a food, I would be bacon and not just because it's tasty. Bacon is powerful. It is distinctive. If you are trying to punch up the flavor of anything—vegetables, appetizers, soups, hell, even desserts—add bacon. Bacon is forbidden, irresistible, powerful, and delicious. It's the superhero of meat. And who wouldn't want to be that?"

I live on Desire Street and that's not an accident. It's a good noun to run your life by, making it a lot more interesting than running it on Piety. The smell of Bywater is equal parts BBQ, patchouli, and weed. It's messy and vibrant and complicated, like everything important in New Orleans. But what makes it home to me is its particular brand of hospitality.

I know pretty much everyone on my street between Rampart and Dauphine, where I make the corner to the Markey Dog Park twice a day. There's Jacques and Mr. Clark and Brandon and the ladies who work in the restaurant and hotel linens laundry service. As I walk by, we all say our "good mornings" and "all rights" and "who dats," and they know my dogs' names and greet them too. I drink my coffee in the morning while they sip their 40s.

One day, while walking back from the dog park, I walk by Mr. Clark's, and there's a huge crawfish pot going. I ask what's in it, and Jacques says, "Coon and rabbit. You want some?" I have never had coon, though I adore rabbit, so I reply, "Yes." They look impressed that I didn't turn my nose up. He goes to get me some "tin ferl," and I peek in the pot. It's ruby red, full of crab boil and meat. The dogs sniff curiously. He wraps me up two big scoops of meat. I say my thank-yous and we go home.

Now I know why most people don't eat coon. My dogs have less discriminating palates and gobbled it right up. The rabbit, on the other hand, was delicious. I was glad to

report the next day that I loved the rabbit, the coon was "strong," but it all was eaten. We all shared that warm glow that happens when you've expressed your gratitude to people who have fed you well.

A few weeks later, my friend Alan, a local who now lives in Seattle, was visiting. I told him about the coon and rabbit, and he laughed and said that would never happen in Seattle. He was pretty sure cooking with an open fire on the sidewalk was illegal and all socialization takes place in the backyard, like the rest of America.

As we rounded the corner, there was the pot, bubbling. The grill was cooking, too. I asked what Mr. Clark was cooking. He answered, "Pork chops. You hungry?" I am always hungry. He assembled the most beautiful sandwich—a pork chop slapped between two pieces of bread. No sauce, no mayo, just the chop with its bone still in. I took a bite. Heaven! I offered it to Alan, who chomped away happily, discovering the bone about halfway home.

Giving food to strangers is an unselfish, life-affirming act that links our humanity in the most beautiful way. For all that is wonderful about New Orleans, it is still a long way from becoming the best city it can be, but I believe these are the gestures that will save us. If there is a heaven I hope it is a place full of Mr. Clarks and Jacques, sitting around on their stoop, drinking their 40s, tending their grills, stirring their pots, and wrapping love up in "tin ferl." And that all of these cooks have been turned into stars.

Elizabeth Pearce with Leon Contavesprie at New Orleans show, October 2010; Elizabeth on Cocktail Walking Tour (Photograph by Emily Ardoin); Elizabeth at Pat O'Brien's Patio Bar (Photograph by Cheryl Gerber); Elizabeth at Mardi Gras as Café Brulot (Photograph by Ann Marie Popko); Elizabeth with Allison Alsup at Mardi Gras

Matt Murphy
Chef/Owner, The Irish House, New Orleans
To Keep an Irishman Out of the Pub, Make Him a Chef of One

"If I were a food, I would be an egg. Eggs work well individually and with other ingredients; they have to be treated gently, and they are always cracking up."

My first real food encounter was collecting apples in the backyard during the summer with my dad on Saturdays—making the pie dough, peeling the apples, rolling out the dough, slicing the apples, adding the sugar, lining the pie tin, and filling it with apples. Then baking it slowly, checking it, and letting it cool down. It took about two hours, but what a satisfying feeling, eating a slice of that pie. It passed the time, but it also made us think about what went into making a simple apple pie.

Next, I remember working in a local hotel at the age of fourteen. We called it Faulty Towers after the famous show where everything possible would go wrong at the most inconvenient time. This was my real introduction to cooking and the kitchen. The chefs found it amusing to soak the plugs in water and ask me very hurriedly, as if it were a life-support machine, "plug in the slicer," "plug in the toaster," "plug in the potato peeler." Each time, the lights would dim and I would stiffen like an electric-chair victim. I was very green and it took about two days of getting zapped before I figured out why people were laughing at me.

I soon realized after a few more interactions with the chefs that I looked up to that you can trade food and get things for it. First, it was feeding the waiters, so they would send beer back to the kitchen, of course saying, "The guest at table two sent some beers back to the chefs." So it became the life of the business. One chef would feed the local food writer and pick up the check,

which always gets positive reviews—a food writer kind of like the guy in *Ratatouille*. I also learned that if you cooked for a charity, they would hold their committee meetings at your restaurant. I continued to absorb the ebb and flow of training and learning from the chef and owners of small-town eateries.

I remember an older chef telling me to "work for the best" and "learn from everyone and don't stop learning." He was old, seventy or something (you don't typically see older chefs; they seem to disappear or vanish). This chef had some wise words for me. He was also a certified Master Chef and would make all, yes all, the sauces for a restaurant that served more than two thousand people a day. I've never forgotten his words or how proud he was of his profession.

When I was twenty-one, I won a scholarship to a culinary school. That's young, right? Well, not really when everyone else in the college was seventeen. I already had experience, and so during the class it was "Michael, plug in the mixer, plug in the toaster." I had perfected the movie *Backdraft*'s opening shot, with flames leaping through the air—leave the back burner's gas on so when the front burner was lit, the victim's eyebrows would be gone along with any hair on their forearm.

To be a chef, you have to be able to hustle. I would finish classes at 5:00 P.M. and jog two miles to the restaurant to be in the kitchen by 5:30 P.M., giving me thirty minutes to set the station. I worked the protein station, which meant exact cooking of filet of beef, lamb, veal, duck, pheasant, venison, skate, sea bass, rainbow trout, salmon, langoustine, scallops—all fresh and delivered daily. Pressure, pressure, pressure cooker! Sometimes it felt like being in a decompression chamber caused the tempo to pick up. Chef would shout "Sa Mache, First course—mussels, asparagus soup, veal terrine, Mâche salad . . . Entrée—one duck, one filet medium, scallops, sea bass."

I spent a number of years moving from chef to chef or restaurant to restaurant, to the point that no situation scared me. In Dublin, I opened an Italian restaurant with my friend. We worked our butts off those first nights. I mean days of nothing but work. On the third day, a Saturday, we were so far behind with orders. A lady walked into the kitchen with her husband and screamed, "We've waited thirty-five minutes for our appetizer," and then hit her husband's arm and said, "Tell them in your own language." He began speaking Italian. For five minutes he spoke, using his hands and looking like he was ripping us a new one. When he finished, the wife asked, "Well, what do you have to say to that?" I looked at her and quietly said, "I don't speak Italian."

I found the other extreme of cooking while working in London and getting to do stages in the famous chefs' kitchens. I would start work at 6:30 A.M., working with standards that were so high I was frightened each day before entering the kitchen of what might go wrong. It was all about the food. We would sleep, eat, and talk food. When I started a new job, it was an opportunity to learn, be present, see how the food was cooked and prepared, and to learn the techniques and the process behind the great sauces. We would work until 11:30 P.M., but it wasn't time to go home; it was the time to write down the vegetable, meat, and seafood orders for delivery the next morning. It was hard to believe the chefs were all veterans of this six-day-a-week love affair of food, and I looked up to them as if they were kings.

Food has taken me to many a place—from Europe to the United States to the Middle East and beyond. I have eaten many types of food, such as grasshoppers, scorpions, hummingbirds, and frogs. When I found myself with the choice of staying in Hawaii or coming to New Orleans, I said, without hesitation, "Let's see what New Orleans has to show."

A chef friend told me to go to Commander's and talk to Jamie Shannon. Most of us find jobs by word of mouth.

When I pulled up outside and saw the turquoise color of the building, I wondered if he was telling the truth or playing a joke! At Commander's I found long-term friends and even more experiences, young cooks making the same mistakes, but always with their own individual flair.

I have lost great friends along the way, including Jamie and other people I have met through food. However, I remember them always and know they are doing the same thing they loved in life up in heaven. In my mind, I see them cooking the fine-tuned dishes that made them who they were.

I took a chance when I left Commander's for the Ritz Carlton. I found a monster kitchen. I had thought hotels were a place that chefs go for some rest and relaxation—not! I took on a twenty-four-hour-a-day, seven-day-a-week kitchen, which cooked food for every type of diet and request you could ever imagine. I loved it—what a challenge! I danced a slow waltz with a huge gorilla, slowly getting faster as I learned how my partner moved.

I met my wife in a kitchen. It was over a dish that she said, "Wow! Who would have ever thought of goat's cheese and chocolate, awesome idea!" We got hitched in the end, and now I have five daughters including a set of quadruplet girls—a nice Irish family, with a big grocery bill!

I've been here twelve years; I have made a lot of friends and a family here. Now I can say 80 percent of my family is from New Orleans. A few years ago, I found out how cooking and food can save you. I fell very ill with a rare, life-threatening disease and was past the point of return when all the people who I have met and worked with stepped up to support me in so many ways. They held a fundraiser at the hotel to help with the medical bills and to support my family and me. To my friends who eat, who cook, who grow produce, who hunt, who fish, who do whatever, thank you for the support and prayers!

It's a miracle I'm here today and that I have made it to this point! If you want "to keep an Irishman out of the pub, make him a chef of one." So stop by and see me at The Irish House and have a pint of Guinness, some fish and chips, bangers and mash, and listen to some Irish music. My experience with food—the personal sacrifices, preparation, thought, design, experiences, and everything else that's part of the ride—has made one hell of a recipe card!

Grilled Pork Tenderloin with Sugar-Cane-Skewered Shrimp

This dish was inspired by the fascination with pigs in New Orleans, and Ireland has pork as a staple in their culture and history. There is a similarity between the Lousiana boudin noir and blanc with the Irish black and white puddings. It was an easy connection to have the pork tenderloin and the sugar cane shrimp, which adds the flavor of the Gulf. The pecan stuffing brings a touch of the many dressing and stuffings used in Southern cooking.

4-7 oz. pork tenderloins
Salt and pepper
6 oz. bleu cheese
2 oz. roasted pecans
1 bread roll, diced
3 sprigs thyme, chopped
3 sprigs sage, chopped
Butter
2 oz. olive oil
1 zucchini, cut into 8 slices on bias
1 squash, cut into 8 slices on bias
1 eggplant, cut into 8 slices on bias
2 oz. shaved Parmesan
1 red bell pepper, quartered
1 clove garlic, chopped
3 green onions or shallots, diced
4 sprigs rosemary, chopped
1 bottle Abita Amber Beer
2 oz. hot sauce
6 oz. Worcestershire
4 oz. butter
4 sugar cane skewers
12-16 medium to large shrimp
1 oz. Creole spice

Slice the pork tenderloin horizontally. Season it with salt and pepper.

Mix the blue cheese and pecans with the bread, herbs, and a little softened butter. Place the stuffing on top of the pork and fold over.

Heat a skillet with olive oil and sear the pork on both sides. Then place it in the oven to finish cooking at 325 degrees for 8 to 10 minutes. Set the pork aside on a plate.

Slice the zucchini, squash, and eggplant on the bias, toss with olive oil, and grill. Take the vegetables off and allow them to cool on a tray. Then layer them on top of each other, placing shaved Parmesan between each layer.

Finish with the red pepper on top and allow the vegetables to warm in the oven for 5 minutes before serving. Sauté the garlic and green onions in a hot skillet. Add in some of the chopped rosemary. Deglaze with half of the Abita Amber Beer. Add in hot sauce and Worcestershire and allow it to reduce by a third. Finish by whisking some butter into the sauce. Skewer the shrimp with the sugar cane and season with Creole spice. Cook these on the grill last and place them on top of the pork. Place the pork on the plate with the vegetable terrine and grilled shrimp on top. Drizzle the sauce around and garnish with rosemary.

Serves 4.

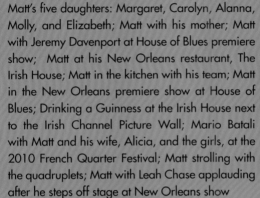

Matt's five daughters: Margaret, Carolyn, Alanna, Molly, and Elizabeth; Matt with his mother; Matt with Jeremy Davenport at House of Blues premiere show; Matt at his New Orleans restaurant, The Irish House; Matt in the kitchen with his team; Matt in the New Orleans premiere show at House of Blues; Drinking a Guinness at the Irish House next to the Irish Channel Picture Wall; Mario Batali with Matt and his wife, Alicia, and the girls, at the 2010 French Quarter Festival; Matt strolling with the quadruplets; Matt with Leah Chase applauding after he steps off stage at New Orleans show

Janet Daley Duval
Actress and President of the Tennessee Williams/New Orleans Literary Festival, New Orleans
A Tasty Bribe

"If I were a food, I would be 85 percent cocoa dark chocolate—all of the pleasure with none of the guilt!"

My earliest food memory is at Moran's La Louisiane, which was on Iberville. It has disappeared from existence, but I bet it lives in the memories of many people. Part of its intrigue was that it was a notorious Mafia hangout. Yet it was a most elegant establishment—huge crystal chandeliers and cream-colored walls with beautiful china and glass wear. But better than all of that was its specialty—pasta. Pasta Asciutta, to be precise. I knew it as Pastashou—one word that brought tears to my eyes and hunger to my belly. Ah, what I wouldn't do for it! Well, my parents caught on quickly after my first experience. So they promised that if I received straight As, then Pastashou at Moran's would be my reward. Clearly, it is only my love of pasta that got me into Georgetown.

The bait worked. I made my grades, and the promised pilgrimage occurred in June of 1965. I'll never forget that moment. We entered through the huge, leaded front doors and slowly sauntered through a smoke-filled bar. I stopped, mesmerized by the black-and-white photographs of Diamond Jim Moran on the wall to the left and the gorgeous copper-topped bar to the right. Though I was all of seven years old, I believed that I was a grown-up and the world was mine!

When the appointed time came, Little Joey, our waiter, in his black waistcoat, paraded out a tray and a stand. With a flourish, the steaming copper pan of hot capellini pasta appeared over a single burner with a low blue flame. And there, in a silver dish, was the magic red sauce (as any true New Orleanian would call it). Perfectly seasoned with garlic, oregano, basil, and a hint of cayenne and strained to the consistency of silk, it resembled a deep-red satin ribbon as it was poured on the waiting capellini. Little Joey took two forks and stirred the delicious ingredients in converging directions so that every last surface of pasta was coated with the Italian potion.

Then came my favorite ingredient—Parmesan cheese. Now in 1965, I didn't know that Parmesan cheese came in huge wheels and that when it was served in its proper state, it had a texture like butter. The only Parmesan I knew was that gravelly substance that came in a bright green can. But not at Moran's! At Moran's it was "fresh from Italy," "grated moments before" Parmesan. Ah, when that luscious cheese appeared in Joey's hand, I nearly leapt for joy. With a wave of his hand, he dusted the pasta with the transcendent velvet dust. By now, I was aching with anticipation.

Little Joey then parceled out our respective servings, and the manna from the gods was placed in front of me. As I slipped my fork into the steaming treat, I knew that every moment spent studying had been worth it.

Well, Moran's moved to the river and then eventually closed. But if you ever want that magic dish, it is still being made. Little Joey struck out on his own. You would know him now as Joey Impastato, and every night you can taste the magic at his restaurant, Impastato's, in Metairie. Oddly enough, it is situated right behind Morning Call— the bookend to Café Du Monde.

Stanwood, David, Anne Gwin, and Janet Duval the night the Saints won the Super Bowl!; In search of orcas off of Victoria, British Columbia; Janet and Stanwood in Bora Bora; With Matthew Payne, for the Stella Shouting Contest at the Tennessee Williams/New Orleans Literary Festival ; Christopher James, Arthur Krystofiak, and Janet enjoying beignets at Café Du Monde; The Duval, Rivera, Daley clan, Christmas 2011; Chris and Irène Daley, Janet's mom and dad today; Janet getting ready for a night out; Performing at the Festival 2008 (Photograph by Ride Hamilton); Amy Dickinson, Janet, Piper Laurie, and Christian LeBlanc at the 2012 Tennessee Williams/New Orleans Literary Festival

Michael Regua
Executive Chef, Antoine's Restaurant, New Orleans
My World of Antoine's

"If I were a food, I would be a Grand Marnier soufflé, as it represents an end of a grand and special meal. It is warm, sweet, and memorable."

Antoine's restaurant opened in 1840 and is the oldest same-family-run restaurant in the country. I have been at Antoine's for more than thirty-six years. I grew up in New Orleans in the Bywater/Ninth Ward neighborhood. When I graduated from F.T. Nicholls High School, I had no idea what I wanted to do with my life. I started working for an air-conditioning supply company. Meanwhile, I had a cousin, Leroy Martin, who was the chef of Antoine's. Every time I saw my cousin, I would ask if he had a job for me at the restaurant. Finally, one day when he was at the cold storage picking up and I was delivering, he said he had a position open at the restaurant. I guess I was at the right place at the right time. The next week I started my job at Antoine's.

I learned from the school of hard knocks; I learned how to cut myself and how to burn myself. I started as a prep cook, boiling lobsters and seafood and preparing escargot dishes. I knew I wanted to advance to the kitchen. I had found my passion, and it was cooking at Antoine's. I was able to learn under veteran chefs. The restaurant business was in my blood. My grandfather was the chef at Morton Brothers, and I was finally going to follow in his footsteps at Antoine's.

I have been a part of many memorable events at Antoine's. One of the most cherished memories is when I was asked to be one of the four chefs to cook for Pope John Paul II in 1989. We went to the archbishop's home on Carrollton Avenue and prepared the dinner for the pope and his cardinals. The Saturday feast included Soufflé Potatoes. In order to prepare the potatoes, a makeshift hood was made by taking a window out of the room the potatoes were fried in for ventilation purposes. The next course consisted of Crabmeat Ravigote and Shrimp Remoulade, an Antoine's staple. The entrée was a chicken broth with vermicelli. The grand finale was Antoine's signature Baked Alaska.

The security for this event was something I will always remember. The chefs and employees in attendance from Antoine's had background checks, without their knowledge, and wherever we went within the three-day period at the Carrollton Avenue property and surrounding areas, the security knew and watched our whereabouts. The pope blessed the chefs in attendance, and he gave us each two blessed rosaries and a blessed medallion.

We have had many celebrities and dignitaries dine at the restaurant. I remember one of the waiters told me Nicolas Cage was upstairs in one of the dining rooms and wanted to meet me. I went upstairs to find him taking care of his young son who was running around the room. It stuck in my head that he was taking care of his son, not a nanny. He was very much at home at the restaurant. This really struck me and made me happy to see him as a father and not the actor we all see in the movies. It gave me great pride that he felt so comfortable at the restaurant that

I love. He started his meal with our famous Soufflé Potatoes followed by Oysters Foch. He is a meat eater and ordered the eight-ounce filet with the Marchand de Vin Sauce. The meal was ended in a grand way with Baked Alaska with Chocolate Sauce and Café Brulot, Antoine's famous flaming coffee.

Antoine's had approximately $10 million of damage after Katrina. We had to buy all new refrigeration because of the spoilage, which was close to $60,000 in inventory. Our goal had been to reopen Christmas Eve, but this proved to be more difficult than we thought. We were able to do a partial opening on December 29, 2005, with quite a few changes because the local vendors were not at full capacity nor was the quality of the food. We eliminated several menu items and had an abbreviated menu. The dress code was changed to business casual to accommodate our clientele that might have lost all of their clothing in the storm. We are very proud and grateful to all of our loyal customers that helped us survive such a difficult time.

One of the highlights of working at Antoine's was going to New York right after Katrina for the James Beard Awards. I made Oysters Rockefeller, our specialty, for one thousand people. Another great trip was going to Jamaica to make gumbo for the ambassador of Jamaica. We also had one of my favorites: beignets from Café Du Monde. But the best thing about working at Antoine's was meeting my wife, Maria. I hired her as a prep chef in 1991 and married her in 1998. She is now the pantry chef, making all the salads, sauces, and desserts. I have three children, Michael Jr., Jeffrey, and Jennifer, who are all from my previous marriage with my first wife, Barbara. Maria is from Guatemala, and when we were married, my two sons stood as our best men and my daughter and Maria's sister as our maids of honor. I have four grandchildren all from my son Jeffrey. My sons both worked at Antoine's at one point and realized the restaurant business was not their cup of tea!

Growing up in the Bywater/Ninth Ward as a young boy, milk and beignets from Café Du Monde were always a treat. As I grew older, I acquired a taste for the delicious café au lait and, of course, three beignets and nothing less.

The storm changed one of my normal routines of having beignets at the Café Du Monde at the Oakwood Mall while Maria was shopping. After the storm, the mall was closed, but I soon found a new way to satisfy my craving. Maria and I would leave the restaurant at night and drive up Toulouse to Decatur. My wife would know that if I took a left onto Decatur it was "beignet time" at Café Du Monde, and if I took a right, it was "home sweet home." Thanks to Café Du Monde, coffee and beignets are now back at the Oakwood Mall.

Chef Michael Regua preparing tenderloin

Crawfish Cardinale

Trout cardinal is a classic Louisiana seafood dish, and this version is a grilled speckled Louisiana trout topped with a rich and velvety béchamel sauce with crawfish. It is a favorite at Antoine's.

¼ cup parsley, chopped
½ cup chopped green onion
½ cup chopped white onion
3 cloves garlic, chopped
1 oz. melted butter
Pinch of thyme
Pinch of basil
2 tbsp. tomato paste
1 lb. crawfish tails, steamed
3-4 oz. white wine
2-3 oz. roux blonde (equal parts butter and flour)
16 oz. half-and-half
Salt and white pepper, to taste
4 7-9 oz. speckled trout fillets, skin off
Parsley

Sauté first 4 ingredients in melted butter until limp, but not brown. Add thyme, basil, and paste. Then add crawfish. Cook until very hot. Add white wine and reduce until the alcohol is gone. Add the roux and half-and-half. Simmer until it thickens, but is not thick. Add salt and pepper to taste.

Rub trout on both sides with salt and white pepper. Cook in a skillet or on a flat grill with a little oil. Cook skin side up until brown halfway through. Turn over and cook the rest of the way, about 3 to 5 minutes. (Thickness will make a difference in cooking time.)

Place cooked trout in the center of a plate and top with Crawfish Cardinale. Garnish with parsley and serve.

Serves 4.

Antoine's Alligator Soup

Alligator soup is one of Antoine's customers' favorites. After Katrina, the restaurant was unable to get turtle meat, and we chose to use alligator meat. We stuck with the alligator because of the wonderful flavor even after it became a lot easier to get turtle meat again.

1 bunch green onion, chopped
4 cloves garlic, chopped
1 medium white onion, chopped
1 bunch parsley, chopped
2 oz. butter
3 lb. alligator tail meat (pre-boiled for 30 minutes in ½ gallon of water, save for stock)
2 bay leaves
½ lemon slice
Pinch of thyme
6 oz. sherry wine
8 oz. tomato juice
1 qt. stock
3 oz. Lea & Perrins sauce
2 beef cubes
Salt and pepper, to taste
3 oz. brown roux (2 oz. butter and 2 oz. flour cooked until brown)
2 hard-boiled eggs, chopped for garnish

Saute chopped vegetables in butter until limp. Add alligator meat and the remaining ingredients. Simmer for 20 minutes. Check seasoning and serve. Garnish with chopped egg and parsley.

Serves 6.

Chef Michael Regua with Alligator Soup, Christmas 2011; In the kitchen at Antoine's; Chef Michael Regua with signature dish, oysters Rockefeller; Antoine's Restaurant vintage picture; Chef Michael Regua in the New Orleans premiere show at House of Blues, June 22, 2010; Chef Michael with his wife, Maria Regua, at House of Blues show; Chef Michael Regua with Peggy at the show; Antoines's Restaurant

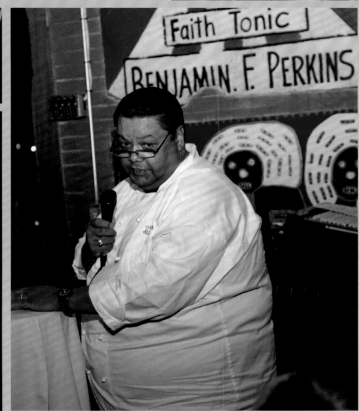

Margarita Bergen
Social Columnist and Realtor, New Orleans
The Dominican Flag—Rice and Beans

"If I were a food, I would be beluga caviar because it is a luxurious delicacy that I start savoring even before I put the delicate roes in my mouth!"

Ever since I was a young girl, I knew I was passionate about food, but cooking was not my passion. I grew up in the Dominican Republic, where the dish of beans and rice is a staple, and we called it the Dominican Flag. Every day we would eat white rice, red beans, and meat or fish, and we would eat it every day, not just on Monday's, as is the New Orleans tradition.

When my father died, my mother immigrated to the Land of Opportunity, New York City. I stayed in Santo Domingo and was sent to live with my grandmother, the matriarch of the family. When I was fifteen, she thought it was time for me to learn how to cook. She took me to her kitchen and told me to start with the beans, which I did. A few minutes later, I left the kitchen, and she asked, "¿Jovencita donde va?" (Where are you going young lady?) I said I was going to the living room, and she replied, "Oh no. You never leave the kitchen until you are ready to serve the meal," which meant at least three to four hours.

Then she told me about the married socialite whose cook unexpectedly left, and she had to prepare a meal for her husband before he came home. So she bought a live chicken, pulled out all the feathers, put it in the oven, and garnished it nicely for the meal. When her husband arrived, she was very proud of her baked chicken until he sliced it and the guts came out. He told her, "I am taking you home so your mother can teach you how to cook." I never forgot that!

Years later, I decided that since I did not have time to cook, I needed to know all the legendary chefs, the maître d's, the sommeliers, and the waiters. Life, of course, became a lot easier since every great chef needs dedicated consumers like me.

One day I went to Chef Paul Prudhomme's K-Paul's to eat their famous blackened redfish, for which I had been salivating all day long. When I ordered it, I was informed that they had run out. I was furious. I had waited in line for a long time. His wife, Kay, was very strict about the line, and I had to wait just like all the tourists, but once there, I immediately ordered the Cajun Martini marinated with jalapeño to help me forget the wait.

So when they told me, "No more redfish," I just stepped out into the street and started jumping up and down to release my disappointment. I reentered the restaurant and Chef Paul, who was sitting in the back, pulled me aside and asked what was wrong. I told him the bad news, and he said, "Darling, I have for you something better than sex: blackened pompano." I ordered it, and when I finished it, I went to him and said, "Sorry darling, but the sex that I am accustomed to is much better than pompano."

I was very fortunate to live for seven years on the third floor of the Pontalba Apartments, facing Cafe Du Monde. I woke up to the smell of coffee with chicory and those decadent sweet little pillows piled up with powdered sugar. No wonder I am called one of the divas of gastronomical delights. How lucky can I be? I am still counting my blessings.

October 2010 show at Ralph & Kacoo's; Margarita Bergen with Leah Chase at the New Orleans premier show, June 2010; Margarita Bergen in New Orleans show at House of Blues, July 2010; Margarita with Chef Matt Murphy and Jeremy Davenport at the June 2010 show; Margarita and Peggy; Margarita's grandmother; Sexy witch at Halloween; Saints fan; Margarita and headliners Jeanne Vidrine, Peggy, Ann Tuennerman, and Nell Nolan

Daron Stiles
Actor, Baton Rouge
A Chicken Pot Pie—My Childhood Comfort Food

"If I were a food, I'd have to be an Italian white truffle: rare, wild, highly sought after, pungent, and expensive."

This is a story about comfort food—that most wondrous category of food that tells us on the deepest and most intimate level that the world is safe and good and that everything is truly going to be all right. Comfort food is especially important to children, who are particularly vulnerable to the seemingly random affronts of a world over which they have no control.

As a child, my comfort food was frozen chicken pot pie. These were not the new, fancy kind that could go from freezer to table in six minutes via the microwave. These icons of frozen culinary bliss had to be baked in the oven for a full forty minutes. The great thing about this was that the crust actually became flakey and toasty brown, just like an old fashioned apple pie. Oh, those hot poultry pastries were well worth the wait. And when that golden pie finally found its way to my plate (hopefully intact, with the crust scarcely broken), all steamy and aromatic, I could hardly wait for it to cool before spooning it into my mouth. The truth be told, I scalded the cleft of my pallet more often than not. I gleefully awaited these pies at least three nights each week, and when that pie was consumed, I was one happy and contented young man, ready for my bedside prayers and a blissful night's sleep.

In the fall of 1959, my family lived in the Villa del Rey subdivision in Baton Rouge. I attended Villa del Rey Elementary School, starting in first grade, the very first year that school opened. Dear Mrs. Rue was the principal;

that larger than life, Nurse Ratchet of a principal knew how to frighten children into submission with just a glance and loved us as if we were her very own. Our house was directly behind Greenlawn Cemetery, a venue for endless forbidden adventures for a child with an active imagination, such as me. Our household attended Florida Boulevard Baptist Church, where the pastor was Roy Stockstill, who later went on to found Bethany Church. I can vividly recall Brother Roy, up at that pulpit, with his mild, soothing voice and his ever present smile. Brother Roy was the type of man who smiled at you from the bottom of his soul and would much rather preach about love and heaven than sin and hellfire. And his style of preaching was pretty effective, too, because he created a fairly steady queue of candidates ready to find salvation. Now, my family members were pretty good Baptists and so, naturally, we attended Sunday morning services without fail. And, being pretty good Baptists, we also attended Sunday evening services, which usually drew attendance of about 30 percent of Sunday morning. And, being pretty good Baptists, we even attended Wednesday evening services, which usually didn't pull in enough bodies to kill the echo in the auditorium. Still, we were pretty good Baptists, so we went.

Now, not many six year olds have a highly enough evolved sense of the afterlife to really appreciate church. But I had accepted going to church on Sunday mornings and Sunday evenings as what the Lord reasonably expected of us on his day (even though if you weren't careful, Sunday evening services could result in missing *Bonanza* on the TV). But Wednesday evening services always seemed to me to be just a little unreasonable of the Lord. I mean, if you think about it, if you go to church too often, it sort of takes something away from the special, holy sacredness of those Sunday services. It all gets sort of diluted—at least that's what I felt at the age of six; and I even advised the Lord of this during some of those tedious, Wednesday-evening-service prayers. I thought it was pretty sound advice.

So this story is actually about one of those particular Wednesday nights when, after a day of school, an afternoon of homework, and vigorous play in the cemetery, I was destined to go to Wednesday-night service. Now, to comfort myself against this miserable fate, I had begged for a chicken pot pie for dinner. And though we were running late for church, Mom had relented and quickly turned on the oven and tossed in the pie. But time was running short, and you simply cannot make a chicken pie cook faster than the immutable forty minutes. So by the time it was cooked, there simply was not time to eat it. With apologies, Mom turned off the oven and told me I could eat it when we returned from church. Needless to say, this did not go over well, and I had some choice words about it for the Lord later on, while Brother Roy was blessing the offering that was about to be taken. The rest of what happened that night is mostly a blur. But I remember being the most miserable of children. I was hungry and bored and not one bit comforted. I demonstrated my annoyance to the Lord by enthusiastically singing the lyrics of a hymn other than the one the congregation was singing. Then, during the sermon, I furiously scribbled on the visitor's cards that were neatly stacked in the hymnbook shelf on the back of the pew in front us, dulling the stubby little pencils stored in the pencil holes. Finally, though, weariness and lack of sustenance caught up with me; my eyes began to grow irresistibly heavy and my will to stay awake evaporated. I lay down on the pew and slid into a deep, committed slumber.

At some later time, my father picked me up and carried me sleeping to the car. I never woke when he carried me from the car to the house. The next thing I was aware of was my mom putting the warmed up chicken pot pie in front of me, at the kitchen table. "Do you want your chicken pie, sweetheart?" she asked. I murmured my assent, picked up my spoon, and stuck it into the precious pie. But that bite never made it to my mouth, for my head was down on the table, and for the first and last time of my childhood, sleep took preeminence over eating a chicken pot pie.

Once again my father carried his sleeping son, this time to my bedroom. Still sleeping, my mom changed me into my pajamas. But no nocturnal coma was so deep that I could escape being awakened for my nightly prayers. My dutiful parents pressed my barely conscious body into the traditional, bedside kneeling position for my nightly recital of "Now I Lay Me Down to Sleep." I do not remember reciting this prayer. And I have only the vaguest memories of my parents falling to the floor, racked in uncontrollable laughter, as I weakly crawled into my warm bed and buried my head in my pillow. I remember feeling deeply injured that, after missing my dinner and enduring a tortuous church service and saying my prayers and doing everything right, they should be laughing at me. These were my last thoughts as I fell into the deep, dreamless sleep of the innocent. And the moment passed.

Years later, as a young man in my twenties, wading through Freud, Jung, Heidegger, and struggling for self discovery, I revisited these feelings of injury and injustice by my parents and confronted them with the question: "Why did you laugh at me, all those years ago, after my prayers?" Like some bizarre, déjà vu event, both my parents again were seized by fits of uncontrollable laugher while I watched, bewildered and helpless. And all those feelings of injury, betrayal, injustice, and abuse came bubbling back to the surface. Finally, when my mother could catch her breath, she cooed, "Sweetheart, you don't realize this, but that night, when you said your prayers, you said, 'Now I lay me down to sleep. I pray the Lord my soul to keep. If I should wake before I die, help me to eat my chicken pie.'"

That's how important comfort food is for a child. Make sure your children get their comfort food.

Cajun Chicken Pot Pie

This recipe started off as an old family recipe for a rather standard chicken pot pie. But in the Gulf South, standard just isn't good enough. I thought to myself, what if I took my (still) favorite food and added the flavors beloved by people in the Cajun lands? So I coated the chicken with Cajun seasoning and smoked it with pecan wood and boiled the potatoes in crab boil. (Employing the drippings from the chicken is key.) Well, the results were enough to please any chef of the line. The first pie was gone in an hour. Everyone came back for seconds, then thirds. Pies three and four followed the next day. Then, alas, pie number four, which I had frozen for a hungry, rainy day, had to come out of the freezer. Guess what I'm making for Thanksgiving? And I'm doubling the recipe!

1 large chicken (about 5 lb.), suitable for grilling/smoking
Cajun seasoning mix, to taste
1 tsp. sage
1 cup diced red potatoes
1 bottle liquid crab boil
1 cup medium chopped sweet onion
1 cup chopped celery
1 cup mushrooms, sliced
1 cup small baby carrots
1 cup broccoli florets
1 cup frozen sweet peas
½ cup fresh parsley, chopped
48 oz. chicken broth
1 can crème of celery soup
1 can crème of chicken soup
1 can crème of mushroom soup
1 tsp. thyme
4 foil pie pans
8 frozen pie crusts
2 egg whites

Season chicken liberally with Cajun seasoning and sage and smoke it with pecan wood until it will easily pull apart. (Smoke it in a pan and save the drippings, to be used as part of the chicken broth. A supermarket, rotisserie chicken can be substituted, if smoked chicken is impossible.) Debone and pull into bite-sized pieces. (Include as much of the smoked skin as is practical.)

Boil small potatoes in crab boil until they will cut easily but are not soft. Dice potatoes. (Go heavy on the crab boil.)

Cook remaining vegetables and parsley in chicken broth until barely tender, then remove, saving broth. Don't overcook!

Expand soups with chicken broth and add chicken and vegetables. Mix and season mixture to taste with Cajun seasoning and thyme. You will get some seasoning from the chicken. Be careful not to over salt.

Place 4 of the frozen pie crusts into bottom of the 4 foil pie pans and fill with mixture. Wet inside edges of crust and put the other 4 pie crusts on top of the 4 pies. Seal top crust with the edge of a fork. Slit a few places on top crusts.* Paint tops with egg whites. Bake at 350 for 75 minutes. The smoked meat and Cajun flavors make this dish distinctive. You won't be disappointed.

Pies may be frozen before cooking but allow time for them to thaw. This is great to make ahead when company is coming.

Serves 6 (1 pie).

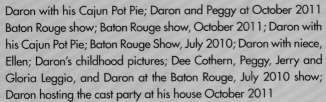

Daron with his Cajun Pot Pie; Daron and Peggy at October 2011 Baton Rouge show; Baton Rouge show, October 2011; Daron with his Cajun Pot Pie; Baton Rouge Show, July 2010; Daron with niece, Ellen; Daron's childhood pictures; Dee Cothern, Peggy, Jerry and Gloria Leggio, and Daron at the Baton Rouge, July 2010 show; Daron hosting the cast party at his house October 2011

Adam Millstein
Owner, SOUTH Bar & Grill, Santa Monica
A Bit of SOUTH in Santa Monica

"If I were a food, I'd be a spicy meatball topped with cheese on a bowl of angel hair pasta. You've got to have a strong foundation—hence the pasta. The spicy meatball comes from always having a little bit of spice. And I'm cheesy most of the time. Put that together and you've got an interesting and satisfying dish."

Growing up in Chicago, I didn't understand the Southern culture of food until I moved to Atlanta when I was eight. There I became friends with our neighbor Janie Newport and another woman named Georgeann. They introduced our family to mac and cheese, green bean casserole, and the list goes on.

I was about seventeen years old when I began applying to colleges and when I visited Tulane, I knew there was something about New Orleans that I couldn't put my finger on, but it was the place for me. I started classes at Tulane and took a job at Copeland's as a busboy. I worked at the restaurant for the rest of my tenure in New Orleans.

New Orleans is truly unlike any other city in the world, and it all comes out in the food. Only in New Orleans can you start a sentence with "Gotta have the Ferdie at Mother's, the oysters at Acme, the eggs Benedict at Commander's Palace, the muffaletta at Central Grocery, the burger at Port-a-Call, the alligator cheesecake at Jacques-Imo's, and beignets at Café Du Monde." It's a place where you can talk about food for hours.

Leaving New Orleans after I graduated was bittersweet. I had fallen in love with everything about the city. I decided I was destined for fame in Hollywood. Being an "aspiring" actor usually means one thing: you will also be working in the restaurant industry. While fumbling through auditions and working a handful of horrendous jobs (from towel boy to dressing up like Batman), I worked in a couple of different restaurants. During this time, I learned a lot about the

industry and met a ton of great people, including the guys who would become my partners in our first restaurant, SOUTH.

SOUTH was a collective idea that came from us being from the South and from the absence of a Southern spot in southern California. We essentially wanted to bring our love and appreciation of the South and New Orleans to Santa Monica. We took the concept and ran with it. SOUTH is a tribute to the people and places we admired. The food was a must. We had to find someone who knew food and more importantly Southern food.

Our chef Jamal Gillespie is just that person. His creativity, professionalism, and knowledge have natives from Atlanta to New Orleans agreeing that we are the real deal. He has enhanced traditional dishes. Pasta Jambalaya, New Orleans Tacos, and Bourbon Street Pizza are just as popular as our traditional po' boys and catfish. Drinks were essential in their authenticity. Abita and Dixie beers were a must, and we pay homage to the mint julep and Pimms' cup. You add all of that together with a staff trained in "Southern hospitality," and you have a destination for everyone.

Owning restaurants can definitely be grueling, but with SOUTH, the payoff is introducing and educating a customer on something that we have such a strong affinity for. Watching someone eat crawfish for the first time, or explaining deep-fried Twinkies, those are the sort of experiences that make it all worth it—passing the love, respect, and experience on to someone else.

The partners of SOUTH Adam, Philip, Robyn, and Chris; Cast of the show at SOUTH Santa Monica, Chef Doreen Fang, Chef Das Smith, Chef Keith Roberts, Peggy, Adam, Lisa Annitti, Lance Spellerberg; SOUTH Santa Monica; Partners of SOUTH: Philip, Adam, Robyn, and Chris; Adam as the Lion with friends at SOUTH on Halloween; Adam and Peggy at SOUTH Santa Monica Show, November, 2010; Adam with his daughter, Peyton, wife, Aurora, and dog, Daisy; Adam with friends and team at SOUTH for Thanksgiving Dinner; Adam celebrating life in California with friends; Adam with Peyton at Disneyland; Adam at Santa Monica Beach with Peyton

Missy Crews
Event Producer and Miss Louisiana 1980, Baton Rouge
Caution . . . Nostalgia Is High in Calories!

"If I were a food, I would be my mother's fried chicken. No fuss, easy to approach, and makes you feel at home."

Oh, Louisiana, home sweet home, place of my most precious childhood memories, a culture I have longed for these past twenty-five plus years of living away. Oh, Louisiana, you are a deep well of intrigue and fascination. Your people, your music, your stories are in my soul. And your cuisine . . . well . . . Lordy. What is a well-meaning, healthy girl to do?

When I left Baton Rouge after college, I headed to New York City without really knowing when, or if ever, the hands of time would bring me back to Louisiana. I lived in New York, New Jersey, and, most recently, Charlotte, North Carolina, where I raised my two daughters. In this past year, I decided that those hands of time were wrapped around mine, and they were pointing me back home! Now, I have loved catching up with old friends, and the ease of being near my family again has been an incredible gift.

But I had a sense from previous visits over the years that a permanent move back would require some concentrated will power on my part when it came to culinary indulgences. The problem is that I truly underestimated just how wildly seductive food would be when it came to nostalgia.

I love stories, always have, and in reflection, I recognize how many of them revolve around the comfort of a meal. My parents are both Mississippi natives, and I loved the tales of cold watermelons on hot Delta days, family reunion spreads on the church lawn, and what the preparation of a holiday meal would mean for the whole family.

I grew up one of six children here in Baton Rouge and have great memories of the round oak table and family dinners, where we talked about nothing much and everything important! So family and the lure of home would have me returning to Louisiana each summer with my own children. It was important to me that they knew their Deep South heritage. Therefore, I made sure they were introduced to the many things I love about the Pelican State, and, of course, favorite foods became a huge part of their education.

As far back as they can remember, we met friends at Jay's Bar-B-Que and had po' boys at Phil's Oyster Bar. We visited Sonny at Calandro's Grocery, and he told them how little I was when he first met me. That is when the old store faced Edison and not Government Street. We visited the legendary Baton Rouge actress and friend Virginia Hill at her favorite place, Giamanco's, and the girls drank Shirley Temples and listened to her dramatic tales. I wish that place were still there; I'd go tomorrow.

Of course, we had to have the unique square pizza called Round the World at Fleur de Lis. Seriously, that place is a landmark! And thinking about it, Government Street should be renamed Temptation Boulevard! I bet I have gained several happy pounds from that street alone!

We toured the LSU lakes, rolled down the Indian mounds, visited Mike the Tiger, and hit the student union

90

for T-shirts. The trip highlight was our favorite snowball stand on Perkins Road on the way home—not too much syrup, please!

They begged to go to Tony's Seafood to watch the fish in the tank, and I can promise you they were the only little Tar Heel girls at their school who knew about crawfish and boudin!

They introduced their North Carolina schoolmates to king cakes and Mardi Gras beads. Grown children still tell me they were sad they never found the plastic baby in their piece of cake. Even though we called North Carolina home for many years, none of us ever became used to putting slaw on our barbeque. Although, I reluctantly tried liver mush and found I liked it.

Now, I am back home and overwhelmed daily by the call of the "just one bite" temptation. Seems that everyone wants to make sure I have the taste of home on a regular basis. My friends are so sweet to me! I hear . . .

"Red beans and rice on Monday. You have to have it for tradition." "You work downtown and you've never been to Poor Boy Lloyds?" "Meet me for the *best* margaritas at this cute new place." "I don't care if you ate breakfast. How can you pass on beignets at Coffee Call . . . oh, just order the fingers!" "You have to go to Georges and Parrain's . . . and Acme (you can just order a salad)." Okay, I'll have the fried catfish but really you can leave off the étouffée, fried eggplant, and crabmeat topping—ugh, but so delicious!

No doubt about it, people in Louisiana love their food, but the beautiful thing is it really is more than that. It is celebrating, sharing, being with friends, and knowing that those moments of menu choices, laughter, and anticipation are all going to be a part of you somehow.

I am happy to say that the move back to Louisiana has made me proud on many levels, and I haven't spent all my time discovering and rediscovering favorite foods. I am thrilled to see the many good things happening in our state, and I am comforted to know that the fun-loving, generous spirit of the Louisiana people is alive and well.

On my first weekend back in Baton Rouge, I went out to Tony's Seafood alone. I looked at the catfish swimming, took in the amazing scent of the seafood seasoning, and talked to locals who won't buy their seafood anywhere else. I bought six boiled crabs and some cold beer. Once home, I spread the newspaper on the table outside like I was preparing an alter. I mixed a sauce, with just the right amount of horseradish, put the beer in the freezer to get it really cold, and found a good blunt knife to crack the shells.

Content with my own company, I sat grateful and in wonder that fate had brought me back to a place I love so much. Boiled crabs and a beer on a perfect October afternoon never tasted so sacred.

Nostalgia—all the places, scents, and tastes that call you back to your memories. I'm not going to kid you; it can be a little high in calories, but oh, it is ever so worth it!

Paul Arrigo, Missy, Peggy, and Lt. Gov. Jay Dardenne at Anniversary Show

Miss Louisiana 1980 in a Mardi Gras parade

Louisiana Buttermilk Pralines

This is a favorite holiday recipe for my family, and we usually make several batches for friends as gifts. Many tell me they look forward to their praline present more than any other. And I should note that I forgive my Northern friends that insist on calling them *pray*-leens.

2 ½ cups granulated sugar
1 tsp. baking soda
¼ tsp. salt
1 cup buttermilk
3 tbsp. butter
3-4 cups pecan halves

Use a large pan (8 qt.) and mix first 4 ingredients. Stir over high heat scraping bottom frequently. If you use a candy thermometer, it needs to reach 210 degrees F for 5 minutes, or note when the mixture begins to bubble and turns a light cream color. At this point, add the butter and pecans.

Keep stirring constantly and mixture will turn light brown. A candy thermometer should show 230 degrees and a small drop of mixture in cold water should form a soft ball. Continue stirring and try a test drop on a sheet of wax paper to see if mixture will "set" and harden. The mixture should not look too glossy before pouring out. Candy should set for 10 minutes on the wax paper.

Makes 24 pralines.

Notes: I love this recipe because the buttermilk makes for a smooth and rich praline. The trick to candy making is to know when to pour the mixture out in drops on your wax paper or foil. Sometimes the batch has to go back on the stove to cook further if you see that the pralines are not setting. I have made lots of mistakes pouring the mixture too late or too soon but always end up with a nice batch of praline crumbles or syrup for ice cream!

Also be careful with the heat when making pralines. Hot boiling sugar can leave a painful burn. I always use a cooking mitt to protect my "stirring" hand!

Missy at First Anniversary Show; Missy performing with the Louisiana Concert Ballet; Missy as an LSU cheerleader, 1979; Missy and Peggy at New Orleans premiere show at House of Blues, June 22, 2010; Missy and her family at her mother's ninetieth birthday party; Olympic Gold Medal Winner Carl Lewis, Missy, and former LSU Coach Dale Brown at "An Evening with Carl Lewis" presented by Jeffrey Marx; Cheerleading; Missy and daughters, Elizabeth and Susannah Howard

Jeremy Davenport
Singer and Trumpet Player, Davenport Lounge, New Orleans
An Evolution of a Midwestern Digestive System

"If I were a food, I'd be a crème donut because I'm sweet and nasty."

Easy does it, I thought, as I boarded the plane from St. Louis to New Orleans on a seemingly average August morning. Jeans, backpack, trumpet, cassette tapes and deck (the '80s), light jacket. I'm hungry; it's not even 8:00 A.M. yet. I think I'll try to make it until lunch. Delf said that I would be in for a real treat.

Outside: Am I in a sauna? Holy mother of a biscuit—this is hot! Sweaty and starved, I climb into a yellow cab headed to Tipitina's to meet Delf. "Hey, man . . . Why didn't you tell me I needed my winter jacket?" As we exchanged laughs and more jokes, Delf and I take off for Mandina's.

Mandina's: Air conditioned, well, thank God.

I'm hungry, and I should have been more aware of the enormity of this sandwich (if it can be called that) as it was placed on the table. They called it a loaf—the biggest loaf of anything I had ever seen. We are talking seemingly hundreds of fried seafood critters, more than your allowable weekly serving size of mayo, a small tomato plant, head of lettuce, and a vat of ketchup—all smashed between a meter-long stretch of warm French bread, coated in a stick of butter that is beautifully melted to connect the mayonnaise and other goodies with the crispy interior.

Half a loaf, a dozen oysters and two beers later, we mosey out and head to Delf's car. Then I hear, "I could go for something sweet. How 'bout you?"

"We're gonna go to the oldest snowball stand in the city; you know what a snowball is right?"

"Is it like a snow cone?" Only laughter.

Hansen's Sno-Bliz Shop: "Two large please, both with condensed milk."

I know I just ate ice, but it is so hot. I think I might pass out. I don't feel right. What is happening to me? I think I need to find a restroom immediately!

Delf suggests, "My folks' house is pretty close."

"No way, man," I say, "I am not meeting the rest of your family on this note."

Do you like to cook? This is the equivalent of running into Julia Child's home, unannounced and in trouble.

The rest is a little foggy. Hi, Grandma Marsalis. Nice to meet you. Okay, bye! Please don't tell Wynton about this. I will never live this down.

How do people eat like this? I'm the poor boy who is going to experience *death by chocolate*, and I didn't even have any chocolate. Stop thinking about food! Something is seriously wrong with me.

Sleep. Next day. Eat. Sleep. Play. Months go by. Play. Play. Sleep. Eat. Years. Eat. Play. Eat. I've evolved! At least my stomach has—po' boys, condensed milk, stuffed artichokes, BBQ shrimp, fried chicken livers, red beans and rice, sauce piquant, crabmeat au gratin, whiskey, and beer. Bring it all on!

And meanwhile, as I sit here, back at Café Du Monde, eating a full order of beignets, drinking a steaming cup of café au lait, and already wondering where I should have lunch, I think how blessed I am to be able to digest this delicious city.

We'll Dance 'Til Dawn album cover (Photograph by Theresa Cassagne, courtesy Basin Street Records); Jeremy ending his monologue with music; Jeremy playing in the French Quarter (Photograph by Theresa Cassagne); Jeremy being introduced at the show; (Photograph by Theresa Cassagne); Jeremy in the New Orleans premiere show at House of Blues, June 22, 2010

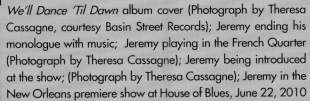

Diana C. Zollicoffer
Writer, Producer, and Director, Los Angeles
The Other Creole Girl

"If I were a food, I would be cheese. Cheese comes in so many varieties from sweet to sharp and goes with almost everything."

I was invited to be in the "Meanwhile, Back at Café Du Monde . . ." show at the Los Angeles House of Blues because I was a Creole girl. No, not Louisiana Creole, but Creole from Seychelles. Say who? Seychelles. Actually, Seychelles Island to be exact. For those of you not familiar with my little piece of heaven, allow me a moment to digress, and for those of you who are familiar, allow me a moment to beam. Seychelles Island is an independent nation. It's made up of approximately 120 islands gloriously located in the beauty of the Indian Ocean. My tranquil island is east of Africa, close to Madagascar. (Feel free to look it up and fall in love.) We are a proud utopian mix of African, European, Indian, and Chinese people. We call ourselves a "masala," which in the Indian culture is a mixture of spices. Yes, we are an easy-going *"Creole" bunch.* Peggy Sweeney-McDonald and I always discussed the spirit of Creole people from all over the world. Unfortunately [for my taste buds], she asked me to go to New Orleans when I was on a very strict diet. I was in the process of losing 118 pounds. I was going to research and develop a script about the famous haunted Myrtles Plantation, which meant my first trip to Louisiana. Many folks thought I was insane to go to the heart of Louisiana Southern cooking and be on a protein-based diet, but I did.

My dad always mentioned when he was younger how much he loved New Orleans-bayou cooking. I joyfully hunted down a roasted turkey leg (protein) when we arrived that first night at the French Quarter Festival and happily chomped on gator for the first time ever. It was pure protein. But when it came time to have a delicious powdery Café Du Monde beignet, I had to restrain myself. In fact, Peggy thought I was nuts when I said I was going to take a few and freeze them to eat when I was allowed to in six weeks. Go ahead and laugh folks, but that's what I did. I bought my beignets, froze them, wrapped them in the most secured amount of aluminum foil, nervously boarded my plane back to Los Angeles, and six-and-a-half weeks later I ate them with a Starbuck's Breve Latte. Sigh . . . it was amazing, but I am looking forward to my next trip to New Orleans, so I can have my beignet and café au'lait the authentic way. Y'all know how—while sitting at Café Du Monde, people watching, and wiping powdered sugar off my face.

My Southern father was a major influence on my cooking and eating. I was seven years old when my mom married the nicest man. Immediately I called him Daddy, not a moment's hesitation. My daddy was much older than my mom. He was thirty-three years her senior, but to see them together, you never would have known. Hosea Zollicoffer was full of spirit, energy, and light. He laughed a lot and gave the best hugs. He grew up in a generation that didn't share their feelings, but there wasn't a day that went by that he didn't tell my brother, Ricky, and I "I love you" and every night ended with a kiss before bed. He always made my mother laugh and discussed every decision with her. He was a "good egg."

He taught me how to cook. Girl, did I mention that my daddy was from Mississippi, so hence he would always jokingly say, "Girl, come down here so I can teach you how to cook, so your husband won't beat you and I won't have to shoot him, so I'm saving myself." My daddy was proud of his and my cooking. We cooked everything! We made Southern food, Italian food, Chinese food, Indian food (my mom's specialty being that we're Seychelles), and things we kind of made up along the way. We cooked desserts, breakfast, lunch, dinner, and snacks. I wasn't afraid to try anything because he wasn't afraid to try anything. I'm still the same way.

I would get a notion to make something, and I would say, "Daddy, we need to go to the grocery store." He would take me three or four times a day if I was experimenting or failing in my experiment. I made and decorated my friends' birthday cakes in high school, and despite all of that cooking, I wasn't fat. Now don't get me wrong, I was never a tiny girl, always had these hips and butt, but never sloppy fat.

When my father died the year I graduated from college, I stopped cooking. Honestly, for nearly fifteen years, I barely boiled let alone scrambled an egg. The oven was only used to keep my apartment warm, and the fridge pretty much stayed empty or stocked with tasteless frozen wares, and even restaurants seemed void of flavor. I ate my mom's cooking because that was the closest to my dad's, but everything tasted like white bread to me.

All that changed a few years ago when my roommate Sarah and I decided to cook Thanksgiving dinner for the boys and a few girls. At that time, we were surrounded by guy friends but no boyfriends, no lovers, just "platonic men space holders." Since Los Angeles is full of transients and these bumpkins weren't going home, we decided to cook Thanksgiving dinner for them. Just like in the Disney movie *Ratatouille*, it was as if the ghost of my dad came to me that day. I felt his spirit. I was inspired to cook again. I was diagramming desserts, conjuring up ideas, and mixing ingredients and flavor. I was me again. The twelve-year-old me was roaming the grocery store, deciding what I wanted to make and changing my mind a "cagillion" times.

The boys ate and came back for the next four days. In fact, the following year they decided to give us money to cook to make sure we did it again. So for the next three Thanksgivings, we were bound and obligated to feed those hungry minions, but I only cooked for Thanksgiving because it was my daddy's favorite holiday, and he would go all out.

About two years ago, I completely rediscovered the joys of daily cooking for myself, not just hungry boys. Cooking brought my youth back to me. I lost a ton of weight cooking fresh foods, and I cooked like my buddies Julia, Yan, Jacques, and Jeff. I commentated to an invisible TV camera as I went along, and I knew it was going to be a good meal if I found myself humming as I cooked. Cooking brought me back to my creative side as well, to my horrible amateur painting, jewelry making, French classes, picture taking, and writing.

I love to cook! I love to cook for friends, and I love to cook because cooking was one of my earliest memories of love from a dear sweet spirit—my daddy.

Hosea's Wine Bottle Buttermilk Biscuits

When I think about the day my dad taught me how to make these biscuits, I crack up. Why? Well it's the method that made me laugh. The recipe is for buttermilk biscuits. I have since added thyme because Daddy always told me, "Girl, if you can add sum'thin to make anything better, go on and do it!" He was a food adventurist. I was a giggling nine-year-old when I learned this recipe because we used a "wine bottle" as a rolling pin. I recently made these biscuits, and my roommate Sarah laughed at me when I used an empty wine bottle to roll out my dough. She stopped snickering when she ate the amazing biscuits, which are simple to make and quick to bake.

1⅓ cups all-purpose flour
2 tsp. baking powder
½ tsp. baking soda
Pinch (or 2) salt
Pinch (or 2) sugar
1 tbsp. dried thyme
1 stick cold salted butter, cut into cubes
½ cup sour cream
¾ cup cold buttermilk (I use low fat; Daddy always used full fat)
2 tbsp. salted butter, to top before baking
1 egg, to use as an egg wash

Preheat oven to 450 degrees and line a baking sheet with parchment paper.

In a large bowl, sift in the flour, baking powder, baking soda, pinch of salt, and pinch of sugar. Add in the dried thyme and the cubes of cold butter. Using the tips of your fingers, incorporate the butter into the flour mixture. The flour should look like coarse crumbs. (If you have a food processor fitted with a metal blade, whisk together or process with 6 1-second pulses.) I mix with my hand.

Add the sour cream and the buttermilk into the flour mixture, just until a dough starts to come together. Lightly flour a large cutting board and start to gently roll out the dough (with wine bottle or rolling pin) to about ½ inch thick or so.

Fold dough in half and gently roll again. Fold dough in half again and super gently roll out again. (Please do not overwork your dough.) Cut the dough and place onto the baking sheet. My dad always cut in squares!

Cut the remaining 2 tbsp. of butter into pieces and dot each biscuit with a piece of butter. Lightly whisk the egg in a cup, and brush each biscuit with the egg wash. Bake the biscuits in the oven for about 13 to 15 minutes or until golden brown.

Makes 10 to 12 biscuits.

Photographs by Diana Zollicoffer

98

Diana at The French Quarter Festival; 2010 Los Angeles Film Festival; Diana and her nephews; Diana and her family in the Seychelles; Diana directing; At the Seychelles beach; Diana with friends: The Food Network Stars Aarti Sequeria, Giada De Laurentiis and Manouschka Guerrier. Diana with her niece; Diana with her Mom, Jeannie Zollicoffer; 2010 Los Angeles Premiere show at the House of Blues-Sunset with Peggy, Lance Spellerberg and Manouschka Guerrier; Diana flying over Catalina Island.

Nikki Thomas
Radio Host, KBLX 102.9, and Creator,
The Nikki Thomas Network, San Francisco
Laissez Les Bons Temps Rouler

"If I were a food, I'd be a sweet potato—low fat, luscious, sweet, and Southern!"

I was born and raised in New Orleans, the city of the best food and parties ever! When you say food and party, what city do you think of—New Orleans! Growing up here was a wonderful experience, and Café Du Monde was my favorite hang out!

I've been doing radio for almost twenty years. I started at WYLD in New Orleans in 1992, and my first shift was the midnight to 8:00 A.M. shift. The first thing we would do when we got off was head to Café Du Monde. My friend Andre and I would head over for café au lait and beignets! "Baby, look at the weave on that floozy over there! It's unbeweavable." He worked strange hours too, so we would be there no matter what time we got off. This was the way we passed the time. And after all these years, Andre is still one of my best friends, and beignets are my all-time favorite dessert.

Now people don't understand that when they go to New Orleans it's like visiting another country. It has its own cuisine and its own language: "Yeah, you right!" "How ya mama 'nem?" And what about "Hey, la bah?" It means "Hey, how you are doing?" "Lagniappe," a little bit extra! But my favorite is *"Laissez les bons temps rouler!"* "Let the good times roll!"

To tell you the truth, as wonderful as New Orleans and the food was, I was always dreaming about going somewhere else and doing yoga as a vegan hippie. I wanted to go to a place where I could live without relaxing my hair and that's how I ended up here in San Francisco.

It didn't really work out the way I wanted right away because I had to go to Buffalo, New York, first. So I left New Orleans with all this great food—gumbo, étouffée, and shrimp Creole—to go to . . . Buffalo wings!

A few years later, I received an offer to come to San Francisco, and I was so excited. I'd be walking down the street thinking to myself, "Oh, this is so beautiful." San Francisco had its own style, its own architecture, and its own cuisine! I was in heaven! It's a place I could finally do yoga and be a vegan hippie!

You see how things evolve? I wanted to do something, ended up somewhere else, and then found a home where I could do what I wanted to do.

Nowadays, I am a broadcaster at the KBLX Champagne Brunch, from 10:00 A.M. to 2:00 P.M., every Sunday at ANZU Restaurant in the Hotel Nikko in San Francisco. Yes, I talk and eat every Sunday. Every now and then someone will come in, look at my skinny self, and wonder where all the food goes. Louisiana genes, baby!

One day ANZU's Chef Phillipe came in and told me he wanted me to taste the new menu items; he brought me beignet dunking sticks. They were really neat little beignets, as they were served with little dunking cups of sauces so you didn't get powdered sugar everywhere. Isn't that the coolest thing?

But no matter where I go, I know that Café Du Monde is always open and waiting! Now, I visit my hometown with my daughter, Marley, who, just like her mom loves the beignets!

Nikki Thomas with daughter, Marley; Nikki Thomas with baby Marley; Nikki Thomas - Yoga Vegan Hippie; Nikki Thomas with Peggy at the San Francisco show at the Razz Room, March 2010; At Jazz Brunch at ANZU at Hotel Nikko; Nikki Thomas as a baby; Nikki Thomas at work

Sandy Davis
Caddo-Bossier Director of Homeland Security, Shreveport

Eleven-Bean Soup

"If I were a food, I would surely be fried chicken because there is nothing more Southern than fried chicken, and I am as Southern as they come. Fried chicken fits in with any occasion, much as I do. It is good hot out of the grease or stone cold from the fridge—ready for any occasion anytime, so am I!"

I worked at Central Fire Station in downtown Shreveport, Louisiana, for several years. At the time, there were twenty-two men working on each shift at this station, so you can only imagine what a big ole "Boy's Club" that must have been. Typically, each shift had a designated cook or members would just take turns with the duty. Well I was the official cook on my shift, which was B Shift.

It had been a cool and rainy week, and my wife had cooked Fifteen-Bean Soup for us at home on the Sunday afternoon before I went back to work the next day for my twenty-four-hour shift at the station. Fifteen-Bean Soup comes in a one-pound bag with a variety of dried beans and dehydrated spices already mixed in. All that had to be done was add a little sausage, bake some cornbread, and the meal was prepared. Nothing sticks to your ribs like a good soup and cornbread on a cool, rainy day.

One advantage of being the cook is that I was able to choose the menu for the shift, so whatever I was craving would be the fare for the day. That Fifteen-Bean Soup was so good that I just could not get it off my mind as I headed up the stairs to report to duty that next afternoon around 3:00 P.M. After reporting in, I immediately went on the intercom and announced that we were having Fifteen-Bean Soup and asked who wanted to be counted in. All twenty-one additional men were hungry, and because I had never let them down when it came to quality and quantity, they all wanted in on that soup.

I made myself a list and headed to the nearest grocery store to shop for the ingredients for what promised to be a real treat for supper. There was only one problem; when I got to the grocery store, there was no Fifteen-Bean Soup! Now I had twenty-one men all excited about this new concoction I had promised, and it was nowhere to be had. Well I fell back on my fireman training at that point; when you are in a bind and don't have the right tools at your disposal, you do what you can with what you have. In the dried-bean aisle right before my very eyes, there were eleven different kinds of dried beans in one-pound packages. I used my outstanding math skills and deciphered that twenty-two men divided by eleven was a half-pound of beans per man. Now when I cooked meat, I figured a half-pound per man as a general rule, so I figured it was meant to be; twenty-two men and eleven pounds of beans—problem solved.

At this point I must bring to your attention that on the back side of a one-pound bag of Fifteen-Bean Soup, it clearly states that it will make sixteen servings; keep that in mind as you envision what is about to take place.

I hurriedly made my way through the rest of the grocery store, picking up sausage, onions, and other ingredients to go with the beans. I returned to Central Station, carried the bags full of fixings upstairs, and began to get excited about just how much my brother firefighters were going to enjoy this hearty meal. I pulled out the largest boiler from under the counter, filled it half-full of water, sat it on the stove top, and turned the burner on "get it" (High).

As the water was heating, I tore open those eleven bags of beans, dumped them into the sink, and started washing them off. They were beautiful with all the different colors mixed together—red, yellow, green, brown, black, and white. When I had all eleven pounds in that sink my captain walked in to the kitchen, looked over into the sink, and asked, "What is that?" I proudly said, "That is Eleven-Bean Soup!" To which he asked, "When are we going to eat it?" My reply, "For supper." He questioned, "Tonight?" Now remember we didn't get to work until 3:00 P.M., I had been to the grocery store and it was now 5:30 in the evening. (For you less-educated readers, "supper" is the evening meal in the South.) My captain said, "You can't cook eleven pounds of beans and have them done in time for supper tonight." I looked him right in the eye and in all sincerity said, "Well, my wife did last night." Now I didn't know that my wife had soaked those beans overnight before she cooked them!

Undaunted by the captain's negative attitude, I poured those eleven pounds of beans into the boiling water. For future reference to all of you cooks out there, eleven pounds of beans will cool off a pot of boiling water considerably. It took forever for that pot to begin to boil again, and when it did, those beans started to swell. Well soon that five-gallon boiler was brim full of hot water and beans. I went on the intercom and hollered for help, "Somebody come help me pour these beans into another pot!" Help soon arrived, and I transferred half of the beans and water into a second five-gallon pot, adding more water. When the two pots came back to a boil, they both filled up with boiling water and swelling beans. A second time I called for help and got another five-gallon boiler to hold the mixture. Now I had fifteen gallons of hot beans, sausage, and spices on my hands; it is a good thing we had a big commercial stove at Central Station.

By now it was well past 7:00 P.M., which was our usual eating time. The crew would one by one slip through the kitchen, look at me sadly, and ask, "When are we going to eat?" Each time I would look at my watch and reply, "In about fifteen minutes."

At 8:00, those beans were still as hard as Chinese arithmetic, 8:30 same thing. I had always subscribed to the philosophy that if you waited long enough and had large enough quantities that you could feed a fireman anything, and he would be happy. So at 9:00, I rang the dinner bell and they all piled into the kitchen. When they were all assembled, I told them to go get their safety glasses because these beans were still "kind of" hard, and when they tried to poke them with a fork, they might just fly out of their plates like a tiddlywinks.

(Note: On the back of the eleven packages of beans, the number of servings that each bag will provide is listed; eleven one-pound bags will yield 117 servings of beans.)

We said the blessing and commenced to chow down. Those beans were about halfway done, so they still had a little fight left in them. I didn't know just how much "fight" until later that night.

In those old fire stations that were built before there were any females on the job, the bedrooms were just big, open dorm-style rooms. Central Station was built in 1922, so the main bedroom was a rather large area with fifteen beds in it, all open with no dividing walls. Fifteen of the twenty-two men that worked on each shift slept in that one room.

Now the "fight" that was left in those beans began, slowly at first, then with much more vengeance, to manifest itself. I will not go into details here as to the sounds and smells coming from those men in that bedroom, but just imagine fifteen men who had consumed eleven pounds of half-cooked beans. I will only say that there is not enough Beano in the world to have counteracted that much gas.

When the alarm sounds at 7:00 A.M. to wake you up at the station, the lights come on at the same time. The next morning when that took place, I sat up in my bed, looked around, and thought that there were fourteen pregnant men sleeping in that room. Oh, the moaning and groaning coming from that group the entire morning!

They made me remove Eleven-Bean Soup from the menu rotation at Central Fire Station.

Fifteen-Bean Soup

After you have read my story, I know you don't want to make my Eleven-Bean Soup recipe, so I'm giving my wife's recipe, which inspired me to cook the bean soup for the firemen. It is delicious and perfect for a cold day. Serve with cornbread, and it will put a smile on your face!

1 1 lb. bag 15 Bean Soup Mix
1 onion, chopped
1 cup chopped carrots
1 cup chopped celery
Dried basil, oregano, pepper, to taste
1 tbsp. olive oil
2 lb. good-quality smoked sausage and/or ham
32 oz. chicken or vegetable stock
2 14.5-oz.cans chopped tomatoes with juice
Salt, only if needed
Parmesan

Rinse and soak beans overnight.

Sauté onions, carrots, celery, basil, oregano, and pepper in olive oil until soft. Add sausage/ham and sauté a few additional minutes.

To stockpot, add stock, soaked beans, and tomatoes. Add vegetables and sausage/ham to beans. Bring to boil, turn down, and simmer for 2 hours, stirring occasionally. (For slightly thicker soup, you can mash with a potato masher.)

Serve with a slice of cornbread and top with fresh Parmesan.

Serves 16.

Family picture. *Back:* Eason, Justin, Patti, Sandy, CJ. *Middle:* Staci, Camon, Jordan, Mandi. *Front:* Ashlynn, Isabelle, Katie, Lacie

Former fireman Sandy Davis at work; Sandy at the Baton Rouge April 2011 show at Juban's Restaurant; Sandy with emcee, Tom Pace at the Shreveport April 2011 show; Sandy at work; Sandy in the Baton Rouge April 2011 show; Sandy with Peggy at the Shreveport April 2011 show; Sandy with Vinni Villicano at the Baton Rouge 2011 show; Sandy with his fifteen bags of beans

Whitney Vann
Anchor, 2une In, WBRZ News 2, Baton Rouge
Tiger Tailgate Tales

"If I were a food, I would be a chocolate chip cookie. It's warm, inviting, full of great ingredients, loved by everyone, never crumbles, and one smart cookie!"

Food is to Louisianans as bourbon is to Kentuckians. For those of you fortunate enough to be born here, you may have thought it perfectly normal to move from the baby bottle to red beans and rice—for the rest of us, it was just rice cereal.

When I moved to Baton Rouge to work at WBRZ sixteen years ago, one of my first road trips was to the Breaux Bridge Crawfish Festival. I didn't know what crawfish were; my co-anchor, Leo Honeycutt, explained that they were like mini-lobsters. When I saw them, I said, "That's bait. I used to catch them under rocks in my backyard creek and fish with them." But once I tasted them and spent the day drinking beer, sucking heads, and eating tails, I proudly proclaimed that after twenty-seven years I had found my people!

However, I quickly discovered that cooking for Cajuns could be intimidating. For our first tailgate party I pondered for weeks what to cook. I settled on jambalaya. It would feed a crowd, easy, and I had the recipe and wisdom of the World's Jambalaya Champion to guide me.

"I'll handle the cooking," I told my husband, Robert, "You handle the drinks." As our new friends gathered, I heard comments on the jambalaya, such as, "unique, surprising, definitely bringing my own Kentucky flair to it." It wasn't until my husband tried it then spit it out that I realized there might be a problem. "What kind of meat is in there?" he asked. "Chicken and sausage," I answered. "What kind of sausage?" he asked. "Oh, that really good kind, we always use!" I proudly answered. "You mean the

kind rolled in plastic that you serve for breakfast?" he inquired. "Yeah," I said. "Is there any other kind?"

Happily, I've come a long way since then. And believe me, I had a long way to go.

I didn't grow up learning to cook from my grandmother, Joy. When I'd spend the night with her and she'd ask what I wanted for breakfast, I played it safe and said "just cereal." That's after she made scrambled eggs the previous visit. I had bitten into something and asked, "Oooo, what's in the eggs?" "I wanted to do something special for you, honey. It's squash."

While my grandmother didn't feed my stomach very well, she did feed my soul. As Kentucky Poet Laureate, she turned language into the bread of life. She wasn't the type of grandmother who'd bake a cake for my birthday, but she would write me a poem. She knew words would feed my soul.

Joy couldn't make great food, but she could sure mix up a good drink. I remember the first time my husband met her. As Joy filled up her wine glass for the third time, Robert whispered, "A few more glasses of wine, and your grandmother's going to be schnockered." I said, "Wine? That's scotch, and you better drink up, too; it's the only way you'll be able to choke down the dinner she cooked."

So while my grandmother didn't teach me a lot about the universal language—food—she did teach me everything about the universal language—love! It wasn't what was served on Joy's dinner table that was important. It was those gathered around it.

WHITNEY VANN

Emcee at the premiere show at the Myrtles Plantation, May 16, 2010; Pat and Daryl Vann (Whitney's parents), Robert, Sydney Joy, Reid, and Whitney; Whitney with husband, Robert Schneckenburger; Sister Judith Brun, Jeff Kleinpeter, Whitney, and Leo Honeycutt at the Lyceum show, May 19, 2010; Mayor Kip Holden, Whitney, and Scott Rogers (emcee) at the one-year anniversary show, May 12, 2011; Whitney with Reid, Sydney Joy, and Robert; Erin Segrest, Leah Simon, and Whitney Vann at the premiere show May 16, 2010 at the Myrtles Plantation; Whitney Vann, anchor for *2une In,* WBRZ News 2 Baton Rouge

Ruffin Rodrigue
Owner, Ruffino's Italian Restaurant, Baton Rouge
Wine and Food through Song

"If I were a food, I'd be a tender, center-cut filet, cooked to perfection because it goes so well with a good glass of wine, as do I!"

My first experience with food was when I was about ten years old, and I had an absolute obsession with the movie *Willy Wonka and the Chocolate Factory*. At that time, I wanted to invent the "perfect" soda by using Louisiana blueberries and chocolate. I came up with some concoctions that I thought would have blown minds, except they only succeeded in blowing up my mother's temper because the kitchen was a mess every day! On one of these days, she asked me what I was doing. My mother then told me, "Son, you are going to be an LSU football player like your father; you are too big to be a soda maker." So naturally, being a young boy who was told by his mother not to do something, I instantly fell in love with the whole aspect of flavors in foods.

I also loved to sing back then, especially the songs from Willy Wonka. When I was a jock at LSU—playing football—I have to be honest with you; I had to give up singing, as my teammates wouldn't have appreciated it in the locker room! After LSU, I went to work with Mockler Beverage, distributors of Anheuser-Busch. I learned so much about food because I called on restaurants and grocery stores to promote Budweiser and Bud Light.

My moment of clarity came when I went to New Orleans for the Sugar Bowl. There were about two hundred people in the main dining room at Galatoire's, and Melvin Rodrigue came over to me and told me that everyone there wanted to hear me sing. So I belted out "Danny Boy," and that moment helped me realize that this was my true calling; I wanted to be able to sing in my own restaurant.

My first passionate experience with wine and food happened when T. J. Moran brought me in to work at Ruth's Chris. I went to their Chicago restaurant. I was given a glass of Chardonnay that tasted sweet, like donuts. I had it with a BBQ shrimp appetizer. And in that moment, I knew I wanted food and wine to be central parts of my life.

I realized I had literally fallen in love with food and wine when I went to Far Niente Vineyards in Napa Valley around 2001. I was with friends sitting out on the lawn having dinner. There was a beautiful sunset and I had a glass of Cabernet with a big steak. It was unforgettable, kind of like my first kiss. After my grandparents' seventieth wedding anniversary, I asked my grandmother, Rita, if she remembered her first kiss, and she said, "Yes, because it happens every day!" That's pretty close to how I'd describe my relationship to food and wine! Once you find a passion, you never let it go.

We all know red wine is a living organism. When we open the bottle, it starts to grow and change. That's what I love about Cabernet, and I'll never forget that first glass at Far Niente Vineyards! I couldn't begin to describe what the flavor and sensation did for the food. It was the first time I was in Napa and the first time I really appreciated food pairings, which is why I have wine dinners at Ruffino's—so people can enjoy and learn about wine and food pairings. Nothing is better, and I can honestly say, "My life is a Cabernet, living, breathing, changing, and simply delicious!"

With Ruffino's executive chef Peter Sclafani; Premiere show at the Myrtles, May 16, 2010; Ruffin with wife Allison and children, Maggie and Adam; Painting of Ruffin (#68) and his father, Ruffin Rodrigue, Sr. (#51); Singing in his monologue at the Myrtles; With Todd Graves at the Myrtles premiere show cocktail party; Ruffin at Ruffino's Restaurant with his favorite glass of Cabernet.

Syrena Johnson
Liberty's Kitchen Graduate, Chefs Move! Scholarship Recipient, New Orleans
Expect the Unexpected

"If I were a food I would be a pineapple. I appear hard on the outside but I'm super sweet on the inside!"

I'm just a regular girl from Uptown New Orleans. My first job was at McDonald's at the age of sixteen, from there I've worked at Domino's, Popeyes, Piccadilly, Vucinovich's, Fit Gourmet of New Orleans, and Lola's, and that's just the cooking places! Everything kind of made a change for the best when I started the program at Liberty's Kitchen. When I first arrived, they were doing things that I had already done before, but there were still things for me to learn, so I decided to stay. The program lasts for twelve weeks, but I completed it in seven, and then I was hired to work at their contracted school, New Orleans College Prep, in the cafeteria.

While there, my program director learned about the Chefs Move! Scholarship program and thought I would be the perfect candidate for it. After a great deal of my own stubbornness and a whole lot of encouragement from others, I filled out the application and was placed in the first round. I didn't think that meant anything; I just thought it was a stroke of luck. From there, I was given the recipe Pumpkin Risotto, which I had to memorize and write in its entirety and complete a food-cost scenario.

Throughout the process, I was very nonchalant and didn't really think that I could win, but I felt very confident about my accomplishments, and then I started becoming more and more serious about it. I advanced to the second round and met with Jessica Bride, the cofounder of the scholarship, and Emery Whalen, executive director of the John Besh Foundation. They wanted to know a little about me and why I love to cook. After the interview, I felt that I had totally knocked it out the park, but my journey was not over yet!

I finally received the call that I had progressed to the last and final round! I was going to interview with the legendary chef John Besh. Nervous was not even the word for how I was feeling. I didn't know what to expect or what to say. I never even thought I would make it this far, but I knew I couldn't fail now. Failing was not even an option. To tell you the truth, I had heard of Chef Besh before, but I wasn't knowledgeable of his work. I did my homework and Googled him before the interview to get myself familiar with his accomplishments. I discovered that he was a cool person who loved New Orleans and did everything he could to uplift it. Knowing that information, I was comfortable with him. We talked and talked and laughed. I told him about myself, where I was from, and why I got into cooking. He told me about himself and his reason for creating the scholarship. At that point, I knew I had to win! I wanted to be a part of this movement! I felt like we hit it off right away, and it didn't feel like I was on an interview. It really felt like I was talking to a friend—my new friend, Chef John Besh!

In the middle of the interview, Chef asked me, "Are you hungry?" I felt like I had opened up enough to be honest and say, "Sure, why not?" So Pastry Chef Kelly brought in one of her specialty chocolate snowballs—ummmm—yummy! At that point, I thought to myself, if I didn't think I had won the scholarship before, then I felt like I knew I would now! After the interview, Chef asked if I had any questions, and I said, "Are you going to offer everybody else dessert?" He smiled and said, "No."

The rest is history! I was announced the first recipient of the John Besh and Bride Mayor Scholarship, which included a full-paid scholarship to the French Culinary Institute of New York, a $250 grocery card, a $500 metro card, a camera, laptop, media training, and mentorship from some of the most famous chefs today, including Chef John Besh. I've been on radio shows, featured in magazines and newspapers, and even appeared on TV. I did a complete 180 in less than a year. I'm now living in New York City and attending the French Culinary Institute. It's a dream come true.

My experience in the Big Apple has been breathtaking. There's so much to see and do! There are so many different nationalities and personalities; it's just amazing. I lived on Roosevelt Island for three days. It was nice, but it is kind of a secluded and a small area. Now I live in Brooklyn Heights, one of the most historical neighborhoods in New York. While here, I've figured out the subway system—just enough to get myself home, to school, and to Target (my best friend at times). I'm totally enjoying myself and plan to see and do so much more.

I had my first day of school! The day we've all been waiting for, and I must say it is everything I imagined and more. When I see my peers together in uniform, it feels unreal, and I think to myself, "Am I really doing this? Is this for real?"

My goals are to work hard at school, accomplish as much as possible, graduate with honors, and be a mentor to the next Chefs Move! recipient. I must thank Liberty's Kitchen, my supporters, and especially Chef John Besh and Mrs. Jessica Bride for establishing the Chef's Move! Scholarship. It will change lives and the kitchens in New Orleans. Everything that has happened to me has taught me to expect the unexpected!

About Liberty's Kitchen

Liberty's Kitchen is an innovative, nonprofit organization dedicated to transforming the lives of at-risk youth by building self-sufficiency and independent living in a supportive community, where they learn life, social, and employability skills in a culinary setting. The organization supports its programs with teaching-focused businesses: a working café and coffee house, catering business, and contract food services. These businesses are designed to give the students practical experience, while helping to sustain the programs. Liberty's Kitchen utilizes private donations and community grants for the balance of their funding needs.

To learn more about Liberty's Kitchen, stop by for breakfast or lunch, at 422 South Broad Street, New Orleans, Louisiana.

Liberty's Kitchen students

With Chef John Besh and Jessica Bride

Liberty's Kitchen Cowboy Caviar
(Marinated Black-Eyed Pea Salad)

At Liberty's Kitchen we served this as a side dish; however, it was so good that our customers would come up to the counter and order more to take home for dinner! Black-eyed peas are a staple around New Orleans, especially on New Year's Day when you eat them for good luck! This marinated version is a nice, light, and delicious twist on the pea.

3 15-oz. cans black-eyed peas, rinsed and drained
1 large Vidalia onion or other sweet onion, small diced
2 red bell peppers, small diced
4 ribs celery, small diced
2 tbsp. cilantro, rough chopped
Cilantro Lime Vinaigrette (see recipe)

Toss all ingredients with Cilantro Lime Vinaigrette and chill overnight. May be served cold or at room temperature.

Serves 10 to 12 as a side dish.

Photo courtesy of Liberty's Kitchen

Cilantro Lime Vinaigrette
2 oz. freshly squeezed lime juice
4 oz. canola oil
2 tbsp. honey
2 fresh jalapeño peppers, seeded and minced
2 cloves garlic, minced
½ cup loose-packed cilantro
1 tsp. salt
1 tsp. black pepper

In a blender, purée all ingredients until emulsified.

Syrena at Liberty's Kitchen; Syrena wearing her new chef's coat with John Besh; With Chef John Besh and Jessica Bride; Cooking at Liberty's Kitchen; With Emery Whalen, John Besh, Jessica Bride, and Omar Buckner; With Chef Besh receiving chef's coat for winning the Besh/Bride Chefs Move! scholarship; Syrena in the New Orleans show at Southern Food and Beverage Museum, October 2011

Smiley Anders
Columnist, *The Advocate,* Baton Rouge
Memories of a Quiet Christmas

"If I were a food, I would be cotton candy because it is sweet but insubstantial, not to be taken seriously."

A rib-eye steak, baked potato, and a green salad—so simple and common a meal that it's almost a cliché. It's the kind of dinner favored by bachelors, because it requires almost no cooking at all. It's certainly not a Christmas dinner.

One Christmas I found myself alone. I had just moved into one side of a Spanish Town duplex, which was furnished in Early American Divorce—the stuff that didn't move at the garage sale. I had celebrated the holiday on Christmas Eve with my grown son and daughter, who had families of their own. The weekend before Christmas I had an early holiday celebration with my mom and my brother and his family in Oakdale.

A few days before Christmas, I learned from a young lady who lived across the street that she was also spending the holiday alone, so I invited her over. Pleased by the invitation, she offered to bring a salad. She was someone I had met earlier in the year at a neighborhood barbeque, and we had been in neighborhood groups that went out to the movies or to parties. I liked her; she was bright, witty, and good company. But she was much too young for anything but friendship.

When I woke up that chilly Christmas morning, I called her to come over for coffee. She showed up in a flannel nightgown and robe. I was in my flannel pajamas, too.

As I was brewing coffee, I heard caroling outside, and a group of my friends descended on us. They had been delivering Christmas baskets to the poor for the nuns at St. Agnes. They were celebrating their good deed with a jug of Bloody Marys. There was embarrassed laughter all around as I clumsily explained how I came to be entertaining in my jammies on Christmas morning. We chatted with them for a while, then they left toting their empty jug, still singing carols with great gusto.

She went home to change into jeans and a sweater, and I did the same. I had splurged on a couple of huge choice rib-eyes, and as I prepared the charcoal grill on the deck, she put the large baking potatoes in the oven and got to work on the salad greens.

We had a leisurely meal. I had also splurged on a really good red wine (you know, the kind with the cork in it), but she told me she was allergic to alcohol, making her the world's only nondrinking Episcopalian. I told her that was too bad and tried to sympathize, but all the while, I was thinking "designated driver!"

After the meal we cleaned up the few dishes, and I made more coffee. For dessert, we had cookies my daughter had made from my mom's recipe—chocolate chips, raisins, and pecans. We sat around talking quietly about our lives, our joys and sorrows.

Before we knew it, we noticed that the sun was going down. We went out to the front porch and sat on the swing, watching the winter sun color the western sky. As we sat there in silence, I suddenly realized that we were holding hands, and that she was more than just a friend.

Twenty years after that Christmas, she still is.

Smiley and Katherine's grandkids and great-grandkids: Glen Wofford, Emma Claire Wofford (baby), Katie Pilgreen Wofford, Ethan Wofford, Mandy Pilgreen Vollenweider, Leah Vollenweider (baby), Corey Vollenweider; Smiley and Katherine on the porch where they fell in love; Jay Basist, Smiley, and Peggy at the Baton Rouge Show, July 2010; Smiley and Katherine at Christmas; Smiley and wife, Katherine, with friends at Spanish Town Mardi Gras parade; Smiley and Katherine's wedding day; Smiley and Katherine at Jazz Fest; Smiley and Katherine; Smiley and Katherine at home with the smiley light

Sal Sunseri
Owner, P&J Oyster Company, New Orleans
Oyster Lover

"If I were a food, I guess the only choice is the delectable Louisiana oyster. I mean the 'world is my oyster, right.' Pleasing the palette is certainly one of the greatest enjoyments in life that I would possess. And then there is that other, more sensuous one. What more could anyone want!"

The oyster business has been in my blood for more than thirty years. My brother, Al; our relatives; and I have owned P&J Oyster Company for more than 135 years. Founded in 1876, P&J Oyster Company has been cultivating and harvesting oysters that are consistently recognized for uncompromising freshness, consistency, and quality of flavor.

My great-cousin John Popich emigrated from Croatia and settled in New Orleans. Like many immigrants at that time, he started working in the seafood industry. He quickly became an oyster fisherman.

I grew up in New Orleans' Ninth Ward. When I was three years old, my mom offered me a raw oyster. I didn't quite like the experience, so she decided to cut the muscle of the oyster and serve it to me on a cracker with seafood cocktail sauce. That was the beginning of my love of our tasty Louisiana delicacy. I started working in the family business when I was twenty. In the beginning, I was still in college at the University of Southern Louisiana, driving my VW bug, picking up oyster gallons from P&J New Orleans before class, and delivering them to restaurants throughout Lafayette. Some of my favorite memories were seeing our wonderful Vietnamese ladies and local shuckers in the mornings, listening to the sound of shucking, and smelling the fresh scent of sea water and oysters. The women in my family were great cooks, and of course, our meals always included oysters. My favorites are Oyster Joseph, char-grilled oysters, and oyster ceviche, which can be found in my mom's book, *The P&J Oyster Cookbook*.

P&J oysters were present at the creation of many legendary Creole dishes, including the most famous oyster dish of them all—Oysters Rockefeller. It was invented in the 1880s at Antoine's by the restaurant's proprietor, Jules Alciatore.

As an industry, I don't know of many others that have been through such devastation as ours. P&J Oyster Company has been through world wars, hurricanes, droughts, predation, manmade disruption through production of canals and tributaries inconsistent to our natural coast, a catastrophic oil spill, and federal regulations. Looking back, I guess Hurricane Katrina hit me the hardest. Losing our home and not knowing whether we would be able to continue the business were certainly major challenges. So right before evacuating, I gathered our photos and videos, then proceeded to say goodbye.

When we returned, our house was under nine feet of water, but we weren't going to leave our neighborhood. So we tore down our devastated home in November after the storm and set the pilings on September 6, 2006. We spent the first night in our new home on September 6, 2007. We plan to retire in the very spot we've worked so hard to rebuild.

Then we had the BP oil spill. From this latest setback, there is a lack of production due to fresh water kill and an uncertainty of the industry's future. But as long as there's an oyster in the sea, P&J will be offering it to oyster lovers throughout the world. P&J will continue to persevere.

Sal Sunseri at New Orleans Show, October 2010; Sal Sunseri with emcee, Poppy Tooker, and Peggy; Sal with his partners: his sister, Merri Schnieder; brother, Al Sunseri; and nephew, Blake Sunseri; Sal with oyster bag; Oyster shuckers at P&J; Sal with the Oyster Festival poster; Oysters on the Half Shell; Sal's father Salvador Raymond Sunseri; Sal at work in his office

Whitney Talbot Cushing
Owner, Culinary Therapy, Baton Rouge
A Unicorn Called Boudin

"If I were a food, I would be a sweet pea. First and foremost, I adore them, but also because they are considered to be the 'Queen of Annuals.' And let's be honest, who doesn't want to be the queen of something?"

My family has a gastronomic style that is so unique it perplexes most people. Many of you foodies may not have heard of the culinary superiority that is the Talbot family, but that's all about to change. I am honored and proud to enlighten you with the culinary brilliance of my family, whom I love and adore, despite what I am about to say about them.

My father's rise to culinary fame occurred on an involuntary grocery-shopping trip. It was, perhaps, his second trip to the grocery. I don't mean his second trip that day; I mean his second trip ever. Dad was diligently searching for the three items on his list, when he stumbled upon an undeniably familiar face. He approached his nameless buddy and said, "Excuse me, sir, I'm so sorry. I know we know each other and that I should know your name, but I'm drawing a total blank. I'm Evert Talbot." The transfixed man stood there silent. Thinking he had totally offended him, Dad offered the man his hand in salutations. You can imagine the horror when my father's forceful handshake sent his allusive friend and the bag of Doritos he was clutching, straight to the ground. It was only then that Dad quickly recollected his friend's name: George Foreman. It wasn't that Mr. Foreman wouldn't speak to my father; he simply couldn't. The champion boxer and his bag of Doritos were made of a piece of two-dimensional cardboard. My father vowed never to go to the grocery store again.

After swearing off all groceries, Dad was now free to wreak havoc elsewhere. My parents met for lunch at their favorite Chinese "boo-fay." As my father made his selections, he noticed another familiar face through the thickness of the protective glass hovering from above. He peered through the sneeze guard and said, "Excuse me, ma'am; I don't mean to bother you, but you look just like my wife." From across the container of crab rangoons, my mother's doppelganger replied through clenched teeth, "That's because I am your wife." Did I mention the time he set his table on fire at Juban's Creole Restaurant?

My mother, Pat, is nothing short of notorious in the area of food to all who know her. I don't have many childhood memories of our kitchen appliances, as they weren't used often, except to allow my imagination to run wild. At our squeaky-clean stove, I often played what most children called "restaurant." I called it "our family kitchen." I would don a hairnet and shout, "Serve you," while serving ice cream scoopers full of imaginary vegetable casseroles just like the ladies did at that place everyone else, for some reason, referred to as a cafeteria. As for the oven, that was more often used as a large ballet mirror to watch myself dance and for storage of small kitchen appliances than it was for actual baking.

Mom covered our kitchen with lovely food-themed decor. There were light fixtures that dangled slices of shiny glass fruits, wallpaper with repetitive patterns of recipes for Crêpes Suzette, and for that special touch that screamed

118

Pat Talbot, a lovely embroidered pillow that read "The only thing I make for dinner is reservations." Enough said.

Most of my mom's actual cooking was done utilizing a phonebook rather than a cookbook. There was Frank's for holidays, Mike Anderson's for gumbo, and, of course, Piccadilly for our daily family meals. In her defense, Mom did cook every once in a blue moon. My favorite was her spaghetti. There is something about my mom's spin on boxed Kraft Spaghetti Classics Tangy Italian Spaghetti that has always stuck with me. Her secret weapon was a few pinches of McCormick seasonings (even if they came from bottles the company hadn't manufactured in more than two decades) and a whole heap of love. To this day, I won't look at someone else's spaghetti, much less eat it. If it didn't come from a box in my mom's pantry, it didn't come from love, and that's all that matters to me.

As for my brother Derek, I can't so much poke fun at his cooking skills or lack there of, because I've never seen him even attempt to cook. It is baffling to me that siblings can be so opposite. He is seven years my senior and is the logical, wise, and responsible child in our family. I am the flighty, live by my heart, not my head—everything is unicorns and rainbows— little sister. Our differences extended into our palates as well. Mom probably spent a large portion of Dad's salary on our addiction to junk food and our Jerry Seinfeld-like collection of cereal. Lord knows we couldn't agree on those things either. Yet, the one thing we do have in common is that the abundance of preservatives ravaging our bodies from our fondness for Little Debbie snack cakes will allow us both to look the age of twelve until we are 104.

And then there's me. I first tried my hand at cooking in 1993 when I invited my family over for the first meal I ever made, lasagna. My dad said, "It tastes like a can." In my disbelief, I replied, "It didn't come from a can, Dad; I made it." My dad said, "No, it doesn't taste like it came from a can; it tastes like a can." My cooking hiatus began that very moment.

My next cooking snafu occurred when I was newly married, and I decided I should learn to cook. I had some andouille sausage and boudin from a recent trip home and decided to use them to make my first gumbo. I followed the recipe precisely—

until I got to the sausage part. A sausage is a sausage, is a sausage, right? Not so much. My new husband, who had been eager to try my Andouille Sausage Gumbo, spent the evening moaning in pain from the concoction of boudin porridge I had created and shouting, "You tried to kill me!" Perhaps that's why we didn't work out.

Fast forward to 2004—I became fascinated with the meal-assembly-business concept that was taking the culinary world by storm. Opening the Supper Studio was literally my first exposure to the food industry. I had never even waited tables. So I pulled up my boot straps and jumped in. I was incessantly in the kitchen learning every aspect of the business. My focus quickly shifted from being intrigued by the business model to being completely enamored with the food itself. I was smitten.

To learn everything I could, I relied heavily on Google, Food Network, YouTube, and the culinary wisdom of my mentor. I had to learn everything from how to dice an onion to layering flavors. What was the difference between sate and sauté? Why do I have to blanch vegetables? Literally, I was starting from scratch. But six years, two food businesses, a dozen magazine articles, a weekly cooking segment on the news, and a monologue for "Meanwhile, Back at Café Du Monde . . ." later, I am still hooked. It has become my biggest passion, second only to that for my daughter, Talbot. My fervor for the culinary arts has gotten me through divorce, the devastating end of my relationship with my greatest love and mentor, tragedy, more cancer in my family than I care to mention, celebrations, and sometimes simply through a night home alone. It is my faithful friend and companion. It is the very thing that inspires the girl with her head in the clouds to do something that makes her daughter, her brother, her mother, and her father proud.

So to all of you doubters out there, namely you, Dad, this is my chance to say, "I told ya so." Someone asked me to speak about food because I may actually know what I'm talking about. So, looka' me, Talbot family of culinary masters. I have finally arrived—even if I got here on my imaginary unicorn named Boudin.

Tagliatelle Pasta with Peas and Truffle Oil

Filet of tennis shoe topped with sweet pea foam? Sold! Anyone who knows me is aware that I simply worship green peas. Many years ago on a trip to Las Vegas, I had what was the pinnacle of my culinary experience. There it was, wooing me from the menu, tagliatelle pasta with truffle oil and sautéed sweet peas. My obsession with the pop and tenderness of sweet peas combined with the hypnotic effect of the exquisite taste of truffle oil made me travel to an epicurean "la la land" I had never visited. It was the first time I realized food could actually create euphoria like none other.

Many years later, I experienced my love affair with this dish again. After a very difficult breakup, my boyfriend courageously re-created this dish in a bold attempt to win back my heart. Brilliant move, it worked! It is the dish on the pedestal to which all others must strive to measure.

¼ cup unsalted butter
1 tbsp. extra-virgin olive oil
3 cloves garlic, chopped
¾ cup dry white wine
10 oz. fresh tagliatelle pasta
2 cups frozen peas, thawed
¼ cup fresh basil, thinly sliced
¼ cup fresh parsley, chopped
2 tbsp. white truffle oil
½ cup vegetable broth
Salt and pepper, to taste
2 cups Parmesan cheese, shaved

Melt butter with oil in heavy large skillet over medium-high heat. Add garlic, stir 30 seconds. Add wine and boil 10 to 12 minutes.

Cook pasta in large pot of boiling salted water until tender but still firm to bite, stirring occasionally. Drain.

Add peas to wine sauce and stir over medium-high heat to warm through. Stir in basil, parsley, and truffle oil. Add pasta to sauce; toss to coat. Add enough vegetable broth to pasta to moisten. Season to taste with salt and pepper. Transfer to bowls. Top with Parmesan and serve.

Serves 4 as an entrée, or 6 as a side dish.

Whitney with her mother and father, Pat and Evert Talbot, at Baton Rouge show; Whitney and her daughter, Talbot; In the Baton Rouge show, November 2010; Whitney with her parents; Whitney with her daughter, Talbot, in the kitchen (Photograph by Jeannie Frey Rhodes); In April 2011 show at Juban's Restaurant; Talbot and Whitney, Irene's, New Orleans 2011; Whitney (baby) with her Aunt Jackie, mom, and grandmother

Tom Pace
Radio Host, Talk of the Town, Shreveport
Why I Love Southern Cooking . . .

"If I were a food, I'd be a ham because I am!"

My love affair with food began in 1947, in Pine Bluff, Arkansas. In fact, it was liquid, straight from the bottle—milk from Elsie the Cow for all I know. Heck, I was just glad to get the nourishment. Then on to my early years: I believe I was about two years old or so when Mom called out trying to find me, "Tommy Glenn . . . Tommy Glenn . . . where are you?"

"I'm in here," I said. "Where?" asked Mom. "I'm under the table," I answered.

"Doing what?" Mom persisted. "Eating dog food with Sissy." I replied, matter of factly. So you see, therein lies the tale. I've tried just about everything in the world, from dog food to beignets to Mom's boiled peanuts, pulled green and cooked fresh from the fertile fields around Pine Bluff.

Don't know about you, but my memories of food hark back to Mom's home cooking—tender, fried chicken; black-eyed peas; and turnip greens (from the gardens, not from the cans). All made with lots of love. Some of my other favorite meals by Mom include chicken and dumplings and, of course, turkey and dressing for the holidays.

Fast-forward to Colton Junior High in New Orleans and the taste of fresh-shucked oysters at Acme Oyster Bar in the French Quarter, and, oh yes, those hot, melt-in-your-mouth beignets from Café Du Monde in Jackson Square. (Can I get an amen?)

When I was all of fourteen, Dad managed a movie theatre at the corner of Dauphine and Burgundy right off Canal Street behind Maison Blanche. When school was out, many times for lunch, we'd go to a restaurant catty-cornered from Dad's theatre. I remember one summer day in 1961, about noon. We walked into that café and on the floor was a white tablecloth, with customers just stepping around and over it—someone had suffered a heart attack and died. The staff covered up the body and was waiting on the ambulance, and all the while, customers were being seated and waiters were delivering the orders. Talk about "food to die for."

You see, I just love Southern cookin', canned dog food notwithstanding. As I started enjoying even more delights of Southern cuisine, my wife, Su Zanne, and I traveled to New Orleans again on several occasions, where (before Katrina) we dined on fine steaks in the revolving Hyatt Regency Restaurant overlooking the mighty Mississippi River. We ate the sloppiest po' boys at Mother's and, of course, always found our way "back at Café Du Monde."

Your "Café Du Monde" can be any place you always go back to. For us, it happens to be several places across Shreveport-Bossier, including Roxie & John Carriere's Cotton Boll Grills, Nicky's Mexican Restaurants, and Strawn's homemade strawberry pies.

Finally, it seems we enjoy the holiday cooking most of all. Su Zanne has mastered most of her and my mother's great recipes. For me, I enjoy taking pictures of the food. I'll even compare the dressings over the years. And so, my kids, now grown, say, "Oh, please, Dad, give it a break. Put down the camera and eat already!" *Bon appétit!*

Introducing Peggy at Shreveport Show, April 2011; Tom with his family. *Standing, from left:* Bert Schmale, Kyle and Sara Stone, Jason Cram. *Seated, from left:* Valarie Pace-Schmale, Tom and Su Zanne Pace, Heidi Cram with grandson Austin; Tom at his radio show "Talk of the Town"; Tom Pace, age 6, with his dad's car, a 1952 Henry J; Tom Pace, age five, with his pet monkey Poko; Emcee at the Shreveport Show, September 2010

Pam Bordelon
Society Columnist, *The Advocate,* Baton Rouge
It's Got Green Stuff

"If I were a food, I would be a lemon cheesecake because it's sweet and a little bit tart!"

Jim and I had been dating for several months when he invited me to accompany him and a group of his friends on their annual beach trip. As the single mom of three boys (ages twelve, ten, and eight), this was manna from heaven.

This group had been vacationing together for several years, and they had a well-established routine. Each night a different couple was in charge of dinner and the first thing everyone wanted to know when we arrived was if Jim was going to make meatballs and spaghetti. Their next question was had I eaten this delicacy? My answer was, "Not yet." In fact, Jim had been eating my kid-friendly spaghetti. You know, doctored up spaghetti sauce in a jar—one of my boys' favorites. Well, when our night for dinner came up, I made a huge salad, and Jim took care of the meatballs and spaghetti. I took one bite, looked at him, and said emphatically, "I'm never cooking spaghetti for you again!" It was delicious!

Several months later, I had started a new job. At the end of my first week, there was a surprise knock on my door. When I opened it, there stood Jim with a grocery bag filled with ingredients to make meatballs and spaghetti. The aromas filling my apartment were mouthwatering, and everyone was getting hungrier by the minute. I fixed the boys' plates and got them started as I returned to the kitchen for Jim and me to fix our plates.

All of a sudden, we hear sniffling. We look over and see middle son David with his head bowed, fighting back tears. Jim asked him what was wrong and got no answer. The sniffling grew louder, and I went to see if I could find out what was wrong. After much coaxing, David picked up his fork, poked at his spaghetti, and, with big alligator tears streaming down his face, said, "It's got green stuff in it."

Yes, it did; there were onions, bell peppers, and olives—all manner of "stuff" my boys weren't used to eating. But how do you tell the man who's made your mom so happy that you don't like his cooking? So I picked out all the green stuff and everyone was happy.

Fast-forward eight years. Jim and I are married and the boys are all coming for dinner. Jim is making his famous meatballs and spaghetti, which they now crave, "green stuff" included. As we're cooking, Jim brings up the incident from years ago, and we laugh at the memory. Then we have an idea, a brilliant idea.

I added green food coloring to the boiling water to cook the spaghetti and, like before, I fix the boys' plates and call them to the table. They doubled over in laughter at the meatballs and tomato gravy piled on top of a mound of green spaghetti. In that moment, I knew we had made a family-defining memory we would all cherish for years to come. By the way, I kept my promise. I haven't cooked spaghetti for Jim since the fall of 1992.

Pam with son Thomas and husband Jim; Pam Bordelon with the LSU cow; October 2010, Baton Rouge Show; Family: Michael, Thomas, Jim, Pam, and David; Pam being interviewed by Tammi Arender, NBC 33, at the Baton Rouge Show, July 2010; October 2010, Baton Rouge Show; Meredith Manship and Pam at 2011 Spanish Town Mardi Gras Ball; Pam with Bert Fife, Joe Liss, and Deborah Todd at the Baton Rouge Show, July 2010

Leon Contavesprie
Actor, New Orleans

An Anniversary to Remember

"If I were a food, I would be a candy apple. You have to break the hard outer shell to get to the really good stuff that lies underneath."

I was born and raised in south Kenner. My entire family was, for that matter. Food for us was more of a quantity thing than quality. Now, don't get me wrong, we had delicious food; in fact, some of the best I've ever eaten. But because Sunday dinners were more traditional Italian and south Louisiana fare, my palette was anything but sophisticated. Truthfully, if it didn't have a red gravy on top of it, I didn't know what it was or how to eat it. So imagine my first time eating haute cuisine.

My best friend of thirty years, Sandy Lussier, and I decided to go all out and treat ourselves to a very fancy dinner at a swank restaurant near downtown for our three-decade "friend anniversary." Our goal, of course, was to expand our urbane palettes (we're both from the 'burbs). I won't mention the name of the restaurant, but I will say that once they found out we were celebrating thirty years together, and we were only thirty-five at the time, we were treated like celebrities—weird celebrities, but celebrities, nonetheless.

Let me set the scene for you: very upscale restaurant, white linen, multiple utensils, and a beautiful ceramic centerpiece in the shape of a quasi-donut, with the outer ring filled with a fluid that, when warmed, gives off a slight aroma. The candle in the "donut hole" was lit when we were seated.

We looked at the menu and decided on, what else, steaks. Our server approached and told us that the chef was intrigued by our "friendship anniversary," and it would be his honor if he could prepare a four-course meal for us. The only catch was we wouldn't know beforehand what the dishes would be. So Sandy said, "Sure, let's be adventurous." I agreed. If we only knew what was about to unfold.

The first course arrived, which was a mixed green salad with sun-dried tomatoes and sweet vinaigrette. While enjoying this first course, our server approached the table with a small demitasse cup overfilled with something pink, along with a small basket of water biscuits. He said, "You'll love this. It's smoked salmon—on the house." While I watched him walk away, Sandy dove into it. But upon looking at it for the first time, I thought, "Wait a minute, this isn't cooked." I knew that neither of us liked sushi, so I attempted to tell Sandy before she shoved a wad in her mouth. I was too late.

The shock of recognition was enough to shake the graceful New Orleans photos on the walls. However, being the trouper she is, Sandy swallowed it down. We both nipped and tucked at it little by little, but the more we ate the more it seemed to reappear. We didn't want to be rude to the chef, so we tried to think of ways to make it go away, because truthfully neither one of us could stomach more than a bite or two. Sandy decided our best bet would be to methodically slip some of it into the "donut bowl" in the centerpiece. After all, who would see it, right? So, we did just that between server visits.

The second course came. He put it in front of us and said, "Sweetbreads. Enjoy!"

I remember thinking, "How strange to serve dessert before dinner. Oh, well, maybe it's a French thing." We dove in.

Have you ever had sweetbreads? Do you know what sweetbreads are? Let me put it this way—it ain't sweet, and it ain't bread.

So, little by little, the pancreas and thymus glands (yep, sweetbreads) found their way into the donut along with the salmon we had already drowned in the fluid. The waiter kept coming back as more and more of the food disappeared, and each time he'd say something like, "Wow, you guys are really enjoying this!" And we'd pretend to be chewing our last morsels and say, "Mmmm, delicious!" knowing full well most of it was swimming in the centerpiece.

The entrée came next: tournedos of beef. This was quite good, but slightly undercooked for our tastes. By that, I mean it was off-the-bone raw. When I made the first slice, it looked as if I had slit my wrists. To add insult to injury, a very decorative scoop of creamed potatoes garnished with vegetables lay adjacent to the bloody meat, which instantly soaked up the crimson brine, making the entire plate look like a crime scene.

Not wanting to insult the chef, we tried our best to eat what was in front of us. After all, it was a special occasion, right? In all honesty, I was ready to ditch the suit, throw on a T-shirt and jeans, and find the nearest crawfish boil. All I could think was, "If the second course was sweetbreads and the entrée was steak tartar, then dessert must be gall bladder flambé."

Speaking of flambé, we were in the middle of our dessert, affectionately known by our server as "Chocolate Foolishness," when we noticed a strange smell. Did you know that smoked salmon, combined with sweetbreads and a certain aromatic fluid, when heated by something as small as, oh let's say a decorative candle—gives off quite the aroma and will ultimately catch fire?

We first saw the flames when Sandy's long blonde hair practically ignited. I grabbed a glass of water and launched it at her, hoping to extinguish her smoldering locks and the now ablaze centerpiece. Fortunately, I put out both fires, but the water diffused everything and the pungent smell quickly made its way across the dining room. We were now garnering way too much unwanted attention by the servers and the other guests.

During the initial staff-wide panic, Sandy quickly whispered that we needed a diversion to avoid being busted for wasting the food *and* burning the place down. Her not-so-subtle solution was to make the whole thing seem as if we were in a horrible fight with each other. Before the word "No!" was out of my mouth, she lobbed a glass of ice-cold water on me. I bolted up and screamed, "What the hell are you doing?" She too jumped up and screamed right back, "What the hell are YOU doing?" Chaos ensued, complete with the chef and security hightailing it to our table.

So there we were, on our thirtieth friendship anniversary: I, waterlogged in my Sunday best; Sandy, blonde hair smoldering; and both of us wildly laughing and unable to catch our breath, being escorted out of the building.

Needless to say, we are no longer welcomed at this restaurant. In fact, I believe we have been blackballed by several other eateries, for fear we may cause the same uproar throughout the city.

But as in all good stories, there is a moral:

Smoked salmon: $12

Sweetbreads: $11

Steak tartar for two: $55

Burned centerpiece: $16

Banned forever from a four-star restaurant and having to spend our next anniversary at a crawfish boil in my backyard: Priceless!

Francesca's Shrimp Mirliton Casserole

This recipe was from my maternal grandma Francesca at her Sicilian best. It is legendary in our family and is always the centerpiece of every holiday dinner. She passed away Easter 2011 at the ripe young age of ninety. Now that Francesca is no longer with us, we compete to see whose version comes closest to her annual masterpiece. It's our way of keeping her spirit in our hearts forever.

6 mirlitons
2 tbsp. vegetable oil
1 medium-size onion, finely chopped
4 stalks celery, finely chopped
½ medium-size green bell pepper, finely chopped
4 cloves garlic, minced
1 lb. cleaned and deveined shrimp, cut into pieces (or whole if small)
2 slices white bread
¾ cup Italian-style breadcrumbs
1 ½ tsp. fresh thyme leaves, or ½ teaspoon dry, or to taste
Salt and pepper, to taste
Butter or margarine for baking pan
2 tbsp. extra-virgin olive oil

Wash mirlitons and boil, covered with water, until tender, about 40 minutes. Drain, reserving 1-cup mirliton stock. Peel mirlitons, seed, and chop pulp into about ¼-inch cubes; set aside. (If "smooth-textured" casserole is desired, use potato masher to smash mirliton cubes.)

Preheat oven to 350 degrees.

Meanwhile, heat vegetable oil in a large (about 5-qt.) saucepan. Add onions, celery, bell peppers, and garlic, and cook over low to medium-low heat for 10 minutes, stirring occasionally. Add shrimp and cook and stir for another 10 minutes. Drain reserved mirlitons (if needed) and stir into shrimp mixture.

Moisten bread thoroughly with reserved mirliton stock, squeeze dry, then break bread into bits, and add to pan. Add ½ cup breadcrumbs and thyme to mixture and season with salt and pepper to taste. Continue cooking over low heat for 10 minutes more, stirring and scraping pan bottom often so mixture does not stick.

Transfer mixture to a lightly buttered 13x9-inch baking pan or dish, spreading it evenly. Sprinkle top with ¼ cup breadcrumbs and drizzle olive oil over all. Bake uncovered until lightly browned and bubbling around edges, 30 to 40 minutes. Serve immediately. Leftovers (as if there will be any) are good reheated or cold. (This dish works well as a dip served with crackers.)

Serves 6 to 8 as a side dish.

Leon at the October 2010 show at Ralph & Kacoo's with friend, Ann Marie Pinkney; Riding the Green Machine; With best friend, Sandy Lussier, at Café Du Monde; With the cast of *We All Scream for Halloween Murder Mystery* show, 2011; With Ginger Pool Avis in *Don't Dress for Dinner* at Mill Mountain Theatre Roanoke, Virginia, 2006; With nephew Andrew Stagni; As "The Gentleman Caller" with Liz Mills, *The Glass Menagerie* at Theatre Marigny, 2009; Leon with his father, Joseph

Carolyn Roy
New Media Content Director, KSLA, Shreveport
Café or Cuppa

"If I were a food, I would be a jalapeño—colorful, an acquired taste, and not to be underestimated!"

I grew up loving the cliché Vermont fare: exquisitely sharp cheddar cheese, freshly picked and pressed apple cider, apple pie, and sugar on snow (that's food, isn't it?). But with an Irish family, there were lots of meat and potatoes on my childhood plate. And pasta! My father cooked massive one-pot dishes as if he was expecting a navy ship to dock at the door and send all its sailors in for dinner.

Besides carrying familial traits and traditions, tastes and hang-ups, food also carries important symbolism—from fasting to feasts, the traditional Seder meal to the final meal of the condemned man, and even the post-funeral tradition of bringing food to the mourning family. These are not traditions dedicated to physical nourishment, but rites of passage, celebration, remembrance, and custom. Most of all, food serves as a common denominator, whether it is for comfort, celebration, or just something to gather 'round; the act of breaking bread together is a unifying experience.

And so it is, even when sitting down for a simple cup of tea or coffee. We called it a "cuppa" in our household. Some of our most memorable and serious discussions came around those cuppas, and our most hysterical laughing fits.

In some form or another, we've all gathered the family together to eat special meals for Thanksgiving, Christmas, and New Year's. We plan entire wedding receptions around the menu, and potluck is practically synonymous with fellowship.

The reception following my wedding to my first husband,

Eric, was a unique, yet practical merging of these concepts. Symbolic of the entire event, it was collaboration among our friends, family, co-workers, and congregation in South Burlington, Vermont. He was six years into his battle with cancer. We weren't interested in going into debt, but we still wanted to celebrate the occasion. Everyone pooled his talents. One committee member took on the creative task of transforming the sanctuary into a reception hall with simple white, but ingeniously draped bed sheets—yes, bed sheets—and white Christmas lights. They gathered wildflowers that echoed my bouquet. A small army of little Lutheran ladies cooked up a choice of baked chicken breast or a finely crusted spicy halibut with vegetable casserole. They laid out a beautiful spread of fresh vegetables, fruits, and more home-cooked appetizers and finger foods.

It wasn't fancy fare, but it was made with love. Their culinary and creative contributions helped make it a deeply personalized affair, topped off with homemade carrot cake, iced with rich cream cheese frosting, garnished with baby carrots and a little bunny bride and groom—symbolic of Eric's mantra to "be the bunny," as in the Energizer Bunny in his battle with cancer . . . and keep going and going.

Eric kept going another year and a half. His funeral was just as intimate and personalized, and yes, there was food. And as it was with the celebration of the wedding, the celebration of his life was catered by love and fellowship.

Emcee, Carolyn Roy introducing Tom Pace at the Shreveport show, November 2010; Carolyn on her last day as a news anchor for KSLA; Carolyn and late husband, Eric Richard Feldes; Carolyn and late husband, Eric, cutting the "Be the Bunny" wedding cake; Shreveport show, September 2010; Late husband, Eric Richard Feldes, doing what he loved best, hiking; Carolyn Roy with husband, Cody Jennings; Carolyn, Connor, and Cody

Paul Arrigo
President/CEO, Visit Baton Rouge, Baton Rouge
New Orleans Restaurants Storm into Baton Rouge

"If I were a food, I'd be an Italian sausage, the process is ugly, but the end result is divine!"

Growing up in a New Orleans Sicilian family meant that food was a celebration. I remember having large family dinners outside under the pecan trees on my grandparents' property. In 1989 when I left New Orleans for Washington D.C., all of my friends and family asked me how I could leave New Orleans and the great food for D.C. You see, the world revolves around New Orleans—just ask a New Orleanian!

Then I left D.C. to return to Louisiana, but rather than New Orleans, Baton Rouge was my town, and again the New Orleans friends and family asked me, "Why Baton Rouge?" They think they are all culture in New Orleans, and Baton Rouge is agriculture!

Then came that tragic weekend in August 2005 when Hurricane Katrina struck New Orleans, and as a result, the two cities had a better appreciation for each other. Do you remember all of the traffic in Baton Rouge five years ago? And New Orleans people trying to buy liquor on Sunday?

Now there has always been a certain exchange of foods between the two cities. They gave us Copeland's and Popeyes; we gave them Piccadilly, Ralph and Kacoo's, and Raising Cane's!

After the storm, things changed.

The first New Orleans restaurant to open was Galatoire's. Galatoire's in New Orleans is in the shadow of strip clubs, and in Baton Rouge, it's in the shadow of the country club!

At Galatoire's in Baton Rouge, we have the country club set of people wearing tennis visors, having one glass of white wine. When they finish lunch, they rush to Martin Wine Cellar Baton Rouge. Another great New Orleans tradition is when they open the door, look around, make sure they don't recognize anyone, and proceed to purchase a case of wine, which they take home to polish off in the privacy of their own home.

I was concerned that Acme Oyster House would have a problem being successful in Baton Rouge—even with those great fried shrimp or oyster po' boys, the kind that explodes in your mouth when you bite one. After all, in New Orleans they have a huge beer-drinking crowd and video poker! How would Acme make it in Baton Rouge? Well, the folks at Acme are quite crafty. When you walk in, they sell you those big nose and mustache glasses— ya'll would look like me when you wear them. That way you would be disguised, and no one would know who you were, and you could have all the fun you could stand!

Then came Lucy's Retired Surfer's Bar to Downtown Third St. They had a great brunch on Sundays, but they had to shut it down because they were selling too much alcohol. They crossed the 60-40 ratio and became a bar. Baton Rouge law prohibits bars opening on Sunday. I suggested that they charge more for food and give away the alcohol, but they didn't take my suggestion.

What will be the next New Orleans restaurant to come to Baton Rouge? Will it be a Brennan's or Camellia Grill? What's your favorite?

Paul's favorite restaurant Acme; Paul with Jay Ducote at the April 2011 Baton Rouge show; Lyceum Ballroom show, May 19, 2010; Paul with his wife, Melanie, and daughter, Lauren August 2010, Baton Rouge show at Ralph & Kacoo's; Emcee at the April 2011 Baton Rouge show, introducing Lt. Gov. Jay Dardenne; Paul on the Myrtles Plantation's verandah before his debut on stage for the premiere show, May 16, 2011; Paul in disguise at the bar at Acme; Paul with Ana Adair and Peggy at the April 2011 show at Juban's Creole Restaurant

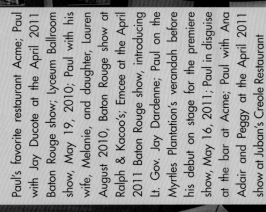

Liz Williams
President/Director, Southern Food and Beverage Museum, New Orleans
The One and Only Food Museum

"If I were a food, I would be pasta. It is a great comfort food, but it can be sophisticated and casual. It contributes to all cuisines. And it just tastes good."

I was lucky enough to grow up in New Orleans in a half-Sicilian family, surrounded by culinary culture. St. Joseph's altars, po' boys, gumbo, the French Market, Solari's, red beans and rice, and muffalettas. Of course, as a child, I didn't realize that I was growing up in a rich food culture. I ate wonderful authentic Sicilian food as well as traditional New Orleans fare. Not only was the food itself extraordinary, but the attitude toward food and living was rich and full of enjoyment.

My grandmother, the oldest of nine children, was eighteen when my great-grandfather brought his family to New Orleans from Palermo, Sicily. She cooked and helped take care of the family. My great-grandfather and my great uncles were butchers at the French Market and would always share bits that would be considered offal (the parts that spoiled first), if not eaten immediately. It is fashionable now, but I remember eating all of the offal from the meat market. We ate delicious and interesting meals. I did not appreciate my good fortune as I thought the whole world ate in the same manner.

I attended Louisiana State University and Louisiana State University Law School in Baton Rouge, where I enjoyed and learned to cook Cajun food in the homes of my Cajun friends. Although this experience expanded my culinary world, it didn't yet make me aware of my good fortune. I awakened to my luck when I joined the army after law school and was stationed at Fort Gordon, outside

of Augusta, Georgia, prior to attending the Judge Advocate General School (JAG). I ordered trout almandine at a nice restaurant, and the meal served by the waiter consisted of fish sticks with almonds on top served with catsup. At that moment, I realized how lucky I was to have grown up in New Orleans. That culinary experience and others like it heightened my awareness that culinary pursuits did not have the same importance the world over.

I studied law instead of anthropology because I did not understand how deeply my interest in gastronomy impacted my worldview. Also, I was not aware that I could study the art and science of food. Perhaps in hindsight that was a positive, as it kept my obsession under wraps while my husband and I focused on completing law school. After graduating from law school, we joined the JAG corps and experienced European cuisine for three years. Along the way, I discovered the gastronomic languages of various countries, learning about a country's culture, history, and politics while dining.

I spent the following years practicing law, teaching at universities, and raising a family, all the while continuing to study and explore food. I not only focused on eating and cooking, but I also studied the culture, economics, and law of food. I learned that food caused the European explorers to travel the world looking for peppercorns and nutmegs, and countries used blockades to starve their enemies. Tracing food around the world revealed trade patterns and migrations that allowed me to view the world through the lens of gastronomy. My experience and findings led me to establish a museum devoted to food.

I had been working as the CEO of the University of New Orleans Foundation (UNO). The UNO foundation had previously opened the D-Day Museum (the present-day National World War II Museum) and the Odgen Museum of Southern Art. When I approached the foundation with my idea of establishing a food museum, UNO was not interested in opening yet another museum. They could not even imagine what type of exhibits would be included in a food museum. Following in the footsteps of my role model, Julia Child, I left my job and embarked on a second career. When I began planning the museum, I was the same age as Julia Child when she began promoting *Mastering the Art of French Cooking* on television.

With the help of a few dedicated people, we opened the Southern Food and Beverage Museum (SoFAB) in New Orleans. It all continues to be very exciting. We are making it up as we go along, as there are no other food museums we can use as role models or guides. I do not have the proper credentials and am not a museum professional, and we have invented much of what we do. We tried to find a catchier name but found that the chosen name gave a great acronym. The museum really is "so fab." SoFAB is the only non-corporate, non-single-focus food museum in the United States that addresses general, cultural, and gastronomic issues. There are no statues of asparagus or wax effigies of cauliflower. We explore cultural food ways, history, economics, technology, and science. We collect artifacts that tell historical and current tales about food and document trends. We celebrate the foodways of the American South by exploring how it was influenced by the cultures of the world and the cuisines of the world. There are endless exhibit possibilities.

We reach our visitors by offering them the world of food, that is, live and love. We operate without the safety net of a sponsoring institution, such as a university or state museum system, which gives imagination free rein and grants us the freedom to develop the museum without bureaucratic obstacles. The trade off is that we must proceed slowly and prudently to survive and thrive. We have started small, but we intend to grow into our full potential.

I cannot fully express how privileged I feel to be able to do what I love. Every day I am excited about this job and the opportunity to continue building the museum into an institution with an even greater library. Currently we have seven thousand volumes in our culinary library and our intention is to develop it into the greatest culinary library. We are well on our way. Our library includes a great menu collection, a vast archive, a significant artifact collection, fabulous exhibits, and wonderful programs, among other great resources.

Other individuals have joined us in this obsession by donating collections developed over their lifetimes to the museum for safekeeping. The seven thousand volumes in our library have all been donated. The thirty-two-foot, mid-nineteenth-century bar from Bruning's restaurant, a refrigerator from 1927, more than twelve thousand beer bottles, and so much more have all been donated to SoFAB.

These artifacts have been entrusted into our care because people understand that our institution will endure and be a good steward of their cherished possessions. I am deeply touched by the trust granted to our institution. It inspires me to work harder to maintain their trust. Establishing SoFAB has also enriched my life through the extraordinary people I have met.

So now that I have described the institution, I would like to entice you to become co-conspirators in this empire building enterprise. Visit the museum and view the collection and the growing exhibits. Be a participant by sending us menus, artifacts, and books. It can be Aunt Sally's recipe box in the garage or that collection of community cookbooks that you don't use. Attend our programs, join our mailing list, and tell your friends to visit, too.

The museum is in its fifth year, and we are looking forward to moving into a new building that will allow us to more than double in size and have a restaurant and bar. We also plan to build an auditorium for lectures and demonstrations.

SoFAB is not supported by the state or by New Orleans. We are developing an independent museum into an institution that will eventually establish New Orleans as the intellectual food capital of the country. We are creating partnerships all over the country and expanding our circle of volunteers. We are also creating a network of corporations, supporters, and fans that will carry us into the future. When I visit older, well-established museums, I remind myself that they too were once new museums. One day SoFAB will be a well-established museum that people will think has been around forever, and I cannot wait.

Four-Generation Olive Salad

I consider this "four-generation" because this is basically my great-grandmother's olive salad, but my grandmother, mother, and I have each tweaked it in our own kitchens to make it the salad below. Of course, it is great to use traditionally on a muffaletta, but it is also great on an antipasto platter or in a tossed green salad.

My great-grandmother's salad was a fairly basic olive salad. My grandmother added the capers and lots of garlic. My mother added the thinly sliced lemon. I added the artichokes and fennel.

1 anchovy fillet

Extra virgin olive oil (use a fruity olive oil)

2 cups coarsely chopped black olives*

3 cups coarsely chopped cured green olives with pimento

1 cup finely diced celery

1 cup finely diced carrot

1 cup finely sliced fennel

1 very, very thinly sliced lemon, including any juice that can be saved

10 baby artichokes, boiled and quartered, fresh is best**

1 cup finely diced cauliflower (optional)

4 minced cloves garlic

¼ cup capers, coarsely chopped

Freshly ground black pepper, to taste

4 tbsp. fresh oregano, chopped, or 6 tbsp. dried oregano

Mash the anchovy with 1 or 2 tbsp. olive oil in the bottom of the bowl you are using. Mash until it totally dissolves into the oil. Add all ingredients except olive oil and oregano and mix the ingredients. Add enough olive oil to just barely cover the mixture and add oregano. Stir well so that the mixture is even, without clumps of like ingredients.

After an hour taste the mixture, and if it needs more acidity, add a bit more lemon juice to taste. Because of the olives and anchovy, this mixture will probably not need additional salt, but add it if you like. Sometimes I throw in fresh basil leaves right before serving. This recipe is very forgiving and flexible.

136

*The better the olives, the better the salad. This does not mean what is sold in a can as chopped black olives; it means black olives that you have chopped.

**This is about 2 packs of frozen artichokes, boiled and cooled. Canned can be substituted in a pinch, but the taste is inferior.

Serves 12.

Photograph by Jordan Zimmerman

New Orleans show, October 2010; Liz's sons, Eric and Mark Normand; Liz and Eric, with friends Oliver Tessier and Tracie Felker at Commander's Palace; Liz prepping for the SoFAB Kid's Cooking Class; Liz's mom Josephine Baiamonte Williams, 1921; Liz and husband, Rick Normand, at her son Eric's wedding in Buenos Aires; Liz at Warren Perrin's farm in Erath, Louisiana, with Food Studies Program students from New York University; Liz and Eric with friends Clarkson and Shirley Mosley at Commander's Palace; Liz's great-grandmother, Francesca Paola Gambino Lecce; grandmother, Elsabetta Lecce Baiamonte; and mother, Josephine Baiamonte Williams; The Southern Food and Beverage Museum

Vinni Villicano
TV Host and President, Advertainment Media, Los Angeles
Real Sugar, Real Butter, Real People

"If I were a food, I'd be a bowl of spaghetti and meatballs because I'm high strung and full of energy like the noodles, sweet and tangy like the marinara sauce, and mixed with diversity and a ballsy attitude like the spices in the meatballs."

My father's parents were immigrants of Latin and Italian descent, and our bloodline came from Italy by way of Mexico. I grew up as a child in Bakersfield, California. I first started learning how to cook from my grandmother, Catalina. She showed me the ways of the kitchen starting at the age of five when she would send me out to her garden to pick ripe Roma tomatoes and peppers, along with chasing her chickens to turn into soup to serve with fresh-made bread and tortillas. We raised sheep, cows, and crops. We worked hard on the farm and used traditional cooking methods by adding "a little of this and a little of that." You will never find measuring cups or teaspoons in my kitchen. Just as Grandma did, I always cook from scratch using real natural ingredients!

I was very innovative as a kid. My three sisters called me their "crazy little brother," as I was always trying to find a way to make a buck. I cut grass for a man who had about thirty fruit trees on his lawn, and when I was done, I would help myself to all this great fruit and take it all back to my farm. Our patio had a tin roof, and with my mom's oven racks, I'd slice the fruit, lay it out on the roof to dry, and sell it to the neighbors in plastic bags.

I went to Los Angeles to become an actor and ended up on the road pitching kitchen gadgets at home and garden shows and state fairs. I have sold everything. I have traveled to forty-nine states, have seen the country, and have eaten all the local food!

In August 2010, my friend Brady introduced me to his friend Peggy. She was producing her first "Meanwhile" Los Angeles show and wanted me to be in it. While I was looking at her website, she mentioned she wanted to produce a television pilot based on the live show. I loved the concept and told her I would like to co-host and produce it. We met the next week, and after ten minutes, I felt like we had known each other our entire lives. Weeks later, I grabbed my camera and jumped on a plane to New Orleans. If you can believe it, in my many journeys in life, I had never been to New Orleans! It was also my first time to experience the live "Meanwhile" shows, and the laughter in the rooms was contagious. These were my kind of people—and they all loved real food, like me! We spent the day with Jeff Kleinpeter at Kleinpeter Farms Dairy, where I tasted the best milk and ice cream that I have ever had in my life! The next day we headed to Hubig's Pies to film Drew Ramsey. My first apple pie was hot out the oven and melted in my mouth. I met the owners of Café Du Monde, Karen and Burt Benrud, and experienced my first café au lait and beignets. Real sugar, real butter, real people, it doesn't get better than that!

The day I left, after a late night on Bourbon Street, I ran out for breakfast in the Quarter before heading to the airport. I ordered two and a half dozen raw oysters for breakfast because I could. They were salty, cold, and simply delicious, and I finally knew the meaning to "the Big Easy!" I can't wait to go back.

Vinni and Peggy at 2010 Tasty Awards in Hollywood; Vinni at Hubig's Pies in New Orleans for pilot shoot; Vinni directing the pilot shoot at Kleinpeter Farms Dairy with Peggy; Peggy and Vinni at the April 2011 Shreveport show; Vinni and Peggy at Café Du Monde with Karen and Burt Benrud, owners; Vinni and Peggy at Café Du Monde; Vinni's first trip to Café Du Monde in New Orleans; Vinni being interviewed with Peggy on red carpet at Santa Monica show

Debbie Allen
Writer, Actress, Community Organizer, and Activist, Shreveport
Dinner with the Wall Family

"If I were a food, I would be sushi because it's fresh, sexy, and raw, and when people think they've had enough, in an hour they're back for more."

I grew up in a very working-class family. My father was a teamster, and my mom stayed home to raise the kids, until I was a teenager. My mother was your typical Louisiana Southern cook. She could make the most amazing meals from hardly anything because she cooked from scratch. I was in my thirties before I conquered her recipe for homemade biscuits. When she would make an apple pie crust, she would take the leftover dough, sprinkle sugar and cinnamon on it, and bake it up separately for my sister, brother, and me—our own version of a beignet!

I can safely say my fondest memories were all happy times around the dinner table. We would always eat together when my dad came home from work. While he was taking a shower and cleaning up for dinner, the kids would all gather at the dinner table. Momma would bring the dishes of food out one by one as we waited.

As I said earlier, I had one brother and one sister. I was the oldest, and then there was my sister, Jamie, the typical middle child. She was quiet and did what she was told and was constantly in the middle of squabbles between my brother and me. Then there was Les, short for Leslie Drew. He hated being called Leslie, and I would tease him, saying Leslie was a girl's name. He didn't take my older sister's abuse laying down either; he was

scrappy and very passive-aggressive. I had to keep one eye over my shoulder all the time!

As a girl, I was a tomboy, active in sports, and usually had quite the appetite come dinnertime. When Momma made my favorite dinner, salmon croquettes and French fries, you had better not get in my way, or you might lose a hand!

I remember one night when we had all sat down at the table. Les must have been around three because I was about ten. As Dad said the blessing, the smell of the salmon croquettes was getting to me and my mouth was watering. Not a minute after the "amen," I reached for the serving spoon, helped myself to a nice portion of the croquettes, poured the catsup, and began enjoying my momma's cooking to the fullest. Dad stopped eating, looked at me, and said, "Debbie! You really need to start eating less!" It was then that Leslie proclaimed, "Please don't eat me! Please don't eat me!" He started bawling; I looked at my dad, then at my mom, and we all busted out laughing, as my mom consoled Les and promised he wouldn't be my dinner!

Needless to say, after that, anytime Les would smell salmon croquettes cooking, we usually could find him hiding under his bed.

The Wall Family; The Wall/Campbell wedding; Debbie and baby sister, Jamie; Brother, Les; With her daughter, Ashley Hazelton, granddaughter, Julia, and her mother, Hazel Campbell; With Sheva Sims at Shreveport show; Community activist; April 2011 show; With Governor Edwards and his wife Trina Grimes Scott at book signing of *Edwin Edwards, The Louisiana Governor* by Leo Honeycutt

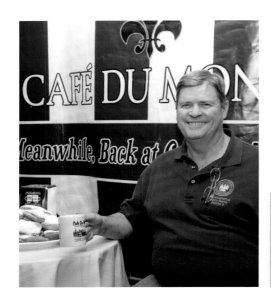

Rep. Henry Burns
Louisiana State Representative District 9 (Bossier Parish) and Owner, the Wooden Spoon, Bossier City
Café Du Cookie Man

"If I were a food, I would be a banana. Although each banana has its own identity, its value comes in bunches. Just like us, it starts out green but develops a bright yellow hue, signifying health, happiness, and greatness of one's productive dreams. It ages much like people, and enters the last of life's cycles ready and available for use."

One of my favorite memories of my childhood centers on the sweet smell of tea cakes and banana nut bread baking at my grandmother's house and at my next door neighbor's house, who lived nearly a quarter mile away from our family's home in the Red Rock Hills of Shongaloo, Louisiana.

Never in a thousand years did I think I would become a baker! In the military, I was an Explosive Ordnance Disposal officer (bomb squad) and a nuclear weapons officer. In civilian life, I was in sales and settled into the oil field until the bust in the late eighties. My transition from crude to Crisco was necessitated by a wonderful wife and four precious children who looked to me to support them and preserve and finance the family unit.

How did I become the "Cookie Man"? Well, first of all it is important to understand that this title evolved over a period of time. I enjoyed being a low dog or under dog, and I have often joked that I am the Cookie Man, spelled with a "C" because with a "K" it would read Kooky Man. I will be the first to admit that I am a "battered man" and that I am at the top of my game when I am totally "mixed up." Few professions can say that with pride.

The Wooden Spoon, a cookie gift basket company, was for sale, and I thought to myself, this had to be easier than the oil field! Boy, did I get a wake-up call! I am convinced that small business owners have to be among the brightest humans on Earth. They deal with inspections,

certifications, permits, taxes, personnel issues, and heaven forbid, trying to produce a marketable product with the ability to replicate it day in and day out for what seemed, initially, to be an eternity. Then as only God can do, I fell in love with the business! I stumbled onto my grandmother's secret. Without question, baking is the shortest route to someone's heart! Even the most jaded and hard-nosed people will melt into a smile and a good mood when they partake in one of our yummy treats!

From day one, I bounded ruthlessly forward into the community, passing out goodies and encouraging those in my path to order cookie baskets. The Wooden Spoon's business doubled, then tripled, and then quadrupled. After two years of 24/7 indulgence, the Bossier Chamber of Commerce awarded us Small Business of the Year, an award still treasured today. I look back and wonder if some of those early orders were just made in gracious support by friends, who were so willing to show encouragement or maybe even pity! I cannot thank everyone enough who played a role in keeping our doors open from the beginning and over these years. The Shreveport and Bossier citizens, family members, employees, and the many wonderful friends truly rescued me and restored my confidence and pride. I discovered an unrelenting desire to serve and give back to the community.

As the Cookie Man, one of my biggest challenges was preparing large quantities of baked items, while still maintaining the quality of home-baked goodness, which requires a balance of appearance, texture, moistness, and taste. Each cookie has its own unique protocol, and each presentation stands alone. We do not use icing or other enhancements to heighten or alter the final product. Using the inspiration from my grandmother, our early campaign slogan was "Grandma, Eat your Heart Out!" We are known for our fabulous brownies, cookies, and banana nut bread!

As the owner of the Wooden Spoon, I was the messenger for thousands of well wishes, which was an unexpected benefit— happy birthday, happy anniversary, I love you, thank you, and the list goes on. The Wooden Spoon was a platform and a vehicle for extending my presence into the community, plus it made me both accessible and approachable. Now, isn't it special how God can use the least of us, especially me, for such a ministry? The old adage of shoot the messenger was transformed into vote for the messenger because I give God the credit for any success that is shared. Only God can bless and transform a dishwashing, floor-mopping delivery boy into a Cookie Man. During my run as the Cookie Man, I have served on the Bossier Parish School Board for fifteen years. I take pride in being just who I am—just a regular guy who has been blessed with a signature name.

I decided to take my brand of service to Baton Rouge, but there was a problem: I had to sell my capability and worthiness to the constituents of District 9. After I narrowly won a four-year term in 2007 as a state representative, I soon discovered that many other state representatives had a similar goal. We were supported by a dynamic governor, Bobby Jindal, who wanted to transform the image of Louisiana as a business-friendly state with lawmakers that were known for their integrity and honesty.

During my first year, I extended my cookie ministry to Baton Rouge and tried to keep my generosity of cookies, breads, and brownie distribution low-key. But over a period of time, this action opened the doors of acceptance and support. The governor selected me, the Cookie Man, as one of his four floor leaders, and my peers supported the majority of my legislative initiatives.

After four years of proactively representing my district, and with the absolute sterling performance of my legislative assistant, Dodie Horton, and God's smiling grace, the Cookie Man was reelected for an additional four-year term without opposition.

I thank God each day for directing my path into this wholesome vocation. For me, baking is a ministry. It's a nourishing, reviving, and energy-renewing way of life, and I'm honored to be called the Cookie Man! That's with a "C" not a "K," as in "Kooky Man!" Being the Cookie Man has given me the honor of being a messenger, spreading love, support, and encouragement to everyone I meet. I am truly blessed. Was it the cookies, the sweet breads, or the brownies that provided me with the humble opportunity to serve and enjoy some level of success? I have limitations, but the God that I serve is not challenged by the frailties and shortcomings of mankind. Daddy, Pawpaw, Representative, and Cookie Man are some of the names that I answer to. Each has its time and place, and on occasions, they are synonymous. A name is a label, the first comes at birth and is a legal designation. Other names, whether positive or negative, are earned. I would like to think that the name Cookie Man has been earned due to the generosity of countless customers and friends that afforded me this opportunity. Without question, I have the "crummiest" job in town, and I will forever be grateful.

Henry Burns' Famous Banana Bread

While some fruits are discarded because of their aged and ripened state, the banana is ready to make its impact on life. It is the main ingredient to the most delicious, gum-smacking banana nut bread. We are known for our banana bread, which uses more bananas than most recipes. When you taste our banana bread, you won't ask, "Is that banana bread?" You will know it's banana bread!

Photograph by Tom Pace

1 cup margarine
4 eggs
4 cups sugar
10 ripe bananas
4½ cups all purpose flour
2 tsp. baking soda
1 tbsp. vanilla
1 cup chopped pecans

Preheat oven to 350 degrees.

Cream margarine, eggs, and sugar together. Add bananas. Start blending and add dry ingredients.

Spray loaf pan with cooking spray and pour batter into pan. The final 20 percent of the batter may need an additional 1 tbsp. of flour to firm up the final serving of batter.

Bake for 20 minutes. Turn pan to ensure even browning and cook until top of center of bread is brown. The larger the pan, the longer it takes. As in all baking, humidity can cause a small variation in time. Trial and error is the best method. To minimize excessive browning during the process, you might want to lower the temperature, which will require a little extended baking time.

The Wooden Spoon version uses more bananas than traditional banana bread recipes, which use approximately 3 or 4. To keep the strength of the fiber of the bananas start by separating the banana into 3 long strips, rather than chopping or mashing. When stirring the bananas, they will liquefy on their own.

Makes 12 small 8-oz. loaves, or 6 16-oz. loaves.

144

Henry Burns in the Shreveport show; Jamie Burns, Peggy, Jay Basist, and Henry at the Shreveport show, September 2010; Peeling the banana at the Shreveport show, October 2010 for his famous Wooden Spoon banana bread; Henry Burns with the his grandkids and future bakers: Emmalyn Burns, Chandler Burns, Kyler Burns, Isabella Burns, Kameron Burns, Olivia Burns, and James David Burns; Henry Burns at the Shreveport show with son, Jamie, showing correct way to peel a banana; Henry Burns at work

Laurie Cothern
Actress, Baton Rouge
Food and Photographs by Raymond Cothern, My Father

"If I were a food, I would have to be my grandmother's homemade cream-style corn—made with corn cut straight from the cob—because it has a tougher exterior but is soft and sweet on the inside."—Laurie Cothern

"If I were a food, I'd be a lemon icebox pie. It reminds me of summer as a kid, plus it's sweet at first taste, and then has a satisfying bit of sour comeback."—Raymond Cothern

At its largest size years ago, a Wilson reunion in Mississippi, usually around the Fourth of July, drew crowds a hundred strong, related to each other no more distantly than third cousins. Farmers, schoolteachers, fishermen, lumberyard owners, mechanics, oil field roughnecks, and nurses, all tied significantly to Onetia Wilson Cothern, my grandmother. She is the last of her brothers and sisters and turned ninety-seven years old in August 2011.

Uncles, aunts, and cousins were always photographed in chairs scattered about under a huge oak tree at the farm. Those reunions started early. And many things were always the topics of conversation—Uncle Roy and his *sugah die-bee-tees*, cousin Sue marrying a Thibodeaux boy from Louisiana, Jimmy Gaines (a third cousin) having a spell with his heart and only forty-two. There were dishes of black-eyed peas, butterbeans, field peas, okra, platters of boiled crabs, fried chicken, bream, bass, rabbit, squirrel, boiled crawfish, bowls of strawberries, cream churned from cows milked before dawn, and pies—lemon, egg, coconut, apple, and cherry.

Other gatherings were sometimes for mourning. Wilson descendants tend to die on Sundays. It's not a family tradition one looks forward to carrying on. But the tradition last continued with Uncle Wayne, who with his last breath blew out his private candlelight early one Sunday evening. So friends, neighbors, and relatives gathered with food, such as delicious chicken wings from Andrew's Food Mart, roast, sausage, meatballs simmering in a Crock-Pot, and string bean casserole.

Inevitably, the photographs came out. One was of Uncle Wayne and Aunt Peggy and friends Eddie and S.J. and their girlfriends with the guys in black shirts and the girls all in matching pink blouses, all leaning against some car with fender skirts, posing like the cast from some teenage movie from the 1950s. And more photographs were passed around, like slick layers of silver to be scooped up and carried away and looked at on laps. If we were at my grandmother's house for a Sunday dinner of chicken and dumplings and homemade biscuits, sometimes the old brown suitcase came out, full of photographs whose colors have faded like a pile of slippery fish in an ice chest.

As a child on Christmas Eve, I remember helping beat eggs in a large bowl for cheesy eggs and toast and later stirring the cake batter and licking the bowl and the beaters with the anticipation of Christmas morning. Photographs now stored in closets and desk drawers are witnesses that we always received everything on our Christmas lists and more. There are so many photographs of us at Christmas, so many Christmases that blur into sentiments we are reluctant to express for fear of being too corny or overly sentimental. But the fact is Christmas, with its attendant food, touches the best in us, wanting to please and make people happy, and to express our love without saying it. Look into a young daughter's eyes as she approaches the tree on Christmas morning and see eternity.

Laurie and mother, Dee Cothern, in New York City; Laurie, Brandon, baby Sarah, and Tanner; Laurie's parents, Raymond and Dee Cothern, Laurie, Peggy Sweeney-McDonald, and her sister, Jennifer; Baton Rouge Show, July 2010; Laurie with her grandmother; Laurie's niece, Rachel, with her cousin, Sarah; Laurie, Peggy Sweeny-McDonald, and Jennifer at Asphodel Plantation Arts Festival, October 1980

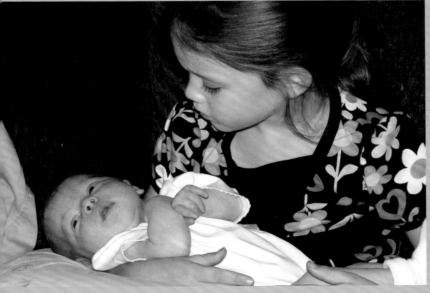

Alan Ehrich
Executive Chef, Audubon Nature Institute, New Orleans
From the Delta to the Crescent City: A Culinary Journey

"If I were a food, I'd be a porterhouse steak, tender and cut sweet on the fillet side, tougher but lots of flavor on the strip side, and grilled on an open flame. This kind of explains my dual personality."

I have always liked the more primitive style of cooking. I love the flavor of smoked meat. It brings me back to my childhood when my dad would take over culinary duties from my mother on Sunday afternoons and barbeque. It was always a feast of chicken, ribs, or steak on the grill.

So this is the evolution of me becoming a chef. I grew up with Russian grandparents, and I came from a very Jewish family living in Clarksdale, Mississippi. Jewish food, although I have a greater appreciation for it now, was not very exciting to me. It often included a brisket that had been in the oven for a long time, accompanied by potatoes and carrots. Matzo ball soup, which is an egg and matzo-flour dumpling-type ball in a chicken broth, and gefilte fish, which was ground up buffalo fish that was cooked, congealed, and served with horseradish were two common dishes. I will say, however, that my grandmother used an old meat grinder, and my first experience with sashimi was when she had me taste the raw fish, onions, salt, and pepper, coming out of the grinder.

My parents could be described as June Cleaver and Marcus Welby. My sixties and seventies household was pre-microwave, but not pre-Tupperware, as Mom has always loved to freeze dishes. Instead of preparing fresh, she would prepare months in advance for affairs of the family. We kid her about this constantly, yet if I tell her I'm coming to Dallas next month to visit she will respond with "I'll start cooking now." Got to love her!

As was typical of the time, Mother did most of the daily cooking. I was brought up on frozen or canned vegetables, pressure-cooked cauliflower and broccoli, and iceberg lettuce with Italian dressing with wedges of tomatoes. Because my father had a heart issue, nothing had salt or spice in it. However, my father took over cooking on the weekends. Because he didn't cook as a chore, but for the love of it, we had omelets, big pots of different types of soups, and of course barbeque. It was through his eyes that I learned cooking was fun and an art to bring excitement to the sense of taste, smell, sight, and texture.

A caterer was hired for my bar mitzvah, and it was then that I clearly remember tasting tenderloin for the first time, smoked and sliced thin on French baguette. There were little homemade rolls, with butter on them, which I would have never had in my heart-healthy household. Still, it wasn't until I moved away from home that I realized that there were such things as foie gras, and I was able to taste caviar for the first time. My father made homemade wine from elderberries, but I never knew the world that was waiting for me until I opened my first cabernet.

When I was fifteen, I started working for a Greek man, which was my first introduction to European food. He had an old-style Greek restaurant, with Mom and Pop Polis watching the door and the cash register at the same time. He was a very passionate man, and when people would ask him if the fish was fresh, he would haul out a huge fresh fish and cut the fillet right off the carcass. He had a bartender who made all of his drinks from scratch—sweet and sour mixes made with fresh lemons, limes, and sugar cubes, Tom Collins's and martinis shaken vigorously. He took a liking to me and taught this eager youth the finer points of bartending.

Long before fusion cuisine as we experience it today, I desired to learn from a wide range of food cultures. I went to school in Switzerland, visiting a variety of countries to study their respective kitchens and culinary styles. Sushi and the Japanese art of cooking and displaying foods also had a very distinct influence on how I see plates, color combinations, portion size, and how food impacts the palate and taste buds. I also became more aware of the effect of the fats, sugars, and acids in foods that I prepare as they combine with wines and sauces.

I followed my passion to the culinary capital, New Orleans, and continued to hone my flair for Creole cuisine with the Patouts. I have carried my eclectic curriculum a step further by combining the distinctive spices and cultural styles with the native flavors and essence of Louisiana. I endeavor to make my food a prettier, healthier version of comfort food. It's classic Cajun or classic French or classic Southern or classic Jewish but with a modern look that I call Southern fusion.

As time has gone on, I think the trend today is that fine dining menus have become healthier. The plates are still small, but restaurant goers are not starving when they leave, as they were in the nouvelle cuisine days; it's still tapas. I am always trying to take into account portion size, color combinations, flavor, and wine pairing.

I have found my home as the executive chef at Audubon Nature Institute, which has given me the freedom to bring my expertise in fine dining to events. With so many different venues, including the Audubon Tea Room, Zoo, Park, Clubhouse, Aquarium of the Americas, and Woldenberg Park, I have the exciting challenge of creating for gatherings of fifty to ten thousand and for all occasions and tastes. I am honored that the Audubon Tea Room was voted Best Place for a Wedding Reception in a recent *Gambit* citywide poll, and the Audubon Clubhouse was voted Best Place for a Wedding Reception by the *Knot* magazine.

I love that I have the flexibility to create both traditional and innovative weddings and a broad range of events. Two recent examples of this variety were a spontaneous dinner we held on the floor of the Superdome and a U.S. State Department dinner for international ambassadors served at the Tea Room. Contrasting the routine of restaurant work, I can, for example, utilize the culinary equivalent of perfect pitch to re-create a client's favorite dishes from sight and taste as well as being able to exercise my continuing fascination with culinary trends, such as molecular gastronomy.

My heart is in sustainability, and I have spearheaded Audubon's certification as Louisiana's first green caterer. I redesigned my menu to focus on seasonal foods available from local vendors and farmers' markets and to use fresh herbs grown in the zoo's gardens. Today I am much more aware of where my fish comes from and whether or not it's on the endangered species list. I know where my produce comes from, if it's being shipped from Mexico, California, an hour away in Mandeville, or southern Mississippi.

As far afield as our education takes us, in the end we always return to what we know and love. I have completed my culinary circle with my latest personal venture, Delta Blue's Barbeque, a catering barbeque truck for festivals and offsite private events. On the opposite end of the culinary spectrum, I have also founded My Personal Chef, Inc., a small, private offsite catering service for the most discerning of our local foodies.

What I love the most about being a chef is that I am always growing, changing, and learning. I am always using both the artistic and analytical side of my brain to craft and accomplish. Most of all, it's the interaction with my team and my clients, of creating and making dreams and visions a reality. A lifetime of exploration into this amazing field means the journey has no end.

Audubon Tea Room Crawfish Cheesecake

I have served and demonstrated Crawfish Cheesecake hundreds of times. This unique recipe is the true essence of Louisiana, starting with the "Holy Trinity" (onions, celery, bell pepper), smoked andouille sausage, and finishing with Louisiana crawfish. This is a twist on the traditional cheesecake recipe; one bites into a savory Cajun delight that lets you know that "you are no longer in Kansas;" you have just crossed over to Cajun Country Louisiana! Perfect for a party appetizer.

1 onion, minced
1 stalk celery, chopped
1 green bell pepper, chopped
1½ tsp. minced garlic
¼ cup olive oil
1 lb. crawfish tails
1 lb. andouille sausage, chopped
1½ tsp. Creole seasoning
1 lb. cream cheese, softened
1 cup heavy cream
¾ lb. Gouda cheese, chopped
4 eggs
1 cup Italian breadcrumbs
3 tbsp. grated Parmesan cheese
3 tbsp. olive oil

Chop onion, celery, bell pepper, and garlic. Sauté vegetables in olive oil.

Coarsely chop crawfish tails and andouille sausage and add to pan. Add seasoning and cream cheese to pan and mix thoroughly. Remove from heat and add the heavy cream, Gouda, and eggs. Mix well.

Combine breadcrumbs, Parmesan, and olive oil in a bowl. Place mixture in the bottom of a spring pan to make base crust. Press tightly.

Pour crawfish mixture into pan. Place pan in a 2-inch hotel pan and add 1½ inches of water and cover. Bake for 45 minutes to 1 hour at 350 degrees until mixture begins to set then remove cover and continue to bake until golden brown, approximately 10 to 15 minutes. You know that it has set when you shake the pan, and the center does not jiggle, and also when you touch the center of the cake with the palm of your hand, and it is firm to the touch.

To remove from pan, run a small knife around the edge of the cake before releasing the latch.

Serves 50 on a buffet.

Alan's company logo, featuring a cartoon of his dog Blue

Alan in the kitchen with Ron Forman, CEO of Audubon Nature Institute; At Mardi Gras Ball with step-son, Dennis Braud; Alan's Mom, Leah Ehrich and son, Jordon; Setting up a candelit dinner on the 50 yard line of the Superdome; At New Orleans Bike week cooking contest; On vacation; Alan with emcee, Poppy Tooker, at the New Orleans October 2010 show; At work; Ground Zero Blues Club, Clarksdale, Mississippi owned by Bill Luckett and actor, Morgan Freeman

Chef
Alan
Ehrich
Audubon
Institute

CAFÉ
...nwhile, B...

Jerry Leggio
Actor, Baton Rouge
Mustard Sandwiches and the Dough Boys

"If I were a food, I'd be Gloria's lasagna, because it's the best and I like being the best!"

Let me take you back a few years to 1944. Both wars (in Europe and the Pacific) would soon be coming to an end. I was nine years old and my friend Lloyd (also nine) said, "Hey, Jerry, let's you and me and Homer go on a picnic to the Boyd Wood." Homer was my other friend, and the Boyd Wood was a little grove of trees about two hundred yards off Boyd Avenue, known today as Spanish Town Road. This little oasis was our private get-away, a place where young boys could go and commune with nature, a place where we could fish in the lake that bordered the wood, simply our little piece of heaven. Today the lake is gone. It was filled in many years ago, but the wood is still there. So we all agreed that Lloyd had a good idea, and we each retreated to our respective kitchens to prepare our sandwiches. We agreed to each make three sandwiches, and then we would trade out. My favorite was mustard sandwiches—just two pieces of bread slathered with mustard—that's all, nothing else. I made three, wrapped them in wax paper, and placed them in a small brown grocery bag—all moms saved grocery bags. When the three of us started our trek to our little paradise, we took inventory. Lloyd had peanut butter and jelly, and Homer had some kind of egg sandwiches. But Lloyd, upon seeing mine, said, "Yuck, mustard sandwiches." Homer felt the same way, so I wound up with three mustard sandwiches.

When we got to our little piece of heaven and started to eat our lunches, we heard some raucous voices off to our right. Coming toward us were six teenagers, twice our ages, twice our sizes, and twice in number. We realized that this was shaping up to be a misadventure, so we decided to abandon our plans for the day and start back toward Boyd Avenue. Unfortunately, our route was the same as theirs, so when we encountered them, they had the audacity to highjack our lunches. Well, we couldn't allow that to happen, so we cut loose with a plethora of child-sized expletives, which of course fell on deaf ears. And not surprisingly our tirades had no effect. The teenagers continued toward our private little oasis while we retreated toward home. How terrible! They were going to desecrate our private sanctuary. But before we got back to Boyd Avenue, we heard, "There ain't no meat on these sandwiches." We looked back and two of them were viciously protesting this absence of meat on the mustard sandwiches—so much so that they took out after us. They were going to beat us up, as if we had deprived them of meat on purpose. They took this very personally. Well, we managed to arrive at the street before they could overtake us, and they wisely retreated as well, obviously not wanting to have any witnesses see them beating up three little kids.

As we proceeded home, Homer said, "Jerry, that was great." "What was great, Homer?" "Making those mustard sandwiches. That was great." Homer, not one of the sharpest knives in the drawer, really thought I had preordained that little bit of trickery, as if I knew that this encounter was going to happen. I didn't say otherwise. I let him enjoy that little fantasy. But we all three looked at each other with mischievous little grins. We didn't need to say a word—sweet justice!

But all was not lost. About a month later, my mother came out on the front porch holding up a shiny silver dime. She said, "I want you and Lloyd to run around to Wolf's Bakery and get a dime's worth of bread dough." Wow, we knew what that meant—fried dough. Mom would fry dough and you talk about good! It was a cross between today's funnel cake and beignets. Delicious! You could eat it with powdered sugar or granulated sugar or syrup or jelly or just plain. Didn't matter. Fried dough, as cooked by my mom, was scrumptious.

Lloyd and I happily bounded off to Wolf's Bakery, about a mile from home. It involved crossing North, Main, and Laurel streets and finally Florida Boulevard. (Two nine-year-old boys walking about a mile and crossing that much traffic alone—I always knew my mother loved me, but—nah.) Anyway, we made our way to Wolf's Bakery (today it is Flowers Baking Co.) and went in the side customer service entrance. I put my dime on the counter and said to the clerk, "My mama wants ten cents' worth of bread dough." He popped open a brown paper sack and began loading a fistful of dough into the bag. He sealed it, and we were on our way. Lloyd asked, "I wonder where his hand had been?" I said, "What are you talking about, Lloyd?" This was before latex gloves had been invented. Lloyd replied, "I just can't help wondering where his hand had been." I said, "Lloyd, Mom's going to fry this dough. So if there are any germs, they'll be fried too." He responded, "Oh."

Now it was midsummer, and I began to experience a strange phenomenon. The sack of dough seemed to be getting larger, not heavier, just larger. The paper sack was splitting open, in fact it was actually shredding as the dough continued to grow. I said "Lloyd, help me." He took half the dough, and as we walked, his half as well as mine continued to grow. I had to put some of my half on my shoulder for fear that I would lose some of it. When we got home, my mother, who had been waiting outside for us, immediately started laughing. She knew instantly what was happening. She said, "Oh my god, I forgot about the yeast." She would later explain about the yeast. She then said, "They didn't put it in a bag?" I said "Yes, but we don't know where the bag is." She said, "Oh." Anyway, we had some delicious fried dough that summer, laced with shredded bits of paper bag. I've often wondered how much of the paper sack Lloyd and I probably ingested.

When I was preparing my "food" story, my wife Gloria said, "Don't you wish now that you had put meat on those sandwiches?" Those of you who know Gloria know how very compassionate she is. When she asked, I must confess that, in retrospect, I do wish those sandwiches had had meat on them.

Gloria's Lasagna

The first time we ever ate lasagna was at a Baton Rouge Little Theater cast party in the sixties. There was a group that called themselves NYOBs (New York or Bust), and they would cater some of the cast parties to raise money to go to New York City. Their lasagna was so good that Gloria couldn't wait to learn how to make it. She made a few changes, but it quickly became a favorite with our family and friends. We like to serve a green salad and garlic bread with lasagna. It was our son, Jerry's, favorite food. We always think of him and wish that he was still with us to enjoy his mom's lasagna.

4 lb. lean ground beef
1 20-oz. can tomato purée
1 20-oz. can stewed tomatoes
20 oz. ketchup
1 tsp. salt
1 tsp. black pepper
1 cup dried parsley
1 cup chopped onions
1 cup chopped carrots
1 cup chopped celery
1 16-oz. package lasagna noodles
48 oz. small-curd cottage cheese
2 lb. sharp cheddar cheese, grated

In a large cast iron pot, brown ground beef. Add tomato purée, stewed tomatoes, ketchup, salt, pepper, parsley, and onions. Cover and cook on low heat. Stir frequently to prevent burning.

Chop carrots and celery and add into sauce. Cover and continue to cook on low heat and stir to prevent burning. Cook approximately 1 hour.

In a separate pot, heat water and prepare lasagna noodles. Do not overcook. You want the noodles to absorb some of the sauce.

In a large 9x13, deep-cooking pan spread a layer of the meat sauce, a layer of cottage cheese, a layer of the sharp cheddar cheese, and then a layer of the lasagna noodles. Repeat. End with a layer of meat sauce, cottage cheese, and the grated cheddar cheese.

Bake at 350 degrees for approximately 50 minutes or until the cheese starts to bubble. The carrots will have a nice little crunch.

Note: Lasagna can be very messy while baking, so I always line a large cookie sheet with tin foil and place underneath the pan.

Serves 10 to 12.

Photograph by Felicia Leggio Braud

Jerry and wife, Gloria Leggio; Jerry with Wallace Merck in the film *Mothman*; Jerry enjoying good weather; Baton Rouge show, September 2010; Jerry Leggio, actor; Gloria and Jerry Leggio with Peggy and Missy Crews at the anniversary show at Juban's Restaurant, April 2011; Baton Rouge show, November 2010; Jerry and Gloria in New York

Wayne Bennett
Actor, New Orleans
Family Suppers

"If I were a food, I would be gumbo; separately the ingredients look chaotic, but all together it's the perfect mix."

As a kid growing up in New Orleans, I was the happiest little boy in town. I had two grandmothers, Granny Myra and Nana Rose, who lived right across the bridge from each other and they used to compete for the best cook over the bridge. But to me, they were the best two cooks in town and were kind enough to let me be a judge in the cook-off that was going on in my mind. Man, those were the days.

I would start at Granny Myra's house, where she would cook breakfast. She made banana fritters (banana pancakes) with butter and sprinkled sugar on top—yes sugar, no syrup. She made them with smoked sausage and hash browns, but the fritters were really thin, so you could still have room for the rest of your food because you had to finish your plate. See down south, oh, you're going to finish your plate. If you can't eat too much you better ask for small portions, because it's an insult if you don't finish your plate! To this day, I won't leave food on a plate; even if I need a quick lap around the house to work some of it off! Sometimes Granny Myra would spice it up and make some veal chops with grits and gravy just to tease you. How many people have dinner for breakfast? It has you thinking it is time for bed by the time you finish eating and its 7:30 in the morning. "You mean I still have to go to school?" I was just so confused! But what topped it all off for me were the eggs! Now look I love eggs, but I have never figured out how she made those eggs.

Nana Rose used to throw down in the kitchen as well, from red beans and rice to the Cornish hen with mashed potatoes. I couldn't ask for a better childhood. But the kick was when they got together for the suppers.

A supper is a fundraiser in the local neighborhood to raise money for your family. We didn't always have money for the bills, so we raised it with food. My grannies would get together and make these plates, and people would line up outside our front door. There were three specials: fish, chicken, and mirliton. I'm talking nice crispy catfish with a smile on its face because even it knew it was cooked to perfection. You haven't had chicken until you've had my granny's chicken! And my favorite, the mirliton plate—a mirliton filled with ground turkey or beef and shrimp. We can't forget about the sides: string macaroni and cheese, string beans, corn on a cob, potato salad, sweet potatoes, and greens. And dessert, the world famous, in my mind, bread pudding! Those were some of the best times in my life; the whole family would come around, eat, and take some to go. It was like a live-in restaurant for me, all day every day until the day came when I left for California to pursue my acting career.

I have searched far and wide for that same style "Rose Myra" cooking in California to no avail. All I want is my taste of New Orleans. I came here tonight to the show at House of Blues Sunset Strip to gain some new "family" and now that we have eaten and shared some stories, I'm going to depart the same way my family would after the suppers. I have my Tupperware ready for my "go plate!" Can someone please lead me to the leftovers?

Wedding day; Wayne with his Mom, Myra Cargill, and brothers, Maaliq and Micaah; Second lining at his wedding; Wayne with wife, Karen Balumbu-Bennett; Nana Rose; Wayne and brothers, Micaah, Justin, Lavell, Maaliq, and Rashad; Wayne and Peggy at House of Blues-Sunset show, August 2010; With goddaughter; With Granny Myra; Football player

Rosemary Delores "Mae Mae" Williams-Churchill

Joanie Rogers Enxing
Wife, Mother, Grandmother, and Educator, Baton Rouge
A Mother's Love

"If I were a food, I would be a peanut butter and jelly sandwich! My dear friends think I can be a little nutty sometimes, but sweet. I love PB&J. Plus, I am usually the one in the classroom to sing to the children, act silly with them, and tease them. I am sure most of the kids think I am a nut!"

When Peggy asked me to be part of the show, I jumped at the chance. I was so excited about being on stage again that I didn't stop to think of what I would talk about. When I asked Peggy about what in the world I would talk about, she simply said, "Just speak from the heart." I instantly knew I had to talk about my mom.

Her name was Jean Rogers, but she went by Jean, Miss Jean, Mom, or Maw Maw; I think Maw Maw was her favorite title! She didn't really do anything extraordinary with her life, except have four children, who in turn gave her eleven grandchildren. However, her love, kindness, sweet spirit, and smile were so special that everyone was drawn to her. And once she got you there, she fed you.

Maw Maw passed away on July 23, 2003, at the young age of sixty-seven. We wish we could have had her longer, but we know the years she spent on this earth were filled with love! Love for her family, grandchildren, and her many friends. She demonstrated her love for us with her food. On September 19, 2010, what would have been her seventy-fifth birthday, we all gathered together to celebrate the best way we knew how—by having a Maw Maw-style dinner with a menu dedicated to some of her dishes that were favorites of her family and friends. Also, we each had to be ready to share our favorite Maw Maw story.

My mom was and still is the sweetest lady I have ever known. She reminded us a lot of Edith Bunker—sweet, unassuming, and sometimes a little ditzy! She called all of her grandchildren her "sweet, precious, baby angels." And she meant it; to her, they could do no wrong.

My mom and dad married in 1957 and, like everyone else in those days, proceeded to have four children in rapid succession: Eddie, Michael, David, and me. My mom always made sure we were well-fed. Thanks, Mom!

We lost our grandparents before the four of us were old enough to remember them, so we never had the large family gatherings for holidays. It was just the six of us, but my parents were determined to make the holidays memorable, so our holiday traditions were born! I still remember Thanksgiving mornings, watching the parades on television, while my parents were in the kitchen putting together a meal of turkey, cornbread dressing, and all the fixings. To this day, if I smell green onions, celery, and onions together I am transported right back to my childhood on Cedarcrest Avenue. We still have the same basic menu, and with the additions of in-laws, we have a few new dishes. Today's holiday celebrations have evolved into big memorable events, and all I can think about is just how much my parents would love to be part of it all. Somehow, I think they must know that they are the inspiration.

My mom's greatest loves after her children were her eleven grandchildren. She delighted in everything they did and could always be counted on for an enthusiastic "Hot dog" for all accomplishments—large or small! That love for her grandchildren was so evident by the fact that she worked some weekends and nights so she could buy presents for birthdays and Christmas. For all of the major holidays, each child was presented with a seasonal cup filled with candy, pencils, trinkets, and sometimes a lottery ticket. She always laughingly told them they had to share if they won big! After her death, while we were cleaning out her apartment, we came across bags of presents for the grandkids already wrapped and tagged!

Sometimes her love was so strong it pushed her to do things normally not considered proper. There was one such situation when she vacationed with my brother Michael and his wife, Janine, and their children, Brandon and Nicole. At dinner, everyone ordered steak except Nicole even though she was encouraged to do so. However, when her order got there, she decided she wanted steak after all, so my mom offered to switch with her, but Michael would not allow it. A few minutes into the meal, Michael noticed Mom cutting pieces of steak and sliding them across the seat to Nicole.

Once when she was scheduled for a surgery, we met at the hospital to see her before the operation. But her main concern was that because we got up so early, we didn't have time for breakfast. So right before she was wheeled away, she handed me a bag of donuts and honey buns! She was always thinking of others, always.

I found out recently that she frequently made my friend Tootie a carrot cake for her birthday because she knew how much she loved it. I don't know how often she did that, but she must have done it quite a few times. And I promise you, you have never tasted carrot cake like my mom made from scratch. She grated the carrots, made her own cream cheese icing, and it wasn't finished until she made little swirls on top of the cake and placed pecans in a decorative design on top.

Every dish she made was someone's favorite. Her pimento cheese sandwich spread was a big hit, especially with my brothers, Michael and David. Although, they say they will never eat another pimento cheese sandwich, as no else can make it like she did. Well, I can, so I will just have to prove it to them.

One summer, the entire family went to Look Out Mountain, all nineteen of us. Our plan was to stop at a rest area on the way for lunch. Because there were so many of us, we spread out to four or five tables, and while I was pulling out my ham and cheese sandwiches, I looked up to see everyone gathered around my mom as she unpacked her pimento cheese.

Every Thanksgiving, Christmas, or other family get-together became a smorgasbord of dishes, traditional and new, but a staple was Mom's Mississippi Mud. Our first Thanksgiving without her, one of the sisters-in-law offered to make the Mississippi Mud, only to realize, too late, that Mom must have been doubling the recipe for years. So there we were, about eighteen of us, trying to stretch a dessert we loved so much, so we could all have a taste. Actually, we wanted to savor the memory of a sweet and loving lady who we wanted so much to keep in our midst.

We're a bigger family now, as five of Mom's grandchildren are married. We have four sons-in-law and one daughter-in-law. She also has five great-grandbabies. I can't wait until the day I too can look at the next generation with a smile on my face and love in my heart and say as I heard my Mom say so many times, "Hot dog"!

Miss Jean's Mississippi Mud

My family really enjoys getting together! With every holiday or family function, we would bring our favorite dishes, but no one could make dessert like my mom. We each had our favorite dessert—carrot cake, heavenly hash squares, strawberry salad—but the one dessert everyone loved was Mississippi Mud! I am not sure when Mom first started making it, but once she did, it quickly became the family favorite. More than ingredients went into her Mississippi Mud; it was made with love, affection, and joy. We all share her recipe, and if I lose my copy, I know I can call one of my sisters-in-law to get it, and now, all of her granddaughters know how to make it. I am positive that when my granddaughters grow up they will make it for their families also!

1 cup flour
1 stick butter
1 1/2 cups chopped nuts
1 16oz. container Cool Whip
1 cup powdered sugar
8 oz. cream cheese
8 oz. instant chocolate pudding
4 cups cold milk

Mix together flour, butter, and nuts and press down in 9x13 baking dish and bake at 350 degrees for 15 to 20 minutes. Let cool. Mix 1 1/2 cups of Cool Whip, powdered sugar, and cream cheese and spread over cool crust. Mix chocolate pudding mixes with 4 cups of cold milk and spread over filling. Top with remaining Cool Whip and chill for 2 hours. Serve with fresh berries. Enjoy!

Serves 10 to 12.

Jean Rogers in her kitchen.

Joanie with her three grandbabies, Catherine, Lydia, and Carter; The Rogers Family: George, Joanie, David, Eddy, Jean, Michael; Joanie with brothers, Michael and David; Enxing Family *From left:* Steve, Joanie, Lydia, Melanie, Paul, Diana, John, Carter, Meredith, Catherine; Joanie and Peggy with the old Cedarcrest neighborhood friends and family at the Baton Rouge show, September 2010; Joanie with Steve Enxing; Joanie with family and friends at the Baton Rouge show, September 2010

Scott Jefferson
Actor, New Orleans
From Mashed Potatoes to Mole

"If I were a food, I'd be chicken mole, because when I had it for dinner on my honeymoon, I knew I was in love."

Like any good tale, there is a prologue to this one. I have relished in being the older brother to identical twin girls, Colleen and Claudia. Of course, whatever I told them was gospel. Born as they were on New Year's Day, no one in the family was really up for an exciting party on their birthday. To spice things up, I told them that every parade on New Year's Day was a special tribute to them to. They believed me, until they were eighteen.

Our family usually celebrated Thanksgiving at my sister's restaurant, where she served an impressive buffet. One year a family tradition was started. We all went to the buffet to load up on Thanksgiving dinner. My young niece was at my side, hanging on every word.

She filled her plate with only mashed potatoes. She had a massive serving, spread across her entire plate. To this day, I don't know what possessed me. Without considering the consequences, I put my hand behind my trusting niece's head and pushed it into her plate of mashed potatoes.

A stunned silence engulfed the table. My little niece lifted her head. Her face was covered with mashed potatoes. The only things you could see were her horrified eyes and her mouth hanging open in utter disbelief. She recovered her composure, lifted a glop of mashed potatoes from her plate, and smeared them in my face. "Food fight!" she happily cried, and the Jefferson family tradition began.

Time passed and food adventures became more memorable. My wife, Alice, and I were on our honeymoon, in Mexico.

My wife's goal was to find one of her absolute favorite food dishes—mole. Thankfully, she explained that mole was a chocolate sauce pronounced "moh-lay."

And so the hunt began. We found a charming restaurant in Puerto Morales. The dish and the evening were delicious, delovely, and all those adjectives that conjure up a Cole Porter song.

Wandering through a village market several days later, we happened upon a jar with a yellow label. It was bottled mole. We were taking one of these treasures back to the States with us, along with other Mexican delights, like the obligatory Cuban cigars.

Going through customs, I filled out the declaration and the Customs agent stamped our visa. While waiting for our bags to clear, amid blaring announcements from the intercom, my wife whispered to me. "What? I can't hear you." A tad louder, she asks if I declared the "Mole, what if they find it?" "Honey, why are you whispering? Customs can't hear you! I can't hear you! Why are you worried about mole? We should be more concerned about our three Cuban cigars!" "Oh."

So we made it back to New Orleans with our precious only -to-be-found-in-Mexico mole. On our next trip to the local grocery to buy the ingredients for our chicken mole recipe, what do we discover? A dozen yellow bottles of our coveted, smuggled mole; the very same bottles we found in a remote market in Mexico. It was actually quite good and much easier to make! However, we still like to make it from scratch.

162

Scott's mom with the twin girls, Colleen and Claudia; Scott and Alice on their honeymoon in Mexico; Scott sailing in Mexico; Scott and Alice's favorite place for Chicken mole in Mexico; Scott and Alice's wedding at the Napoleon House May 21, 2011; Scott in the show October 2011 at the Southern Food and Beverage Museum; Scott as "King Lear" in *King Lear* with Martin Covert as "the Fool."; Scott Jefferson and Peggy, October 2010 at Ralph & Kacoo's; Scott as "Chekhov" in *I Take Your Hand*

John Gray
Music Educator and Musician, The J Gray Jazz Trio, Baton Rouge

Hangin'

"If I were a food, I would be popcorn, because when the heat is on, whether in teaching or performing, that's when I pop to life!"

The year is 2000, or 2001, um, 2002? Anyway, I'm in my early twenties and somewhere in the middle of my college years. I'm a proud student of the Southern University Jazz Program, and the fall semester has started. Everybody is back on "the Yard," as we called it, and along with my friends and classmates, I'm ready for another exciting year.

My friends are all students of the Alvin Batiste Jazz Program, and we love to hang in New Orleans. So when we hear that there's a "killin' set" happening at Snug Harbor—a famous jazz club in New Orleans—we make plans to head to "dat city." It might have been Nicholas Payton, Wes Anderson, Donald Harrison, or some other great jazzman we admired performing that night. Doesn't matter, we knew it would be "killin'," and we were gonna be there.

Since I was the only one with an SUV, I take a few of the cats with me. We get to Frenchmen Street, spend about thirty minutes drivin' 'round waiting for a parking spot to open up, and park.

So we make our way to Snug. "Man, that sure does smell good, where is it coming from?" asks one of my friends. "Ahh, the Praline Connection!" says another friend. "I ain't got the bread for that tonight, we ballin' on a budget, man," I say.

We walk into Snug Harbor with our instruments. I look at the marquee, the cover is $15, and I start doing the math. I've got $22 on me now, and a quarter tank of gas. After I pay the cover and order a cold drink, I'll

have $5. Man, that gumbo smells good! Ok, I'll get a cup of gumbo and an iced tea. That's all my money. So as I start figuring out how much the cats will need to give me for gas, George, the owner of Snug Harbor, walks down the stairs. He recognizes us as Alvin Batiste's students and tells the hostess, "Let these guys on through. Ya'll doin' alright tonight?" "Yeah, thanks, George!" "Enjoy, guys!"

Now I've got some breathing room with my $22! The show is awesome, and, as is customary, the bandleader invites cats on stage to "sit in." My friends were always better jazz musicians than I. So as we make our way onto the bandstand, I'm praying that they don't call something like "Giant Steps" or "Cherokee." Please let it be a blues they call, I think to myself. Blues it is, yes!

We all hop up on the small stage and start swingin'. It's late, but the musicians in the audience would stay until the final note was played. We all played, I manage to pull off a decent solo, and we head out.

It's after 1:00 A.M. at this point. "Hey, man, let's go to 'We Never Close'," says one of the cats. "Man, you know their po' boys go off." A short ride later, we're there, and you can smell the grease from the outside. We eat; talk about the music, how good the po' boys are, the classes we won't be making it to the next day; and then head back home.

We're all feelin' good about the night, feelin' good from the food, feelin' good that my car didn't get towed, and I'm feelin' good that I still have more than $5 to my name!

John playing his trumpet; With wife Ebony; Closing the Baton Rouge show, October 2010 at Ralph & Kacoo's; In the show; In the studio recording; At the Kingfish Lounge; Playing with his students at Fest for All in Baton Rouge 2007; With the Soul Jukeboxx Band with Greg Darville and Esco Mc Collum; With the Soul Jukeboxx in the studio.

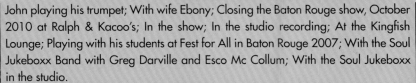

Celeste Landry
Events and Marketing Director, Firebelly Concepts, Baton Rouge
The Fig Tree and Me

"If I were a food, I really want to say something chocolate. Not only is it my favorite ingredient, but I truly believe it is a food group. However, I'd have to say that I'd be a big pot of seafood gumbo. What's in a gumbo? A whole lot of ingredients completely unrelated, but together, they make something delicious."

Here's my smorgasbord of traits: I have a degree in business marketing from Louisiana State University. I minored in sculpture, specializing in metalsmithing. I am a classically trained chef. I love to run and finished my first marathon a couple of years ago. I am currently taking up soccer. I have a seventy-five-pound pit bull, Jolie, that I would kill for and have picked up and adopted out more stray dogs than I know what to do with. And yes, I'm a Catholic girl from south Louisiana who grew up along the bayous of Thibodaux.

Now, I've been going with my dad to LSU football games since I was about three, all dressed in my cheerleading uniform. But, I remember my first LSU game as a student, sitting in the student section with my new friends, trying to learn all the cheers, and sipping on bourbon and coke. (Yes, we smuggled this into the stadium in ways you probably don't want to know). I remember looking around and thinking, "Oh, my god, there are four times more people in this stadium than in my entire city."

I know what you're thinking; Thibodaux is actually a city and the only actual city in Lafourche Parish. They are a very forward-thinking bunch; the mayor is one of my dad's best friends. We have to drive thirty minutes to go to the movies. The only Mexican restaurant is La Casa, the school for children under kindergarten age is the Little School, and, you guessed it, some of the best seafood is served at Bubbas, the one on the 308 side of

the bayou, not the Highway 1 side. Thibodaux is one of those places where going to the store to pick up toilet paper takes two hours because you run into everyone you know. As a high schooler, I could never do anything wrong because my parents would always find out about it before I even got home. It was an amazing place to grow up, and I wouldn't change it for anything.

You can imagine the shock from my parents when I announced that after graduation I'd be moving to Houston, the fourth largest city in the country, alone, to go to culinary school. I tell you what; I had a huge leg up on all the other students in my class because of the French influence on Louisiana food. All of the other students were from the Dallas/Houston area with a couple being from out of state.

This was a small, privately owned school called Culinary Institute Alain and Marie LeNôtre. The LeNôtre family had a huge dynasty in France, and Alain was ranked as the top pastry chef in France. He recruited all his buddies to teach at this school, and since it was private, you basically sign your life over to them. Interestingly enough, it was similar to the Catholic schools I attended. The chefs were allowed to yell and throw pots, and since they were all French and probably just off the boat, they had terrible tempers.

I remember this one time a girl nearly sliced her finger off and ran out of the room crying. The chef ran after her yelling,

"Emileee, come here! I'm going to kill you! Stop crying babee!"

We cooked everything from beef tongue to delicate sauces and learned to fillet every sort of fish under the sun. I had this one chef, Chef Laurent, who was from Calvados, France. This is in the Normandy region, and I was actually lucky enough to take a trip there a few summers ago. Now Chef Laurent looked like the chef in *Ratatouille*; he had huge eyes that were constantly swollen and red. He blamed this on the television show *The First 48* and his serious insomnia.

He would stomp around and smell everything, and if you were lucky, he would nod his head and move on. What you didn't want is the wide-eyed, nostrils-flaring look. This meant your dish was so bad that he had no words for you. This usually resulted in being sent to the library for the rest of the day to read cookbooks and think about how miserably you failed. Thankfully, my food never reached that point; I only watched from afar, as my classmates sulked out the classroom to solitary library confinement.

I actually graduated with flying colors at the top of my class and taught my friends a thing or two about how Southern cooking really tastes. One girl thought she knew what to do because she had a grandmother that lived in northern Mississippi. Needless to say, she had never heard of Tony's or Slap Ya Mama.

After culinary school, I took a job with Chef John Folse as his media chef. I had the privilege to work alongside him and handle all food preparation for the TV and radio shows as well as handle research for some of the cookbooks.

I later worked as a personal chef, specializing in my favorite type of cooking—local, organic cuisine. There is nothing better than waking up on a Saturday morning and going to the farmers' market to see what delicious, fresh goodies the farmers have. There was one man, the pecan man, who had grilled okra sometimes. It was pretty amazing.

I found my way back to the marketing and event world with Sean Malone and Andy Blouin of Firebelly Concepts, where I am the director of marketing, catering, and events. It's such an amazing job and an amazing company. I still get to do menu planning, but I leave the cooking to our corporate chef. I still cook a bit on the side (mostly experimenting at home) and teach private cooking lessons.

Now before I call it a day, I have to tell you about the man that lit the cookin' fire for me; I called him "the Papa." He was my maternal grandfather, self-proclaimed cook, and retiree from Chevron. He could cook better than anyone I've ever met. He used a cast iron pot for literally everything (except cornbread, for that he used a cast iron skillet). If you asked him what margarine was, he'd probably say some kind of pesticide or pharmaceutical drug. He used only real, salted butter; whole milk; and full-fat cream cheese. He made the best root beer floats and always had a huge jar of gingersnaps. He made this special toast called Papa's Toast, which he put slabs of butter on the bread before toasting.

Now in Papa's life, first came grandkids, second came his fig tree. He loved this thing more than imaginable. My cousins would climb to the top and eat all the figs; he attributed the disappearing figs to birds and kept adding more and more inflatable animals to the tree. The blow-up snakes and owls didn't do much good since the little birds were only my cousins and me. Figs, next to chocolate, are probably the best thing in the world. I'm not sure if I was born with the fig-loving in my blood.

I do think it's fitting that the breed of fig that my papa grew and the ones found most in the south are called Celeste Figs. He would make fig preserves and hand them out to everyone. After he died, I remember I was down to my last jar of preserves. I literally licked the jar and cried the whole time. Thankfully, the recipe stayed in the family and my second cousins always stash a couple jars in my purse at "cousin weekends."

Next time you see a delicious fig, think of an old man in suspenders with a big smile carrying a jar of preserves and a cast iron skillet.

Fig Preserve Cake with Chocolate Ganache Icing

This recipe includes my two favorite ingredients, chocolate and figs, and is a delicious treat, perfect with ice cream. For a great breakfast item, add 1½ cups oatmeal and don't glaze with the chocolate ganache.

1 cup fig preserves, chopped, saving ¼ cup preserve liquid
1½ cups white sugar
2 cups all-purpose flour (can substitute whole-wheat or gluten-free flour)
1 tsp. baking soda
1 tsp. sea salt
½ tsp. fresh ground nutmeg
1 tsp. fresh ground cinnamon
½ tsp. ground cloves
1 cup olive oil, extra virgin or vegetable oil (EVOO goes well with figs)
3 eggs (I prefer brown, free-range eggs)
1 cup buttermilk
1½ tbsp. vanilla extract
8 oz. dark chocolate chunks, finely chopped
½ cup walnuts or pecans (optional)
2 tbsp. raw brown turbinado sugar

Chocolate Ganache Topping

1 cup whole whipping cream
8 oz. dark chocolate or semisweet chocolate chips

Preheat oven to 375 degrees.

Butter and flour a fluted tube pan. In the bottom of the fluted pan, pour ¼ cup fig preserve liquid. (Use a ½ tsp. if making mini cakes.)

Combine sugar, flour, baking soda, salt, nutmeg, cinnamon, and cloves in a large mixing bowl. Add the following (beating well after each addition): oil, eggs, buttermilk, and vanilla. Fold in chocolate, fig preserves, and nuts. Pour into fluted pan and bake for 1 hour and 15 minutes (or 25 minutes if using mini Bundt pans). Remove from oven and let cool 10 minutes. Sprinkle top with brown turbinado sugar.

While cooling, make the ganache. Combine cream and chocolate in nonstick skillet and cook over low heat, while stirring until smooth. Keep on low heat.

Invert Bundt pan onto serving dish so that fluted section is on top. Drizzle cake with chocolate ganache.

Makes 1 cake, or 24 to 30 mini cakes

168

Celeste at Mount Saint Michele in France with cousin, Julie Chauvin; Celeste and her sister, Rachel Landry at South Beach Miami; Celeste's beloved dog, Jolie; Cooking at Culinary Institute Alain and Marie LeNotre in Houston; Celeste and fiancé, Andrew Baer and their dogs, Jolie and Duke (Photography by Aaron Hogan); With Andrew in the French Quarter after running a marathon; Celeste and family in the kitchen at Thanksgiving; At the Baton Rouge show, October 2011 with Andrew, her mother, Dot, and cousin, Nita LeBlanc

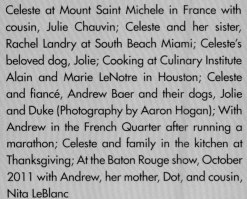

Kimberly Patton-Bragg
Bartender, New Orleans
Best Laid Plans

"If I were a food, I would be shrimp and grits. They are as Southern as can be and can be as sophisicated or low as you wanna make 'em—just like my drinks."

So it was Christmas in New Orleans, the fourth one since moving from New York City with my husband. I was riding my bike home from work to edit my story, but as with all holidays, it was a time of reflection. Great memories of my time as a bartender in New Orleans came flooding back to me as I made stops along the way. My random night seemed like a better idea. Best laid plans.

New Orleans is a city of incredible cocktail history—the Sazerac, New Orleans' official cocktail, is considered by many to be the first cocktail ever and created right on Royal Street by Antoine Peychaud around 1838. Seems silly, but that drink is one of the reasons a bar nerd like me was attracted to this city.

I rode past the stalks of bamboo on Gravier and Carondelet, where the great Henry Ramos created and shook those magical frothy fizzes in the 1880s, which I have found to be the perfect hangover remedy. This reminded me that Glassberg's working one of his last nights at the Roosevelt. The decorations were beyond stunning and the historic Sazerac Bar was there. I could edit my story later—best laid plans.

If you haven't seen the Roosevelt at Christmastime, I can tell you, as someone who has lived in New York for ten years and has ooh'd and aah'd over stuff I'll never be able to afford in the Fifth Avenue windows, the lights in the Roosevelt Hotel are so simple and spectacular it's almost disorienting. This crystalline lobby is where another barkeep friend of

mine, Chris Hannah, from Arnaud's French 75, has the tradition of writing his Christmas postcards. The postcards are a real treat. On the front is a picture of Hannah in a particularly iconic New Orleans spot, such as in front of the old D. H. Holmes with the statue of Ignatius J. Reilly from *The Confederacy of Dunces* serving the cocktail. The recipe (his gift to you) is on the back.

So I've made it to the Roosevelt, gotten my drink from my curmudgeonly partner in crime, Glassberg. I've passed by the French 75 and said hello to the postcard writing Hannah. I've ridden through Jackson Square past the gutter punks, tarot readers, and vampire tours. Then I parked my bike, poured a whiskey, and sat on my balcony thinking about my bartending friends who welcomed me with open arms and open bottles. Chris and Laura McMillian who hold the court for all of us at the Museum of the American Cocktail; Paul at Tujague's, who keeps the bar true to what it was in 1956; Ann and Paul Tuennerman, creators of the Tales of the Cocktail, the largest cocktail convention in the world; and amazing bartender and cocktail historian Neal Bodenheimer, who brought Cure to New Orleans, which has paved the way for more bars and restaurants to take note that what we do is a true craft.

And to all my other liquor-pouring and swilling barkeeping pirates who have made my time in New Orleans so colorful, if a little fuzzy, I was supposed to be an actress in New York City. Best laid plans.

Kimberly Patton-Bragg with Jeanne Vidrine, emcee, at the New Orleans show, July 2010; Chris Hannah's Christmas Postcard; Chris Hannah's Christmas Postcard; Kimberly Patton-Bragg in the New Orleans House of Blues show, July 2010; Saints Fan and Fabulous Bartender

Jim Urdiales
Owner/Chef—Mestizo's Louisiana Mexican Restaurant
Baton Rouge
Journey of a Cajun Mexican

"If I were a food, I would be bread pudding; the only way day old bread tastes so good!"

I was thinking that the only difference between a sopapilla and a beignet is the honey. Both are pieces of pastry dough that are fried and then topped with powdered sugar. The only difference is that a sopapilla has honey. So goes my journey. My sopapilla side comes via my father, Carlos, who was raised in Lake Charles in his father's restaurant. My beignet side comes via my mother, Jean, from Lafayette.

My parents met in Lafayette, and their fateful union brought them to Baton Rouge, where together they opened Carlos Cajun-Mexican Restaurant. The whole family was brought up in the restaurant business early on. One of my earliest memories is of standing on top of an upside down Kleinpeter Farms Dairy milk crate scrubbing pots. I was paid $3 for the night. Talk about cheap Mexican labor.

One day when I was in the third grade, it was raining after school and my mom was coming to pick me up. One of my classmates saw my mother in her grand long Cadillac Sedan de Ville and her big overteased blonde hair and her big blue eyes. My classmate saw her and asked if that was my stepmom since I have jet black hair, olive skin, and dark eyes. I was horrified, so I demanded that my mother dye my hair blonde like hers. My mother, by the way, had been a hair dresser for years, so she agreed to color my hair. Now, I will give you one guess on what color my hair turned. I freaked out when my hair turned bright orange. Mom quickly drove me back to the local K&B store, where she promptly colored me back to black.

Eventually, I moved up to server at their restaurant, and one of my fondest memories is the night that Chef Paul Prudhomme passed through. He was on his way to a book signing at Goudchaux's at Cortana Mall across the street. He came in with his companion and asked my dad to bring him an array of his specialties. Dad brought out his best items, such as Crawfish Chimichangas, Shrimp and Crab Chili Rellenos, and his Crawfish and Spinach Enchiladas. Chef Paul sat there and enjoyed every last bit, and then he proceeded to tell my father every ingredient in his food. I was so impressed that he could taste each spice and ingredient. Thus, my own culinary career began.

I opened my own restaurant, Mestizo Louisiana Mexican Restaurant in 1999 in an old donut shop on Sherwood Forest Boulevard. I stayed there for seven and half years until it was time to move to a larger site. My new location on Acadian Thruway was formerly an old Denny's. I had to spend a lot of money to remodel this location, but next time, I am going to shoot to remodel an old Waffle House, that way I will have made the trifecta of breakfast places.

Anyway, I made my restaurant my own from the name to the menu. Mestizo is a Spanish word that means "of mixed blood" or "two cultures." I took my menu forward and added items such as Grilled Shrimp & Portobello Quesadillas and a Mexican Stir-Fry. Now you may ask yourself what makes a Mexican Stir-Fry. Well, it's a combination of items pan sautéed by a Mexican!

172

I have been blessed that my partner, my brother, and my sister-in-law all work with me in my restaurant. My parents stop by all the time, mainly to critique me. They like to keep me humble. You know it's very interesting that when you grow up in this business, your whole life revolves around it. Every holiday dinner was spent referring to our crazy restaurant stories or experiences from all the years in the business.

My parents just recently reopened their restaurant after a short four-year hiatus. Dad said he was ready to get back to it. When I questioned his sanity, he looked me in the eyes and stated that he would rather die on the floor of his kitchen than on the sofa at the house. There is a certain passion one has for this industry and the personal connection with the customers. Who was I to question my dad? The only thing that scares me is the reality that I might have the same tough decision to retire one day myself. I have one son and two nephews who have started their restaurant careers bussing tables on the weekend. I tell them all the time to find a lucrative career, but I know that if one of them gets the bug, then we will have the fourth generation of restauranteurs.

Oh, the memories I could share! Regardless of what people say, the only difference between a sopapilla and a beignet is the honey, but nothing is sweeter than the love and respect of your family.

Jim's Mestizo's Louisiana Mexican Restaurant, Mestizo sculpture by Joseph Jilbert

Mestizo's Guacamole and Margarita

This recipe for guacamole is a family recipe. It is unique because you add Italian dressing at the end for a great flavor. My margarita recipe is also distinctive in that I use lemon juice instead of lime juice. Lemon juice is less acidic and allows you to taste the great tequila instead of overpowering it. You should never get that tart taste that fresh lime juice sometime has. Try it out and enjoy!

Guacamole

10 Haas avocados, ripe
2 onions, chopped
2 vine-ripened tomatoes, chopped
½ cup Italian dressing
Salt, pepper, garlic, to taste

Blend all ingredients in food processor or mash. Enjoy with tortilla chips and a margarita.

Makes 1 pt.

Margarita

2 cups tequila
1 cup triple sec
1 cup fresh-squeezed lemon juice or lime juice (prefer lemon)
2 cups simple syrup*
½ cup fruit, such as mangos or strawberries (optional)

Shake all ingredients together. Serve on the rocks or blend with ice for frozen margaritas.

*Simple syrup is sugar water. Mix 2 cups water and 2 cups sugar. Heat in saucepan over medium heat. Stir until dissolved.

Makes 4 10-oz. margaritas

Jim and Peggy at the Myrtles Plantation premiere show, May 16, 2010; Baton Rouge Ralph & Kacoo's show, July 2010; Jim as a teen with his mom, Jean; dad, Carlos; and brother, Carlos, Jr.; Jim with Tip Pace and Y'zell Williamson at the Myrtles Plantation during the cocktail party; July 2010 show at Ralph & Kacoo's; Jim and his mom, Jean Urdiales, on stage as she tells her Cajun joke and steals his thunder; Lyceum Show, May 19, 2010 with a margarita in his Café Du Monde cup complete with lime wedge

Dr. Richard Flicker
Industrial/Organizational Psychologist
and Management Consultant, Baton Rouge
How Air Fresheners Saved Me From Going to Hell, Maybe?

"If I were a food, I would be a New York cheesecake because I'd be rich beyond belief, women would want to lick me off their plates, and just the thought of cheesecake evokes feelings of guilt—a Jewish mother's calling card and a psychologist's dream."

I used to live at 415 Lincoln Avenue, which was a thirty-family, four-story apartment house in the City Line/East New York section of Brooklyn. My parents lived in the same rent-controlled apartment for almost their entire fifty-eight and a half years of marriage. We had the largest apartment in the building—a three bedroom, ground-floor apartment in the front. There was no elevator and our door was just a few feet from the staircase and even less to the mailboxes. Everyone had to pass our door to get their mail or to their apartment.

When the new A&P Supermarket opened a few blocks away, my mom began doing most of her grocery shopping there. Everything we needed, they had, except kosher meat. Mom never would buy meat from a regular grocery store; instead, she continued to patronize Diamond's Kosher butcher a few blocks in the other direction. Kosher meat was just better and the slaughter of the animals was done humanely under rabbinical supervision. The A&P didn't sell kosher meat and Diamonds didn't sell ham, pork, or bacon.

For my entire life, I've suffered from a hereditary disease afflicting a large percentage of Jewish people worldwide—PDS. There's no cure for Pork Deprived Syndrome, but it is treatable and usually satisfied in Chinese restaurants.

Torn between Judaic dietary laws and the love of her youngest child, Mom was in a bind whenever my PDS kicked in and I needed a bacon fix. Not wanting to be caught with bacon in the nearby A&P checkout line, Mom would have my dad drive her miles away to a grocery store in another neighborhood. There, Dad would wait in the getaway car with the engine running while Mom (disguised in sunglasses and a kerchief) would commit the crime with the precision of a seasoned bank robber. Before jumping back into our 1958 Oldsmobile 98, she would look around to be sure that there were no witnesses who recognized her.

My dad drove the getaway car, but my mom was the real brains of the operation. Anyone with a nose can tell you that the smell of sizzling bacon is distinctive. Nobody was going to smell bacon coming from apartment 1A, from the only Jewish family in the building! Mom would open our apartment door, peek out, and, if the coast was clear, would empty a can of air freshener with only her arm extended outside the door. She knew exactly how much spray it took to fill the huge hallway all the way up the stairs to the fourth floor and how long it would remain effective.

Mom would head back into the kitchen, turn on the stove, and start frying that bacon before the air freshener began to lose its effectiveness in the hallway. I've always wondered if my mother was fooling just the neighbors, or if she also was fooling God. If God is all-knowing, why wouldn't he know about the bacon? I've never received a satisfactory answer from a rabbi regarding this perplexing theological question. The good news: Nathan's kosher hot dogs are now available in supermarkets like the A&P in my old neighborhood.

Richard Flicker leading a Jewish blessing with a hushpuppy at Baton Rouge show; Bar Mitzvah with his parents; Richard's family apartment building in Brooklyn, NY; Bar Mitzvah; with his parents at his Bar Mitzvah; at the Baton Rouge Show – October, 2010 at Ralph &Kacoo's; Posters of Richard growing up on stage at the shows

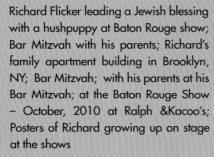

Hannah Blomquist
Actress, Baton Rouge

Tasty Travels!

"If I were a food, I'd be Pop Rocks because they are sweet, a little bit zany, and add a special burst of laughs and energy!"

I have never been one to stay in the same place for long. Before I turned ten years old, we had moved eight times, and anytime I get the chance to travel somewhere, I go! In my twenty-one years of life, through all of my travels, food has always been a link to each place. I make a connection to every stop with some type of local delicacy.

Trips with the Blomquist family were always entertaining! If we were road tripping, my mom would always have the Styrofoam cooler, filled with all sorts of goodies, in between the driver and passenger seats, which would squeak the entire trip. We made many road trips in the old van, but I always liked the times we would fly.

Boarding the plane, I would become excited for two things: the window seat and the food. Strange, I know, since most people relate airplane snacks to cardboard, but for some reason I love them. For my family, the second the stewardess rolled that cart down the aisle, it was an ordeal. As my parents tried to wake us up followed by the frantic decision of what to drink, I would always sit wide-eyed wondering what could be in the little black plastic tray that day. It could be a small turkey sandwich or a strange cheese/cracker concoction. These days all you get is a measly bag of pretzels! I would look forward to the mini-candy-bar package poofed out from the air pressure.

The most vivid memory of a flight meal had to be Christmas Day (also Leah's birthday) of 1999 on a small flight from Florida to Colorado. Midway through the flight, when the "Fasten Seat Belt" light was off, my mom popped out of her seat and headed to the cockpit! Before I knew it, my mom and sister were marching up and down the aisle leading the thirty-person plane in "Happy Birthday," with a cake my mom brought to share with everyone. I died with humiliation, but now it's a joyous memory I will treasure forever.

My most recent adventure was to France and Italy. While there, I tasted fresh-pressed cheese, caramelized onion mousse, fresh chocolate croissants, and Caprese salad! But even with this culinary bliss resting in my tummy, I couldn't help but peek over the seat in front of me to see what the international flight could offer me as a meal for the trip home.

Hopping off the planes has been exciting too! When we hit Denver, we head to Beaux Jo's Pizza, dipping the crust of the pizza pies in sweet honey. In Florida, I still refuse to leave that airport without getting a yummy, gooey Cinnabon. When I go back to Houston, I head straight for delicious, sizzling Tex-Mex fajitas at Los Cucos.

The last four years I've spent in Baton Rouge at LSU have been fantastic. From tailgating and Pi Beta Phi sorority events to running down to New Orleans for Mardi Gras and Jazz Fest, I have really had the chance to experience all the great culture and Louisiana food! Wherever I bop to in the next step of my life, I know that the minute I step back into Louisiana, I will be craving jambalaya, gumbo, fried shrimp po' boys, and as much Slap Ya Mama Creole Seasoning that I can get my hands on!

Baton Rouge show, September 2010; Baton Rouge show, October 2010; Hannah with her dad, Bill Blomquist; Hannah on the beach with her friend Sara Owen; Hannah with her mom, Beverly Blomquist; Hannah in Rome; Hannah with her roommate, Mackenzie Segrest, and Peggy at the Baton Rouge 2010 show; Hannah in Rome making a wish at the Tivoli Fountain

Davis Rogan
Actor, Musician, Writer, New Orleans
Turkey Necks and Foie Gras

"If I were a food, I'd be a crawfish; as I have eaten so many, I really feel a need to replenish the supply so others can enjoy them!"

I think it's fair to say that of any city in the United States New Orleans has the highest percentage of guys who love to cook. I'm not talking about game-day chili; I'm talking full-blown culinary magic I'm actually more comfortable behind the stove than I am behind the piano, as I've been cooking since I was eight and didn't start playing until I was seventeen.

I went to college out of town, and like any homesick New Orleanian, I mastered signature dishes, such as red beans and gumbo. Proselytizing about the food was as important to me as telling non-New Orleanians about the Meters or Professor Longhair. As soon as I graduated, I moved straight home. I began playing piano with my friend Kermit Ruffins, who was starting a group outside of the Rebirth Brass Band. We had played a jam session on Monday nights at a postage-stamp-sized club called Little People's Place in Treme.

It was here that I tasted Ms. Pat's red beans. I was completely blown away. They were so creamy and unrepentantly porky. Little People's Place was shuttered around 1993 and didn't reopen until right after Katrina. Ms. Pat was living in Baton Rouge and her brother-in-law, Rodney, ran the bar. Through the New Orleans Musicians' Clinic performance fund, I was able to bring in my band and reintroduce the Monday-night jam session. Rodney made the most amazing turkey necks. Boiled in a big pot full of spices, they are fall-off-the-bone tender. Money was tight, and I remember taking home a few pounds of turkey necks and stretching them across the whole week.

One of the things that makes New Orleans such a great culinary city is the combination of high and low cuisines. From the free red beans at Little People's to the fried oysters with brie at Clancy's, and every po'boy joint we've got it covered.

I taught music in the public elementary schools. One year, I decided I'd been hit upside my head with my last crayon and I would switch to cooking professionally to support my music habit. I spent six months on the line at NOLA, working my way from salads to hot appetizers before I decided that I do love to cook—at home. Line cooks work harder than schoolteachers and make less money than musicians.

In 2006, my luck took a turn for the better. David Simon, a writer and producer from HBO, bought my record *The Once and Future DJ*. He liked my work so much that he based one of the main characters in his series *Treme* on me. This has led to my getting work as a consultant, scriptwriter, songwriter, and actor on the show.

When David first asked me to consult, there was no guarantee that the show would be picked up. I decided the best way to ensure some remuneration was to do all the consulting at the finest restaurants—Bayona, Herbsaint, Cochon, Brightsen's, and Gautreau's.

I'm not rich yet. I'm very much still hustling, but I keep the lights on. And it's nice to have the means to head out to the farmers' market in Westwego and to the great new restaurants in town.

Saints Fan; Davis Rogan's album cover, *The Real Davis* (Photograph by Zack Smith); Davis Rogan with Jeanne Vidrine and Jeremy Davenport at the New Orleans premier show at House of Blues, June 22, 2010; Davis Rogan with his "piano" (Photograph by Zack Smith); Davis Rogan teaching his friend, Ida, how to play the piano; In the band; Davis after the New Orleans show; Davis performing his monologue at the New Orleans premiere show at the House of Blues, June 2010; Davis with his "piano" (Photograph by Zack Smith)

Tip Pace
Owner, Feliciana Seafood and Deli and Carriage House Restaurant at the Myrtles Plantation, St. Francisville
Where Do You Want To Eat?

"If I were a food, I would be steak and shrimp because the steak is strong, hot, and sizzling, and shrimp are God's sweetest candy of the sea."

Being in the food-service arena, part of the job, at least we make it part of the job, is to try different foods at different venues, so we can learn about what the competition is doing and learn more tricks of the trade. I've been married to the best mother, companion, and lover for twenty-seven years, but most of all she's the best business partner a man could have. My wife loves me and/or tolerates me (depends on the week); thus, I get to make all the decisions around my place. Well, that only works out because my wife agrees to it, that is, as long as she reserves the veto power just like the president! And tough as it may be, veto power is used quite often on my decisions.

The veto power thing seems to pop up more and more as we age. Maybe it's my waning memory or my percentages of right and wrong when it comes to directions or routes to take. When I'm wrong, my wife is very thoughtful, always points out my mistake, and usually informs me of what the correct decision should have been. And, if I'm really wrong, she'll even point out why! It's usually with comments such as "How far are you gonna drive before you admit you're lost and stop to ask someone? It's that male ego again!"

Well, after a long day of filing, cleaning, bill paying, and prepping for the next day's service, we eventually get to the part of the day when it's time for my favorite sport—"dinner," as food is one of my passions. When its mealtime, I'll ask, "Where do you want to go eat?"

She'll say, "Oh, it doesn't matter." Well, I'm slow, but not stupid, and *I know it matters*. Now it's time to decide *what I want to eat*, so then I can decide how to ask or answer the question in a manner that ensures the end result that I desire. You see, I know her veto is out there, and it always comes into play at dinnertime.

Now, I know this is a bit confusing, but just like the cunning politician, I know there are ways to get what one wants. If I say steak, she'll say, "Don't you ever get tired of eating the same thing over and over?" If I really want a steak, I have to suggest two or three places that I know serve a good steak, but I can't say, "Let's eat steak." I'll name the three restaurants, and she narrows the focus by killing off a choice or two—"That place is too loud" or "I don't want to go that far." However, I'd be happy with any of the three, so if she doesn't kill off all three, then I've won, and off we go to a good steak place. If she does have one of those many valid reasons, then I fall back to plan "B," which is, "Okay, then what kind of food do you want to eat?"

It is so nice living in Louisiana because it really doesn't matter what the food choice or country of origin, because in south Louisiana, you can usually have several choices of restaurants if you can reach the basic category agreement like seafood, Chinese, Greek, or whatever.

Many years ago, when my wife and I lived Uptown in New Orleans, we met some boys from Zwolle, Holland;

this must have been around the late seventies. Now, these two boys were brothers, Bert and Albert Peters. They decided to take a trip around the world on their bicycles, and we met them on the streets of New Orleans. They had planned to just stay the night, but we convinced them to stay through the weekend, as it was New Year's, the Sugar Bowl was in town (they played it on New Year's Day back then), and the French Quarter was hopping. As you can imagine, these were strapping young Dutchmen, and they ate a lot. They loved the seafood, the ribs, the Port-a-Call burgers—you name it, there wasn't much they did not eat and we took them to all the local dives and music clubs. Their English was broken, except at mealtime, as they knew food and how to enjoy lots of it. What a wonderful cultural exchange, describing the food from the menu, comparing it to something they knew or had eaten, tasting it, and comparing the previous comparisions to see if what hit their mouth was what was in their mind. The language barrier was always lost when food was put on the table. The smiles told it all. They especially liked walking in the French Quarter with a beer in hand and a Lucky Dog stand on every corner.

So it was New Year's Eve, and this was an Arkansas and Alabama Sugar Bowl, so the Quarter was a sea of red. The Tide fans kept offering to BBQ the Hogs, and eventually the Danes asked us what this meant. So we explained it. They asked about the Roll Tide too, but being an LSU Tiger fan, I explained I had never figured that one out either! We partied until the wee hours of the morning and then, at about 3:00, decided to hit the Hummingbird Café on the way back Uptown. We piled everybody into two cars and headed up St. Charles Avenue for a drunken breakfast. Upon arrival, we discovered we had lost Albert back down by Jackson Square. So I jumped in the car and headed back to the Quarter hoping to find the wasted Dutchman and save him from wandering the streets all night. As I turned by the old Chart House (now Muriel's), where Albert was last remembered as being with us, there was no Albert! I'd hoped he'd stayed near the area, so I whipped around the block to Decatur, and as I reached the crosswalk at Jackson Square, there he was. He was covered in white, his beard white as snow, his blue jeans and shirt a mess, as he was covered in powdered sugar. When he saw me, the international language of happiness and relief, with a smile ear to ear, was quite evident because he had discovered Café Du Monde. Happy from the beignets or from being found, I'm not sure, but I was relieved. Since that day, it has always been a moment of meanwhile, back at Café Du Monde.

Tip Pace making welcoming everyone to the Myrtles Plantation at the show

Tip with his wife, Beth

Carriage House Romano Cheese Grilled Oysters

The Carriage House Restaurant at the Myrtles Plantation is pleased to share with you our version of grilled oysters "plantation style." Now these are best cooked in a commercial kitchen or outdoors on a hot grill because they tend to be a bit messy and flare up quite a bit! Be careful when you grill them. Like most south Louisiana residents, we've tried grilled oysters at numerous locations and decided we could tweak them to a recipe to suit our "country" taste buds. We worked as a team and as competitors to come up with a recipe we could all agree surpassed the ones we'd eaten elsewhere. After numerous blends of sumptuous herbs and spices, we settled into agreement on Chef Chris Caten's recipe as the best, and here's what he's come up with!

2 tbsp. freshly chopped garlic
2 tbsp. vegetable oil
3 tbsp. white wine
2 tbsp. Hot Sauce
2 tbsp. Worcestershire
1 lb. unsalted butter
2 doz. fresh Louisiana oysters
Salt and freshly ground black pepper, to taste
1 lb. grated Pecorino Romano cheese
Layer rock salt for "plating"
¼ cup freshly chopped parsley
Fresh sliced lemon, to taste and to garnish

In a small saucepan, roast garlic with vegetable oil on medium-low heat, making sure not to burn the garlic. Add wine, hot sauce, and Worcestershire sauce; reduce by half.

With the heat on medium-low, add butter and melt. As soon as the butter has just melted, transfer out of pot and leave at room temperature until oysters are shucked.

Spread 1 tbsp. butter mixture evenly over each oyster, add salt and pepper as preferred, and place in cooler until butter "sets." Just before grilling oysters, add 1 tbsp. Romano cheese per oyster.

When the grill reaches its highest temperature, grill oysters. Cook until they bubble and oysters "curl," approximately 2½ to 3 minutes. Place oysters on heat-safe platter layered with rock salt. Garnish with parsley and lemon and serve immediately. *C'est bon!*

Serves 4 to 6 as appetizers.

Buffet on the patio at the premiere show, catered by the Carriage House Restaurant

184

"Duck!"; Tip making turtle sauce piquant; Tip and Beth Pace, proprietors of the Carriage House Restaurant at the Myrtles Plantation; Hunting with sons, Kaine and Kody; Tip with wife Beth, Ruffin Rodrigue, Todd Graves, Peggy, and Cane at the Myrtles premiere show; With good friends at the Myrtles: Beth, Chef Joey, Tip, MJ, and Kody; Tip in the premiere show at the Myrtles Plantation, May 16, 2010

Tammi Arender
Anchor, NBC 33, Baton Rouge
A Taste of Tallulah

"If I were a food, I would be an apple pie because no one can resist the all-American dessert! It's sweet and patriotic; people love it plain or dressed up with ice cream. It even has some nutritional value. The apples may be covered in butter and sugar, but they're still apples!"

Being raised on a farm in a tiny town called Tallulah, Louisiana—known more for its cotton than its cuisine—I learned to like different types of foods. And by different, I mean anything that ran across the field or crawled under the house. Daddy caught it, skinned it, and put it in a skillet. Because of this "anything goes" type of meal preparation, I acquired a closeness to condiments. If I had enough ketchup and mayonnaise, I could eat anything.

After a childhood filled with venison, squirrel, rabbit, and any other type of wild game, I decided I'd never leave home without my condiments. And that proved to be a good decision. After entering the TV news business, I discovered I'd be attending many a luncheon or banquet that served rubber chicken or shoe-leather-style steak. So I carry exactly what every other woman carries with her, a makeup bag. But my little pouch doesn't hold lipstick, it holds my lip-licking servings of special sauces.

Only once did I have a date get up and leave a five-star restaurant when I opened up my pouch of ketchup and slathered it on my filet mignon. I would have understood my date's embarrassment had I asked the waiter for ketchup. Instead, I quietly dug in my ditty bag and discreetly put my simple red sauce on my steak. I don't think he understood my condiment craving bordered on addiction. That was our last date. I knew then I would never marry a man who didn't share my love of lycopene (the antioxidant found in ketchup)!

You might think being dumped over a high-dollar piece of meat in a hooty-snooty restaurant would cause me to be heartbroken and lose my appetite. But *au contraire*, my daddy not only taught me to love "different" types of food, but he also left me with a passion for pleasing my palate. Being heartbroken was no reason to skip a meal. Heck, unless I have the stomach flu, I just love good food. I'll go to great lengths to get my food fix too.

I remember before I earned my driver's license, I would ride my horse about two or three miles to the little country store south of Tallulah, called Fortune Fork, and buy a bologna sandwich, bag of Cheetos, and a bottled Coke. It didn't matter if it was raining or blue blazes hot; when I got a burr under my saddle for a hand-cut bologna sandwich (with mayo, not mustard!), I trotted off on old Trigger to get it.

Trigger is long gone, and I've transitioned from four-legged horses to iron horses. I started riding Harleys several years ago. So these days what I do for fun is jump on the Harley in search of what else? Good food!

After relocating from north Louisiana to Cajun country and being exposed to some of the most scrumptious cuisine in the world, I've found I don't have to poke around in my purse for my mayonnaise and ketchup packets nearly as often. But do not doubt for a second, that if I'm ever served a dry-as-Sahara sirloin, a parched piece of poultry, or a bag of French fries whose drive-through order-taker forgot to throw in ketchup, I'm prepared!

Tammi with Tim McGraw at a fundraiser for Rayville Youth Baseball, Rayville, Louisiana; Tammi's first cycle; Jay Basist, Tammi, and Peggy at the Baton Rouge show; Tammi and Kenny Chesney at the Bayou Superfest; Tammi's childhood home in Tallulah, Louisiana; Tammi with Trigger and Dad; Tammi on her Harley (Photograph by Lane Photography); Fortune Fork, Tallulah, Louisiana; Tammi's condiment pouch (celebrity photos by Curtis Hilbun)

Dian Bulen Lusher
CEO, Dynel, Inc., New Orleans
I Love Me Some Okra!

"If I were a food, I would be a shrimp, so I could swim around freely and then wind up in a delicious dish like shrimp and okra."

Okra is a tall plant, and when it begins to grow, it produces a beautiful flower. It is related to a few plants, but the hibiscus family comes to mind because of its similar flowers. According to most histories, it came from Africa. I like the story that reads about how the African people stuck it in their hair to carry over their family food. I imagine they had many stories that revolved around their food. Familiar food reminds you of family and your heritage.

Family is important all over the world. New Orleans is no different and food creates an even stronger bond here. We revolve most of our family events around food. And we had a typical large New Orleans family. There were seven of us kids, plus an extended family including our grandparents. We so loved being with our grandparents. We loved their small house. We loved that they loved us when we came screaming in the door. We loved how they told us we were the best, the smartest, and the cutest. We loved their garden, well, most of us did.

My grandfather, PaPere, grew a little garden patch in his backyard in Gentilly. He was a local barber in that area. The old folks seemed to grow everything then—tomatoes, strawberries, shallots, and okra. I am the oldest of the seven children. Usually this was a good thing because I could give the orders and could choose what I wanted to do. But being the oldest wasn't always a good thing.

Every Sunday, we joined MaMere (grandmother) and PaPere for Sunday dinner. When we were all young,

we always ate at their house. As we got older, we ate at Morrison's Cafeteria a lot. PaPere said it was because he liked the apple pie there. I believed that until I had three children of my own—two of them boys.

On the Sundays when we did eat at PaPere's, we would help him pick whatever was growing in his garden. We fought over who was going to pick the strawberries. Strawberries were the most fun; you could eat half of them. We liked to pick the tomatoes too. PaPere stopped letting the boys pick the tomatoes, as he could only use them as stewed tomatoes after the boys finished throwing them around.

I always wanted to pick the strawberries, but I would hear, "Dian, get the paring knife so you can cut the okra. You know you can't just pull them off." Why do I always have to pick the okra? Then MaMere would say, "Honey, you're the oldest and the tallest, and we want it done just right. I love me some okra." As I told you earlier, being the oldest was not always a good thing.

Okra! Goodness, even the thought of it still makes me itch and itch. And you know you can't sample it as you go. Of course, much to my horror, PaPere would get one of his old barber gowns to drape across to catch a summer breeze and maybe cut down on the itching. I was sure glad he lived across town and in a neighborhood where no one really knew me. Thank goodness PaPere only grew a small garden.

I never really knew what PaPere did with all that okra. Sometimes we saw it in gumbo, and we would all sneak it out and hide it in a napkin to dispose of later. I would often hear my grandparents say, "This gumbo sure is good, even better with the okra Dian picked for us. We sure love us some okra. We all love our oldest grandchild for helping us." I always thanked God for napkins when we said the dinner blessing.

My mamere and papere are long gone now and their Sunday dinners are a fading memory. I worried that I would never remember all of their stories to tell. Little did I know how my memories would come back to me.

Time changes what you think is important. As a young adult, I didn't cook much. There was too much to do and too much fun to be had in my city of New Orleans. But of course, those are stories for another time.

Once I married, I cooked the foods I knew how to cook, such as seafood, beans, chicken, and more beans. I had never really learned how to cook gumbo, but my husband knew how to put it together. He too is a New Orleans native, and strangely, his papere was a barber in another part of the city. His papere also had a garden. I guess some things are meant to be.

And so the gumbo unique to our house was created. Y'all know everyone has their own unique gumbo, which is another story indeed! I remember the first one we cooked together, and as we were adding the last of the chicken, out from the freezer came a bag of okra. Wow! And boy, I was so glad not to have to pick the okra. My husband told his stories of his papere's garden and the fun he and his threes siblings had there. My husband so loved his papere; he was the best man in our wedding. We declared our gumbo to be the best and often used frozen okra along with the fresh ones from the farmers' market. We loved us some okra!

And that has always been the way we got our okra until this past summer. We now live across the lake from New Orleans. We are up north in a rural area with several acres of land. In the late spring, I noticed my husband way in the back clearing a very large patch. It seemed to have the appearance of a garden, but we had never really planted one. But sure 'nuf, he walked in one day and announced, "I'm going to grow a garden. My papere always did. I just want to see what happens. I only planted a few seed packets, you know, the regular garden stuff."

Every morning before work, he went in the back and weeded and watched. He would comment, "Some corn coming up, plenty squash, and wait until you see the okra. I may have gotten a bit carried away with the okra. We probably didn't need such a long row. But you'll see; we'll use it in many ways."

Okra! What? I don't remember seeing those seed packets. When did the okra sneak in the garden? And when did so much of it sneak in there?

The hot New Orleans summer arrived. We did get a little corn and enough zucchini to make the neighbors run when they saw us waving. We also had some tomatoes, shallots, and an herb here and there. But the okra was unbelievable—tall and plentiful with beautiful flowers. We both laughed over how we could pick it all, and then the next day, there it was again. And when it rained, we would groan, "Here comes the okra." The neighbors still avoid us.

In the late afternoon, we would go out to the garden and pick it. We would always return itchy and sweaty from the okra. Then we would cut it and freeze it for gumbos. We would tell each other stories about our grandparents—some stories we had shared already and others were new to hear. We would chant as we paraded back from the garden, "We love us some okra!" I know it helped us get through the itchy part.

Our children thought we had lost our minds, and we would ask them to join us. I really think they feared losing their cell phone receptions in our woody patches. But they certainly did enjoy the gumbos we all prepared. And being raised on okra, they never once hid their okra in a napkin. When we were all together, we shared our grandparents' stories with them—some we had told them already, others were new to hear.

My husband became possessed by his papere and obsessed with the okra. He was determined not to let one pod go to waste. We had okra every way known to prepare it and more—stewed, in gumbo, with rice and meat and shrimp. I could hardly believe it when one Sunday on TV, *Iron Chef America* had okra as the secret ingredient. My husband learned how to fry and grill it. Some of his attempts were good, and he says he loved them all. He's always trying a new way to eat okra. I'm not so sure about some of them, so I keep my napkin close at hand.

As you can see from the pictures, we have the family trained to embrace okra, and once, the grandchildren danced around, making up a tune, "I love me some okra . . . okra! Okra! Okra!" Our paperes would have been proud. My husband turned and glanced at me with a look that I interpreted as "see I told you it had many uses."

After all of the okra meals and ideas, I have decided there is only one way I really like okra. I learned all about it in my young-adult days. And as I said before, those days are for another story. Yes indeed! Picked okra with Sunday Bloody Marys is definitely the way to go! So a toast to you and my beloved grandparents as I say, "I love me some okra!"

Photograph by Diana Zollicoffer

Dian's Love Me Some Okra and Shrimp Casserole

MaMere loved okra and shrimp. It was an easy dish to prepare, and we always had okra! We kids loved it because when we tired of eating the okra; we could pick out the shrimp and enjoy the dish!

2 large onions, chopped
4 cloves garlic, minced
2 tbsp. olive oil
1 lb. chopped okra
2 14.5-oz. cans stewed tomatoes (spicy preferred)
2 lb. shrimp, peeled

Dian Lusher with her family and their okra

In large pan, sauté chopped onions and garlic in olive oil. Chop okra into bite-sized pieces and add to pan. Add 1 can of stewed tomatoes with juice. Cook until okra is tender. Add second can of stewed tomatoes. Cook another 10 minutes. Add shrimp last and cook with lid on for 10 minutes. Entire dish takes 30-35 minutes.

Serve as side dish or over rice with green salad and hot French bread.

Serves 10 to 12 as side dish, or 6 to 8 as main dish.

Dian in her okra garden

190

Dian with friends Ellen LaRocca, Ann Marie Pinkney, and Jax Frey at the October 2010, New Orleans show; Dian with emcee, Jeanne Vidrine, at the October 2011 show at the Southern Food and Beverage Museum; St Tammany 2011 Professional Woman of the Year; Dian's PaPere's barbershop; Dian Lusher in the New Orleans show; October 2011, at the Southern Food and Beverage Museum

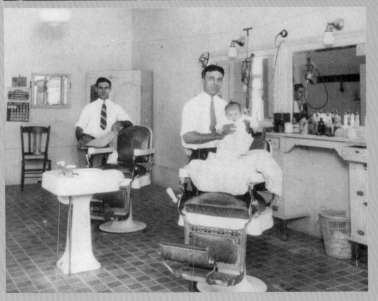

Dr. Corey Hebert
CEO, Social Health TV; Medical Director, Louisiana Recovery School District; and Chief Medical Editor, WDSU, New Orleans
Creamed Potatoes

"If I were a food, I would be an ackee, which is the national fruit of Jamaica, because if I'm perfectly ripe and picked at just the right time, then I am a delicacy and unrivaled in my intensity and flavor, but if you pick me at the wrong time or don't eat me just right, I might kill ya!"

Food has always played an integral part in my life and the lives of my family. From traditional family gatherings like Thanksgiving to the more traditional New Orleans crawfish boil, my life has revolved around a great meal.

My family has an interesting way of preparing foods. Decadent most closely describes this preparation style. My first memory of this decadence was a poignant one that set me on a course of never being satisfied with mediocre tastes! I was a mere child of four when I started formal schooling. As the first day progressed, I was happy about the fun lessons and the smiling kids, so it was obvious to me that lunch at this institution would also be great. As I stood in the cafeteria line awaiting my reward for legibly writing my numbers, what appeared on my plate surprised and saddened me. The cafeteria staff told me that the white lumps on the plate were creamed potatoes. I tried feverishly to reconcile in my mind what I knew creamed potatoes to be. In my house, they were luxurious mounds of warm, fluffy, yellow, creamy goodness speckled with orange and black flakes of the freshest Creole seasonings. What I saw on my plate was the anti-creamed potato—white, gritty, bland, and hard. I voiced my concern, "Ma'am these aren't creamed potatoes. Creamed potatoes are yellow." She grinned and said with the utmost nurturing tone, "Baby at yo' house dey yellow, at this school dey white." This was the beginning of my journey to indulge in only the best epicurean delights. My happy, satisfying journey continues.

After a few years passed, my father decided to use our family's love of decadent cuisine in a commercial venture. He opened the Gill Net Seafood Restaurant. I vividly remember when he told my sister and me that the restaurant would specialize in the succulent jewels of the Gulf of Mexico. The *spécialité de la maison* included fried oysters, shrimp, catfish, the famous po' boy, andouille gumbo, and crawfish etouffee. I was so excited. I imagined being ensconced in fried crab claws and oysters on the half-shell. I could see myself drenched 'til my heart's desire in shrimp Creole and swimming in a magnificent pool of turtle soup. When I got tired of swimming, I could float on a slice of hot buttered French bread. But alas, these dreams were not to be. I never really understood that seafood is not just food, but also an industry. So as my fingers were repeatedly frozen to the bone from peeling pounds of shrimp and cracking crabs soaking in icy cold water every Saturday, I realized that Creole food has been part of my life, my family culture, and tapestry. I was truly thankful that I was able to participate in the continuum of providing this cuisine to people around the country.

As a man that can still consume his weight in shellfish, I was horrified by the BP Oil disaster and how it impacted the citizens of this region and the seafood industry. I have continued to be the strongest advocate for promoting the lore of Gulf seafood and all stories, history, and people that accompany it, but most of all, I enjoy creamed potatoes. The yellow variety.

192

Dr. Corey Hebert with his famous bowtie; In the studio at WDSU; In the House of Blues New Orleans show, July 2010; Childhood picture; Filming a segment; With the boys club; In the hospital; With Dr. Sanjay Gupta; With Dr. Mehmet Oz taping *The Pulse* segment on the *Dr. Oz Show*; With his son, Corey Hebert, Jr.

Jim Engster
Owner and President, Louisiana Radio Network, and Host, The Jim Engster Show, Baton Rouge
Life at Louie's

"If I were a food, I would be coffee because it's strong, works fast, and keeps you alert."

Louie's Café has been perched in the shadow of the Campanile just yards from the gates of Louisiana State University since 1941. It was originally located on Chimes Street, but since 1986, it has been the anchor of West State Street. The restaurant has had its grill in operation through thirteen presidential administrations.

When I enrolled at LSU in the fall of 1977, I remember the first time I dined at Louie's. It was a small place with a few seats and a cat was patrolling the counter. I realized this was not a typical eatery, but every omelet and burger was seasoned with an abundance of charm. The feline mascot was no threat to loyal customers, who never squealed to the health department.

When Louie's moved a block away, I began eating there on a regular basis as a young journalist. Louie's is open twenty-four hours a day. Hurricanes come and go, as do governors and LSU football coaches, but Louie's is always there. It is a constant in my life, and breakfast at my favorite table centers me for the rest of the day.

Louie's is a fascinating place and a microcosm of our city. Baton Rouge is a college town and people from all over the world reside here. Louie's represents that gumbo of nationalities and the ethnic melting pot that is our city.

Through the decades, people from all walks of life have been seated at the counter where head chef Marcus "Frenchie" Cox presides. Frenchie entertains his subjects with constant banter about the news of the day. Frenchie's business card reads "Warrior, Statesman, Fry Cook." Athletic luminaries such as Shaquille O'Neal, Bert Jones, and Bill Walton have swapped stories with the loquacious cook in anticipation of a breakfast prepared by the maestro of State Street.

It is not unusual for titans of society, including politicians of renown, to receive sustenance from Louie's as they dart off to the next stop on the campaign trail. When the establishment first opened, a young graduate student in political science named Hubert Horatio Humphrey dined at Louie's on occasion and infamously bounced a check.

Louie, the original owner, once displayed an array of bounced checks on a bulletin board on Chimes Street. For a generation, the check of Hubert Humphrey was visible for the world to see—even after the fabled LSU graduate became vice president of the United States. Perhaps this explains why Humphrey lost Louisiana in his 1968 quest for the White House.

I generally begin my day with egg whites prepared by Frenchie, and on special days, they are accompanied by the world famous Louie's biscuit. The legendary baseball announcer Harry Caray would often moan when a slugger reached the warning track with a fly ball, saying another biscuit for breakfast would have enabled the batter to hit a home run. I never make that mistake when I need a morning pick me up. I can feel my biceps expand with each bite from a Louie's biscuit.

Breakfast at Louie's; Jim in the Baton Rouge October 2010 show at Ralph and Kacoo's; Jim with Louie's waitress, Crystal Wheat; Frenchie making Jim's breakfast; Louie's Café, Baton Rouge, Louisiana; Jim Engster with Frenchie outside of Louie's Diner; Breakfast at Louie's; The *Jim Engster Radio Show*, interviewing actress Lynn Whitfield

Chef Tenney Flynn
Executive Chef and Co-Owner, GW Fins, New Orleans
Reopening a Restaurant in Katrina Zone—BBQ at Zydeque

"If I were a food, I would be a blue crab because they are hard on the outside and sweet and succulent on the inside."

I don't usually evacuate for hurricanes. I had a girlfriend from Atlanta visiting, and I felt some responsibility to get her home. I do remember a newscast remote from the roof of a house where the announcer said, "Okay, the wind and rain have stopped, and here is what you have to expect: flood waters up to the roof, filled with ants, rats, snakes, roaches, dogs, and cats all competing for space. No water, no electricity, no food, and no one coming to help you." Special emphasis was on the things that were forecasted to be swirling around in the filthy floodwater, including toxic chemicals and disinterred caskets. I think this sort of prompted me to move some belongings upstairs before I left. I packed a couple of changes of clothes and went to the restaurants.

We had stocked up for the upcoming Southern Decadence weekend at Zydeque and loaded up on briskets and pork butts—about fifteen hundred pounds of fresh meat. I remember considering grabbing a few steaks at Fins, but since we'd be back in a couple of days, I thought not to bother. We headed out of town across the Causeway and looked for back roads through Mississippi and Alabama; between the traffic and the route, it took us about ten hours to get to Georgia. The next day, we heard the "we dodged the bullet again" news about the severity of the wind and rain.

Everyone knows what happened next. My new house in Lakeview, which I'd been in for six weeks, was about a half-mile from where the levee broke. The neighborhood was soon under about twelve feet of water. We watched what little news there was. The 504 area code was not working, and my son and his mom were in St. Tammany Parish. So I headed back a few days later with a generator and a chainsaw and lots of gas and water cans.

This is the point where the story begins: when we started trying to get back in the city. Anyone who's ever flown into New Orleans and looked out the window knows about the amount of water there is here. Between the lake and the river and all the drainage canals, the land is a series of islands on dry days and now there were only a couple of above-water roads into town. These were patrolled by the New Orleans Police Department and the National Guard, and after waiting in long lines, we were often turned back. We wanted to see what had happened to our restaurants. Usually the Guard was easier to get past.

Everyone who lived here remembers all the refrigerators dragged out to the street, filled with rotted food and impossible to clean. Our walk-in coolers were that to the tenth power. We had gas at Fins, but at Zydeque, a block away, there was only electricity and no potable water. We had no employees, just Gary Wollerman and myself, and we filled our noses with Vick's VapoRub and started cleaning out the spoiled food. We also had no business interruption insurance, so I'm sure that was some motivation for us to get to work.

We needed work. I couldn't even visit my house in Lakeview; the whole neighborhood was cordoned off, and Gary was commuting from Baton Rouge, where he had moved his family. I was living in a trailer in Folsom and driving one hundred miles a day as well.

We switched the smoker from natural gas to propane and made plans to open with disposable plates and flatware. Sysco was able to supply us with almost all of our raw materials. We did get two health inspections, one from the CDC and another from the FDA. Apparently, they had been instructed to get some restaurants open, and we were one of the first five in the Quarter to do so. We gathered some staff from Fins, and we all did all the jobs. Besides law enforcement and the Guard, every insurance adjustor in the world was here as well as FEMA, and all the open hotels were filled. The streets were surreal—a cross between martial law and a gold rush—a few bars and strip joints were doing a land office business. You didn't have to get far away from the Quarter to be in the land of no electricity—no traffic lights or streetlights or populated homes or open businesses. At night, it got dark.

If you've never eaten an MRE (Meal, Ready-to-Eat, armed services field rations), you're not missing a lot. After living on them for a few days, you lust for real food. Besides needing to work, we were responding to a real need in the community. Our pork BBQ sandwiches with warm cane vinegar sauce and spicy slaw, topped with pickled onions and jalapeños; slabs of ribs; split chickens; andouille sausage; dark gumbo with potato salad; brisket; skillet cornbread; and freshly baked mini pecan pies were like manna to customers who needed to eat real food. Julia Reed, a local writer of some repute, had been in Fins but didn't know we had a BBQ place. She brought in her husband and some big wines and it was an oasis of comfort for them. She wrote about it in *Vogue* and later in her book about post-Katrina Uptown, *The House on First Street*. I had never picked up an issue of *Vogue* before.

It's really hard to describe what the town was like to someone who wasn't here. The importance of breaking bread together in a public place can't be overemphasized. Food is more important here than most places, perhaps, but we all needed some place we could come together and relax and refuel and escape from the chaos that surrounded us. I firmly believe that those of us who provided that did a lot for the recovery of the city, and I'm proud that Gary and I were a part of that.

I now live on the third floor of a building in the lower Quarter, and I'm never evacuating again.

GW Fins' Sautéed Pompano with Melon and Mango Salad

This is a great summer melon salad. The exotic melons are usually available from the end of July through August but the recipe can be made with just cantaloupe, honeydew, and ripe mango. You may want to buy the mangoes a few days ahead and ripen at home.

If pompano is unavailable, lemonfish or redfish would be great substitutions; just bear in mind they need to be durable enough for the grill.

½ cantaloupe, julienned
½ honeydew, julienned
1 mango, julienned
2 tbsp. honey
½ cup seasoned rice vinegar
2 tbsp. chopped cilantro
1 tbsp. chopped mint
¼ tsp. chili paste
1 cup large-diced seedless watermelon
1 cup large-diced honeydew
1 cup large-diced cantaloupe
1 cup large-diced casaba melon
½ tsp. salt
1 tsp. sugar
Juice of 1 lime
2 tbsp. chopped cilantro
6 8-10 oz. pompano fillets, scaled and scored, pin bones removed
Salt and pepper
Flour
2 tbsp. canola oil
2 tbsp. butter
6 banana leaves (for presentation)

Julienne half of the cantaloupe, honeydew, and mango. Mix together the honey, rice vinegar, 2 tbsp. chopped cilantro, mint, and chili paste. Toss with the julienned melon and mango. Set aside.

In a separate bowl, mix together the diced melons and gently toss with the salt, sugar, lime juice and remaining cilantro. Set aside.

Season the pompano fillets with salt and pepper and dust with flour. Divide the 6 fillets, skin side down, in 2 large preheated sauté pans with 1 tbsp. canola oil and 1 tbsp. butter. Cook over medium to high heat for about 3 to 4 minutes. (Cook longer on the skin side so it's nice and crispy.) Turn and continue cooking for an additional 2 to 3 minutes.

Line 6 large, heated plates with a section of banana leaf cut to fit. Place about ½ cup of the diced melon mixture slightly off center and shingle the julienned melon/mango on the side. Plate the pompano so that some of each melon is showing. Serve immediately.

Serves 6.

Photograph by Sara Essex

198

Chef Tenney Flynn in his restaurant GW Fins; Chef Tenny in the kitchen; Preparing fish (Photograph by Sara Essex); Cooking demo at Jazz Fest; Chef Tenney greeting guests; Chef Tenney serving oysters; Chef Tenney with blue crab (All photographs by Sara Essex)

Victoria Greene
Actress, Host, Baton Rouge

My Intimate On-Going Relationship with Food

"If I were a food, I'd be a Strawberry Napoleon: lovely to look at, challenging and difficult to eat, but in the end well worth the effort."

Everyone loses a job at one point in her life. It's not cancer. It's just a job, right? Although I knew that intellectually, when I lost my job, I was emotionally devastated. I lost my career, my financial security, my confidence, my self-respect, and my direction. I simply lost my way.

After a few months of unemployment, I read an article about the privately owned company that I had worked with for twenty-five years titled "No Layoffs Ever." I was fuming. Immediately I rushed to the grocery store, bought candied-covered almonds, Kleinpeter's Ice Cream, and a bag of Zapp's Potato Chips. After stuffing my face for a few hours, I was suddenly better. From that moment on, I no longer felt desolate, desperate, or sad. True, I was unemployed, but I never lost my love of food, my appetite, or the ability to make reservations. What a relief! I realized that regardless of what might go wrong in my life, food remained the only constant, besides, of course, the love of my dogs, family, and friends. Simply put, I have an intimate relationship with food. Every special moment in my life is intertwined with food.

I grew up in Los Angeles, and my very first night in New Orleans my dad took me to the French Quarter. First it was Felix's for raw oysters, followed by coffee and beignets, only to be topped off with a black Russian at our hotel. Imagine going out for a drink with your father at only fifteen. In New Orleans during the seventies, that was the norm.

Two weeks before Hurricane Katrina, I got a call from the basketball coach at Parkview Baptist High School. He asked me, "Do you know of anyone interested in taking in an exchange student from Australia for the year?" After taking a moment, I blurted out, "What about me? I am Jewish." He said, "That's okay, the kid isn't Baptist." I was sold!

Heath Weischman and I met a few days later, and when he shook my hand, I knew I was going to be a "host family" for the school year. Heath moved two days before Hurricane Katrina, and because schools were closed for a week, we were able to get to know one another. It was an opportunity for me to practice my culinary skills, which up to that point were not very good. At least four times a week for eight months, I cooked dinner. Only once did Heath tell me that he wasn't very hungry. It was a meatloaf, and it was obvious that he did not like it.

For Christmas, Heath wanted a traditional dinner, so I cooked a ham. I do eat pork but had never cooked it, but because that is what Heath wanted, I did it. I even put up a Christmas tree, decorated with basketball bulbs.

Having Heath in my home allowed me to experience being a mom. And as it was with my family, we discussed everything while eating dinner. We talked about his aspirations, how he was going to be a better basketball player, and so forth. So I got to be a basketball mom and rent myself a son for a year. I will always be grateful for Heath and our wonderful times around the dinner table.

At the April 2010 Baton Rouge show at Juban's Restaurant; With friends at LSU tailgate party; Nike and Reebok; With exchange student, Heath Weischman; Victoria, Heath Weischman, Nike, and Reebok at LSU, December 2005; Victoria with Whitney Vann at 2010 Alta Vista Club Academy Award Party; With friends at the Baton Rouge show. Back: Boyd Gautreaux, Shannon Manning, Angela Gregoire, Victoria, Richard Flicker, John Bigelow. Front: Regina Gautreaux, Joyce Rodrigue, Sue McDonald; Victoria in New York City

Michael Martin
Actor, Baton Rouge
Out of State

"If I were a food, I'd be coconut shrimp with hot mustard sauce—sweet, spicy, and simply divine!"

I've traveled a bit and even spent a year living in southern Spain. Everywhere I go (and I think most of us are like this) I find that two things always stick out: the people and the food.

Now, before I came down here last August as a Louisiana State University transfer student, I was just a small-town Illinois boy who had never been to Louisiana. I'd had jambalaya and gumbo though, and if that wasn't reason enough to come down, then my Cajun friend Dave's grilling did the trick. So I came down to Baton Rouge, a big city with a small-town complex—don't worry, that's a good thing. And what did I find when I got here? Oh, boy.

I had heard that you have to make a trip to the Chimes. Well I did, followed by countless more. Now I know it's not your maw maw's special homemade roux, but for this out-of-stater, that seafood gumbo always does the trick. The Chimes is also where I first discovered Abita beer.

Then there was my first trip to New Orleans and Bourbon Street. I could tell a few stories about that night, but I'm too afraid they might make it back to my mother, and she lives eight hundred miles away.

Speaking of crawfish, my dad and his friend Dale made a trip down to New Orleans during the 2010 crawfish season. Neither of them sounded too enthused about trying the little red critters, but I managed to get both of them in a restaurant and an order was placed. When the dish came out, Dale promptly ordered a plate of oysters, and I won't even try to describe my dad's expression. He did try the

crawfish though, and while he kept mistaking the tails for the heads, he claimed that he enjoyed them. I imagine they stopped by McDonald's on the way back to the hotel.

My friends and I are a little more suited to adventure and excitement than my father these days. One day, I called my friend, Maui, and told her we were heading to Mulate's. I'd heard they had a dance floor, and I wanted to try Cajun dancing. After a lot of gawking, we did actually make it onto the floor by the end of the night, but never have I been so intimidated by grandparents dancing with their six-year-old grandkids.

I named this monologue "Out of State," and I suppose I should end by summarizing what my experience this past year has been like, having come down to the bayous as an outsider. Everyone knows the saying, "Home is where the heart is." Well, I don't hesitate to say that from the very first day I spent in Louisiana—despite the August heat—Louisiana stole this here heart.

I'm now graduating magna cum laude from LSU with a degree in theatre (and a minor in dance). While my immediate plans take me away to Washington, D.C., I have no doubts that I'll be making my way back to Louisiana. The food, the people, the football, the shade of stately oaks and swaying moss in the setting August sun, the thrill that comes simply from sipping on a Café Du Monde café au lait in the cool night air, these are the Louisiana memories that I'll never forget, and I'm convinced that they are only the first of many.

202

Michael waiting for class at LSU; Traveling in Edinburgh; At Mardi Gras in New Orleans with friends; At LSU dance class with Chelsey Payne; Michael with Alicia St. Romain at the Chimes; Michael at work at the Kennedy Center; Baton Rouge show, September 2010; At LSU game with Alicia St. Romain; Baton Rouge show, July 2010

Lance Spellerberg
Actor and Father, Los Angeles
Miss New Orleans

"If I were a food, I would be corn, because of my Midwestern upbringing and my sense of humor."

Meanwhile, back at Café Du Monde, they have a take-out window. Now I don't know why they have a take-out window. Well, um, of course I know why they have a take-out window; it's just that I don't know why anyone would want to enjoy those hot, powdered-sugar-buried pillows of goodness anywhere but at those glazed, sometimes wobbling tables in the heart of Jackson Square with all the chaos close at hand. There's magic there, a flavor enhancing aura and ambience that cannot be duplicated, no way, no how.

Now, you can get beignets at other places, and they're fine, even delicious. But it's not the same. And you can take home all the boxes of beignet mixes and cans of chicory coffee your little o' heart desires, but you're never gonna get it right. Hell, there's even other Café Du Mondes—down at the Riverwalk, in Metairie (pronounced Met-tree), and even way out in Kenner (pronounced Kennah), but it ain't the same. Maybe it's the patina of chicory lining those ancient coffee urns, or perhaps it's the seasoning of the deep fryers from the twenty-four-hour-a-day, nonstop demand over the decades. But I think it's the spirit of the place. Anthony Bourdain will tell ya; it's not just the food. It's the city, the place, the people, the company, and the soul that makes certain places great. And dawlin', Café Du Monde's got soul.

Yeah, you right. New Orleans's got soul. You can neglect her, you can rob her blind with casino scams and crooked politicians, you can buffet her with Katrina and ignore her afterwards, and you can slather her livelihood of Gulf seafood with earl (what y'all call oil), but somehow, some way, her soul lives on. I don't know how she does it. But I do know that's why she's my favorite city.

When I was young, before I lived in the Big Easy, it was New York, the Big Apple—fast, energetic, with anything and everything available at any time. And this is my third time living in Los Angeles. The universe keeps putting me back here, and I'm not fighting it anymore. But the seven years my wife, Mary, and I lived in New Orleans were different. Peggy and Jimmy would introduce us to their friends, and the next time we saw them, they were our friends. You've heard of six degrees of separation? In New Orleans, it's one. When you meet someone there, they either know you, or most likely, are related to someone else you know. It may take a while to find the connection, but it's there.

And then there's the food, from backyard crawfish boils to breakfast at Brennan's; muffalettas only from Central Grocery, please; BBQ shrimp at Pascal's Manale; po' boys from Mother's slathered in debris; and the Palace Café's white chocolate bread pudding is to die for. Now do y'all know about debris? Debris is the little scraps of roast beef in the chafing dish that have been soaking in, um, well, the fancy phrase would be au jus, but let's face it, it's the fat. And we all know that the fat is where the flavor is, and this stuff has got flavor galore. So they take the debris and slather it on a ham po' boy, fully dressed with lettuce, tomato, and mayonnaise, and it is wicked good. There's a little po' boy shack out on River Road that makes a French fry po' boy. Mhmm, that's right; a hunk of French bread layered with French fries, cheese, and drowning in debris. I didn't have the nerve to test my cardiovascular system, but one of the customers swore by it.

Sometimes the food is defined and enhanced by the time or place. Crawfish bread and crawfish pasta taste best while strolling from stage to stage at Jazz Fest. There is some form of festival every weekend from mid-April through October, and each has its own culinary surprise, from the Ponchatoula Strawberry Festival to the Oil Field Chili Cook-Off. At the St. Bernard Crawfish Festival, you can eat the losers (and the winners) of the crawfish races! Try to give someone king cake in July, and they'll look at you like you're crazy, but if I don't get a piece during Mardi Gras season (even when I'm in Los Angeles), I feel deprived. And everyone knows you only eat oysters in a month with an "r" in its name. Each Thanksgiving I had to figure out how to con my Cajun buddy Dave Guidry into deep-frying a turkey for us. O-o-oh, it's unreal, and with oyster stuffing and pecan pie, you have a lot to be thankful for. But I think my favorite meals were some of the simplest— grilling shrimp, chicken, sausage, and fish on the back patio of our house on Upperline Street, with side dishes brought by friends and family, and the house bursting with music, laughter, friendship, and love.

So while other places I've been to around the world invite me to return, New Orleans *pulls* me back. Mary will turn to me and say, "I'm overdue," and I know just what she means. We need us some New Orleans. When we get there, we'll make a beeline to Café Du Monde. It's my son's favorite. Oh, I didn't mention the *best* thing about New Orleans. It's where our only child, Ellis, was born. You can't get better than that. When Mary found out she was expecting, she set out to eat healthy, which is a herculean task down there, but she did an amazing job. The hardest part was at the hospital, where they served her iced tea, mac-n-cheese, and chicken broiled in butter with the skin. That was the health conscious option. Well, she kept it up through breast-feeding and the transition to solid food: fruits, veggies, whole grain, no processed sugar, or corn syrup, etc. When Mary went back to work, my mom came to visit, and I took her to Café Du Monde with Ellis in his stroller. Well, Grandma took a corner of her beignet, all deep-fried and coated with powdered sugar, and popped it in my son's mouth. His eyes grew wide, and I could see his understanding of the universe expand as he strained forward for more. Another satisfied customer! And he's been hooked ever since, right son?

So meanwhile, back at Café Du Monde, we'll probably use the local technique of sliding into an empty table, while the tourists stand in line waiting for the table to be cleared first, or for someone to gesture for them to sit down. (They'll be waiting a while until they figure it out.) Then we'll laugh and say, "Meanwhile, back at Café Du Monde," the phrase Peggy came up with over our myriad visits there. We'll get a couple of orders of beignets and, depending on the weather, either hot or iced café au lait (though I prefer the hot even when the city is doing its best imitation of a steam bath). And while watching the uninitiated cover themselves with powdered sugar, we'll recall the crowded morning visits, the afternoon pick-me-ups to get to the next social event, or, our favorite, the 2:00 A.M. nightcaps when the real New Orleans comes out in all its bizarre and enchanting finery.

It's like no place else in the world. If you've been there you know. If not, you gotta go. I know what it means to miss New Orleans. Do you?

Miss Sherry's Corn Maque Choux

My first time tasting this dish was at Pascal's Manale, when my in-laws were visiting from Los Angeles for Thanksgiving. My wife's mom was a Louisiana girl from Elizabeth, and when she saw maque choux (pronounced "mock shoe") on the menu, she said we had to have it, and it was quite good. But I think I really only had maque choux when Peggy's mom, Miss Sherry, made it for Thanksgiving one year, and I went back for more. They say good actors borrow, bad actors steal, so make up your own mind, but I have basically lifted this recipe from the Sweeney family cookbook. I have added hot sauce for a little more kick. The frozen corn can be a real time saver. For heaven's sake, don't pull back on the butter! You'll miss the point entirely. It's a real Southern dish!

1 large onion, chopped
1 medium bell pepper, chopped
1 medium red pepper, chopped
1 tbsp. cooking oil
½ stick butter
1 package frozen corn, or 6-8 ears fresh corn
¼ cup milk, if using fresh corn
1 14.5-oz. can spicy or regular tomatoes with juice
¼ cup water
¼ tsp. sugar
Salt, pepper, and Creole seasoning
Hot pepper sauce

Sauté onion and peppers in cooking oil and butter. When soft, add frozen corn and let it stick to the bottom of the pan. Once the corn is thawed, add tomatoes and let it all fry down. (If using fresh corn add a ¼ cup milk, but lower heat so milk doesn't curdle.) Add a little water at a time and smother until corn is tender.

Add salt and pepper. If you used mild tomatoes, add Creole seasoning to taste. If you want a little more kick, add some hot pepper sauce to taste in the last 10 minutes before serving, or serve as is with the bottle on hand for guests to use to their taste.

Can be served immediately or pour in an 8x8 casserole dish and refrigerate overnight. Remove from refrigerator and allow dish to reach room temperature before reheating.

Recipe can be doubled for buffets (pronounced "boo-fay").

Serves 8.

Photograph by Diana Zollicoffer

206

Lance with baby Ellis in New Orleans; Lance at Mardi Gras; Lance, Mary, and Ellis at the Baton Rouge show November 2010; Mary, Peggy, Lance, Ellis, and Peyton Segrest at the Baton Rouge show, November 2010; Lance and Peggy at the Santa Monica show, February 2011; "Raise your hand if you miss New Orleans"; Best friends at Mardi Gras: Mary, Lance, Jimmy, and Peggy; Mary and Ellis at the Baton Rouge show November 2010; Old New Orleans home.

One Year Anniversary Show
Juban's Creole Restaurant,
Baton Rouge

May 12, 2011